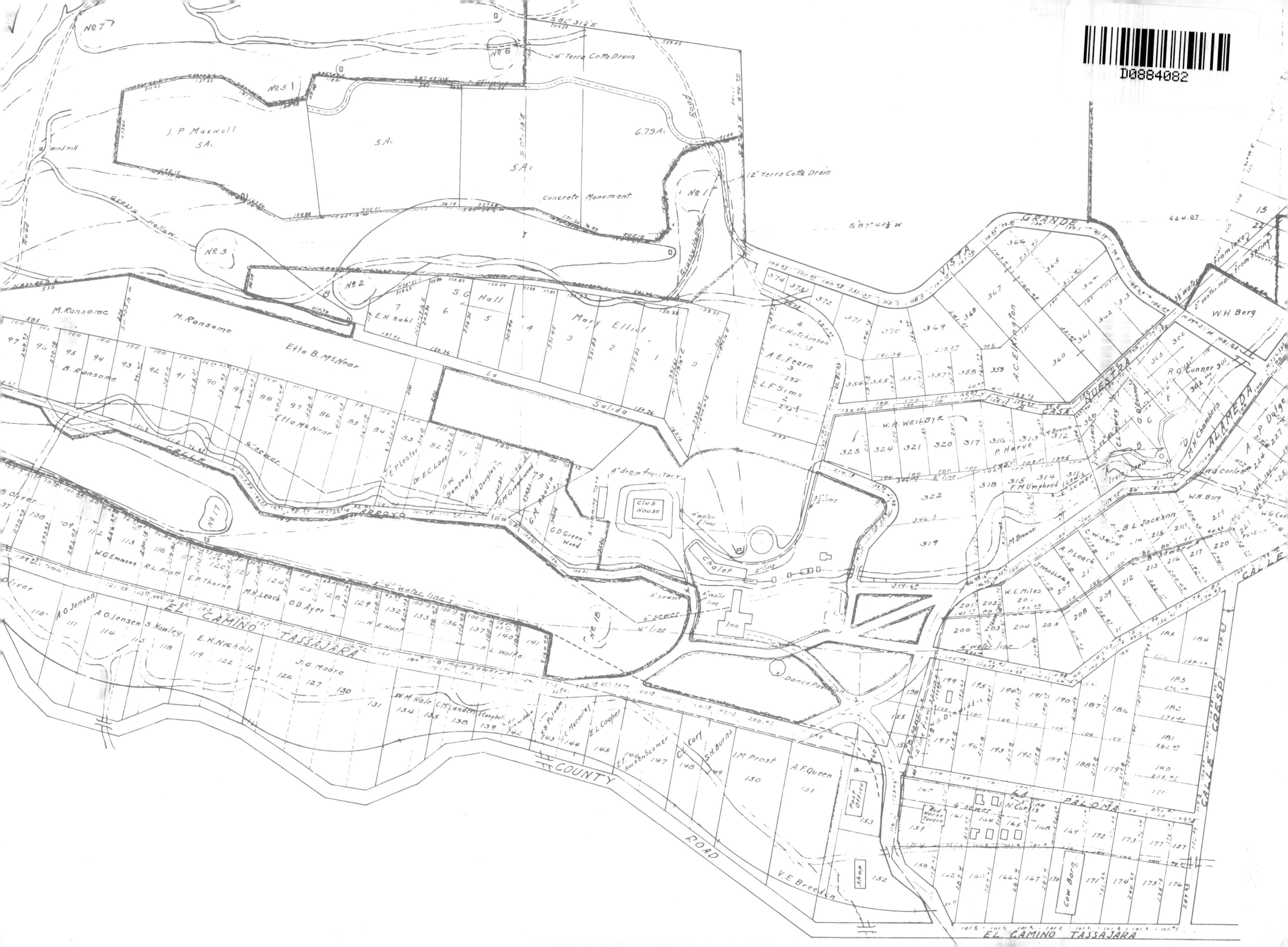

D0884082
No 7
No 6
24" Terra Cotta Drain
No 5
J. P. Maxwell
5 Ac
6.79 Ac
Wind mill
Concrete Monument
12" Terra Cotta Drain
No 1
No 3
No 2
S.G. Hall
E.H. Kahl
Mary Elliot
M. Ransome
B. Ransome
Etta B. McNear
Ella McNear
La Salida
VISTA GRANDE
E.C. Hutchinson
A.E. Fearn
L.F. Sims
A.C. Elkington
W.H. Berg
CASA NUESTRA
ALAMEDA
M.H. Chambers
Club House
Chalet
Inn
Dance Pavilion
ARROYO
No 17
No 18
E.F. Lester
Dr. E.C. Love
N.B. Douglas
G.D. Greenwood
F.M. Umphred
B.L. Jackson
A.P. Leach
W.E. Miles
W.G. Emmons
R.L. Pratt
E.P. Thorne
M.H. Leach
O.D. Ayer
H.E. Hunt
F.L. Wolfe
A.O. Jensen
S. Hawley
E.K. Nichols
J.G. Moore
W.M. Hale
E.L. Cooper
C.L. Cory
S.H. Burns
I.M. Prost
A.F. Queen
V.E. Breeden
EL CAMINO TASSAJARA
COUNTY ROAD
Post Office
Shop
Red Horse Tavern
LA PALOMA
Cow Barn
CALLE CRESPI
6" sewer
4" water line
8" main sewer

DIABLO'S LEGACY

SITE OF OLD
MOUNTAIN
HOUSE
HERE STOOD THE MOUNTAIN
HOUSE, FAMOUS PIONEER
HOTEL, A MILE BELOW THE
SUMMIT OF DIABLO, CLIMBED
FROM HERE. STAGES REACHED
THE HOTEL DAILY FROM
CONCORD AND DANVILLE.
BUILT IN THE '70s
THE MOUNTAIN HOUSE WAS
DESTROYED IN 1901.

DIABLO'S LEGACY

RECOLLECTIONS
&
REFLECTIONS

1912 – Present

James C. Stone

Miller Freeman Inc., San Francisco

Published by Miller Freeman, Inc.,
Book Division, 600 Harrison Street,
San Francisco, CA 94107

Editors: Audrey Barrie and Larry Ives
Marketing Directors: Margaret and Marshall Freeman

Sponsors: Don and Audrey Barrie, Dick and Gail Breitwieser, Paul and Judy Cortese, Larry and Betty Curtola, Roland and Caroline Davies, Bob and Marcia Field, Marshall and Margaret Freeman, Max and Linda Gray, Larry and Connie Ives (Chairman), Phil and Lilan Kane, Bill and Ginny Rei, Jim and Dorothy Stone, Rich and Ruth Swanson, Bob and Lyn Tiernan, Rett and Lou Turner

Cover and Text Designer: Brad Greene, Greene Design
Cover Photo: Stephen Joseph
Title suggested by Ginny Rei and Lois Blemer Lippincott
Printed in Hong Kong

ISBN 0-87930-348-4

MAP OF MT. DIABLO CLUB (Inside front cover)
DeWayne Ryan discovered this map in the rubble of the basement of the Chalet when his father Vern and he were redoing the foundation for Paul Cortese in 1979. DeWayne had the map mounted and framed and hung it on the wall of his home. It is undated but probably was made as early as 1912 because RN's original layout of the Club and the Community is well diagramed. Note portions of the golf course, clubhouse (Casino), Inn (Club, farm house), Chalet, dance pavilion, Red Horse Tavern, Post Office, cow barn, railroad and the owners of the original lots. This map was used in the early '20s when most of the lots were purchased. Note that the Thomas' house built in 1929 does not show Thomas as an owner so sometime before '29, the Mt. Diablo Park Company stopped updating the map. Some of the street names have changed. La Salida is now Club House Road, El Camino Tassajara is Alameda Diablo, Vista Grande is no more and the country road El Camino Tassajara is Diablo Road.

TABLE OF CONTENTS

	FOREWORD: Larry Curtola	*vii*
	PREFACE: Jim Stone	*viii*
Chapter I	PRELUDE TO DEVELOPMENT	*1*
Chapter II	WWI–FORE & AFT	*6*
Chapter III	THE ROARING TWENTIES	*22*
Chapter IV	THE DEPRESSION THIRTIES	*38*
Chapter V	THE WAR–TORN FORTIES	*54*
Chapter VI	THE NIFTY FIFTIES	*72*
Chapter VII	THE STRIDENT SIXTIES	*90*
Chapter VIII	THE INFLATED SEVENTIES	*112*
Chapter IX	THE ENTERPRISING EIGHTIES	*132*
Chapter X	TWENTY FROM THE TWENTIES	*154*
Chapter XI	COMMON CAUSE	*176*
Chapter XII	EPILOGUE: THE NINETIES	*194*
	AFTERWORD	*212*
	FOOTNOTES	*213*
	BIBLIOGRAPHY	*219*
	APPENDIX	*220*
	INDEX	*228*

In 1948 when I was looking for an investment, a friend showed me a nearly deserted Diablo. Most of the Club members lived in Oakland or San Francisco; the clubhouse was abandoned and only a few local residents attempted to use the golf facilities. There was little or no maintenance. A few who lived adjacent to the golf course used hoses from their homes to water the bone-dry fairways.

As I continued my examination of the property on a beautiful July day, I began to visualize the restoration of the faded elegance all around me—the beautiful old barns, the lake and the great oaks, the stately old homes and the smaller cottages set among the trees. I appreciated the traditions, the sense of history and the beauty that make Diablo such a unique area.

After lengthy negotiations with Club officials, an agreement was reached. With the help of the Bank of America in San Francisco and over the strong objections of my father, I bought the Diablo Country Club and Club properties.

My family and I will always have a special place in our hearts for Diablo. We are all indebted to Professor James C. Stone, a resident and Club member for 38 years, who has given his time and talent to provide this story of a surviving social institution—the Diablo Country Club—and a vibrant social network—the Diablo Community.

LARRY CURTOLA

PREFACE

I was appointed Club Historian by the Diablo Country Club in 1989, the result of Director Rudy Frucella's interest. As I conducted my research, I wrote articles for the Club's monthly organ, the *Inferno*. Audrey Barrie and Larry Ives were the Editors. Audrey returned my first manuscript with the admonition, "You're no longer writing for college students. Now your audience is people who aren't necessarily interested in, or don't particularly care about what you have to say. Try again."

Bristling with professional pique, I tried again and my third attempt was found acceptable! Article by article, month by month, I learned to write like a journalist instead of a college professor. The result was totally unexpected: people liked my articles. A year later Shirley Hare showed me how she had put them into a notebook that she kept on her coffee table to show friends. Thus the idea of this book was born.

Moving from idea to reality was the work of many devoted and caring people. Larry Ives worked the telephones and obtained a group of sponsors. Margaret Freeman's enthusiasm was contagious and

we had a publisher — Miller Freeman — with the company's President, Marshall Freeman, as our marketing director. Mari Burnison computerized the manuscript with consultant backup from Don Barrie. Literally dozens of others such as Beth Hearn jumped in with copy, contacts, informants, leads, sources, documents, and pictures. Now that the book is finished, I'm still getting calls and letters with additional data — perhaps enough for a Volume II?

Behind the scenes has been my loving, "silent" (ha!) editor, Dorothy, who has guided and edited, weeding out sufficient prose for yet another volume.

To her, my editors, sponsors, publisher, helpers too numerous to mention, I am truly grateful.

JIM STONE

Diablo's pastoral surroundings with an inset of the clubhouse.

Before the white settlers came this far west, Native Americans worked, played and fought on Mt. Diablo.

Artist's conception of the battle between Balgone warriors and Spanish soldiers. Note the great warrior Puy. COURTESY OF EGON PEDERSEN

Chapter I

PRELUDE TO DEVELOPMENT

The history of Club and Community can not be separated from that of the Mountain. Diablo came into being because of the influence the Mountain exerted on all who saw it, especially the early Spanish Dons.

Before California's gold rush days of '49, Green Valley—now the location of Diablo and Diablo Country Club—was a rancho owned by Spanish Dons. It was a part of the original Spanish grant covering the vast area at the foot of Mt. Diablo.

Father Juan Crespi and Captain Don Pedro Fages, Governor 1782-91, visited Green Valley in 1782 and climbed Mt. Diablo. Their view from the summit gave the Spanish their first glimpse of the beauty and potential of Green Valley.

INFLUENCE OF NATIVE AMERICANS The Balgone Native Americans lived in the mountain forests. From its peak they viewed the great central valley, San Francisco Bay, the Sacramento and San Joaquin Rivers, Half Dome in Yosemite, Mount Lassen and Mount Whitney. From its peak, they also viewed their enemies.

Their enemies were mainly Spanish soldiers plundering for riches. In 1806, the two sides fought a fierce battle near Green Valley. In the heat of the conflict, a great chieftain bedecked in war paint and hawk feathers, appeared on the mountain above the warring Balgones. He turned the tide of battle, driving back the invading Spaniards. According to Native American tradition, this super-human leader was "Puy" or "Spirit of the Mountain." In their exasperation in defeat, the Spanish soldiers translated "Puy" as "Devil" or "El Diablo." (1) And so the name became Mt. Diablo.

Early settlers realized the importance of the mountain as a starting point for surveys. As early as 1851 government surveyors used the summit as a base meridian. A toll road was built to the top in

The Mountain House was popular with tourists, as was the stage coach that left from the Red Horse Tavern to take passengers up the mountain. But neither the Mountain House nor the coach was popular with ranchers, who put an end to it all by setting fire to the Mountain House in 1901.

The 16-room Mountain House was a popular tourist attraction.

The Base Meridian, opposite page.
COURTESY OF THE STEIN COLLECTION.

MT. DIABLO
BASE-MERIDIAN
MONUMENT
ELEVATION 3849
Monument at Summit of Mount Diablo

Toll rates fixed by the Contra Costa County Board of Supervisors to use the Mountain road were: (3)

Two passengers and car	**$1.00**
All others	**$1.50**
Two horse vehicle	**$1.50**
Four horse vehicle	**$2.00**
Six horse vehicle	**$2.50**
Individual person	**$0.25**
Cow, horse each....................	**$0.10**
Sheep	**$0.025**

1873 and a 16-room hotel, Mountain House, was erected about a mile from the summit.(2) It opened the following year and enjoyed a flourishing tourist business for a time. In 1901 the hotel was burned to the ground and the road closed by local ranchers bent on preserving the mountain for grazing.

The road was reopened in 1915 and public spirited individuals and organizations began clamoring to have Devil Mountain become a State Park.

In 1931 the crown of El Diablo and the west and south slopes were acquired by the State for $168,000. Seventy thousand of the total was raised by residents of Contra Costa County. The remaining value was in land gifts.(3)

The March, 1956 *Inferno* said: "We're most fortunate to have El Diablo State Park in our backyard. First, because its physical structure and beauty will always be maintained and second, because the park offers recreational facilities for overnight camping, barbecues, horseback riding, hiking and nature studies."

INFLUENCE OF ANGLO AMERICANS Settlers looking for prime ranchland were also attracted to Devil Mountain. Among them was William Cameron who began buying acreage for a large ranch in Green Valley in 1873. Several railroad companies also purchased various parcels. In time a single owner emerged. It was the Central Pacific Railroad, whose "Big Four" were well-known—Charles Crocker, Mark Hopkins, Collis Huntington and Leland Stanford. (4)

The Big Four appointed David Colton(5) to manage the ranch and he was given Mark Hopkins' share. In time he bought the shares of Crocker, Huntington and Stanford.(6) These 10,000 acres became known as "the Railroad Ranch."

The old racetrack was used for race horses—thoroughbreds and trotters—and was where many came to see, buy, and cheer on the best. Today the track is marked by the row of eucalyptus trees around its perimeters.
COURTESY OF THE STEIN COLLECTION.

Colton died in a horse accident in 1878 and his daughter, Caroline, and her husband, Dan Cook, inherited the property. By now it extended from Green Valley School to Sycamore Valley and from Green Valley to Curry Creek, taking in the headwaters of Marsh Creek, the south summit road and the Mountain House Hotel.[7] Both Colton and Dan Cook are credited with introducing blooded horses and cattle. Seth Cook, Dan's brother, installed the race track[8] and changed the name from Railroad Ranch to Oakwood Stock Farm.

By today's reckoning, the racetrack was located between the 16th fairway on the east, Cameo Acres on the west and the 14th and 15th fairways on the north. The 'ole' racetrack was remembered for the green patch in the center. This was the vegetable garden that was maintained by a Club gardener and supplied the fresh produce to the Club kitchen.[9]

When the Cooks passed on, the Farm went to Seth Cook's niece, Laura, and her husband, John Boyd. Through John Boyd's efforts the Farm gained its great reputation as a stock-breeding center. "It produced more than a dozen of the finest thoroughbred race horses of the period and its trotters and carriage horses were among the best."[10] Boyd also introduced purebred shorthorn and Devon cattle and shipped breeder stock to many parts of the world.[11] He adorned the mile-long racetrack with eucalyptus trees along the perimeter, built stalls for 24 fleet-footed trotters and erected a viewing stand for race judges.

The lush setting dominated by Mt. Diablo offered temperate weather, a railroad and proximity to major cities, all of which contributed to making this area an ideal place for recreational living. To a man of vision, the development of a small secluded community and a country club seemed promising. Enter RN Burgess!

Chapter II

WORLD WAR I FORE & AFT

Racing up the Mountain was a favorite sport of the day.

IN THE BEGINNING: RN: 1878-1965 Robert Noble Burgess, nicknamed "RN," founded the Club and the community of Diablo. He owned Blackhawk and part of Mt. Diablo State Park. His book, *Memoirs*, was published privately in 1964. Elizabeth Ann Burgess Cox, his granddaughter, and Edward Burgess, his grandson, who both grew up in Diablo, lent copies. This chapter dealing with the founding of Club and Community was crafted from RN's book and interviews with his family and friends.

Born on February, 10, 1878, in St. John, New Brunswick, Canada, RN moved to San Francisco when he was six. Two years later, his father, a Presbyterian minister, was named pastor of the Danville Presbyterian Church at a salary of $1,000 per year. RN wrote, "I don't know how we lived unless on borrowed money." Reverend Joshua Burgess purchased a 20-acre parcel 2-1/2 miles south of Danville, built a house and barn and planted the land in almonds, apricots, pears and prunes. One of RN's jobs was taking care of the fruit trees and this early interest later became his first business as a fruit merchant and broker.

Rising at 4:30 a.m., he and his two older brothers Will and John cared for the orchard, pruning, budding, grafting, spraying and harvesting. He wrote, "Ranch work is like woman's work—it runs from here to there."

He attended the Danville Grammar School, completing it in 1893 at age 15. It was a one-room school with one teacher, A. J. Young. "He was a fine man, and also taught our Sunday School," remembered RN. "He was the entire staff and carried us through eight grades, ending with Algebra."

RN's perpetual hunger often made him late for school. He wrote, "I would stop at the bridge under which there was a small stream and a beautiful supply of frogs." He caught a mess of them, built

Billboard advertising both the train and the toll road to the top of Mt. Diablo.

En route up Mt. Diablo Scenic Boulevard to the top of the mountain. This road was both a race course and a road for tourists.

Around the Nation

San Francisco is still rebuilding from the disastrous earthquake and fire of 1906. Pullman sleeping cars, named for their manufacturer, are as popular as railroad dining cars with their spotless white linens and efficient service.

A radical economic system called Communism is firmly rooted in Russia and now there is also an American Communist Party.

A former Princeton University History professor promises to "keep us out of war." But when elected President in 1916, promptly leads us into war to "save the world for democracy." It ends on Armistice Day, November 11, 1918, at a cost of 8,500,000 killed, 21 million wounded and 7.5 million prisoners or missing. America's trains are recognized for their successful movement of troops and materiel to ports and ships on both coasts.

While men are at war, the Women's Christian Temperance Union pressures Congress to pass the Volstead Act requiring the Feds to enforce Prohibition(1) and organizes voters to ratify the 18th Amendment, thus closing America's breweries and bars.

Sinclair Lewis' *Main Street* hits the streets. The movies' Mary Pickford is America's sweetheart.

At the Mt. Diablo Country Club, 200 Oakland Rotarians and their families spend a day "with sport and jollity" racing and swimming in the Lake, playing baseball and quoits, racing up the mountain in cars and picnicking under the oaks.(2)

a fire and roasted them. "They were delicious. I can still taste them," he recalled.

While his two older brothers continued their schooling, graduating from the University of California, RN's interest turned him directly to the world of business and finance. By the time he graduated from the eighth grade, he had saved enough money to buy 20 acres of hay land adjacent to his father's farm, presaging his entrepreneurial interest in land development.

At about the same time, with the help of his brothers, he built a two-story warehouse to process and store fruits and nuts. "We lived simply," wrote RN, "but the real need was for hard-working people like me who put in long hours." While still a minor, he opened a fruit-packing house in Concord. In addition to being in the fruit business, young RN sold sacks and twine to farmers, also insured their grain and later purchased it.

Reverend Burgess' home looked towards the Railroad Ranch, then owned by two old railroad contractors, Seth and Dan Cook. (The Railroad Ranch later was renamed the Oakwood Stock Farm.) As a young man, RN and his cronies often hunted on the Cook's 10,000 acres.

RN remembered Seth and Dan Cook as "rough, hearty fellows." On Saturday afternoons, his father would stake him and John along the front of their orchard road. Along would come Seth and Dan, pull their horses to a stop and yell, "&#$! %!?*, you youngsters, come here." Dan would produce a double eagle $20 gold coin and say, "Give that to your old man. He is the only &#$! %!?* preacher I ever knew that was any good." This happened many times and long before RN began to dream of owning the Cook's extensive ranch that stretched to the top of Mt. Diablo.

MARRIAGE As a single man of 30, he lived at the Athens Club in Oakland and was beginning to take an interest in social affairs. He was invited to join the Oakland Cotillion and there met Anne Fish of Lafayette. They were married on July 20, 1909 at the Fish's home. Just before the wedding, an old express wagon arrived carrying a single bale of oat hay. The expressman was waiting for his pay, as it had been sent C.O.D. "Of course," wrote RN, "I thought it was for Anne's horse so I immediately paid the bill. Then I saw a card addressed to Anne Fish which read, 'all of Bob's wild oats.'" RN knew it was brother Will's doings. He wrote, "If it had been Will's wild oats, there would have been many more bales."

MOTORING AROUND On a sunny day in the spring of 1912, RN was leisurely motoring around Danville and Tassajara.(3) He dropped in at the Oakwood Stock Farm, which he had known

RN Burgess. Courtesy of Elizabeth Burgess Cox.

Oakwood Stock Farm. The Stein Collection.

from his boyhood as the Railroad Ranch. He now was 34 years old and knew of the Farm's fame, its top quality race horses and cattle. He had watched the horses racing around the track where St. Timothy's Church now stands. Today, entering Diablo, the property on the left (1699 Alameda Diablo) displays four Gothic columns from the race track's original viewing stand.

The Oakwood Stock Farm had been inherited by the Cooks' niece, Mrs. John Boyd, who lived in San Rafael. Burgess learned from the current lessee that she was interested in selling the ranch for $150,000 but that her attorney had recently refused such an offer "...for reasons of his own."

Armed with this pearl of wisdom, Burgess suddenly knew exactly how to purchase the 10,000-acre ranch at $15 per acre.

He drove to San Francisco, telephoned Mrs. Boyd and made a tea-time appointment with her that very day at her home in San Rafael. En route, he stopped at the Crocker Bank and purchased a $10,000 cashier's check payable to his order. Over tea, Mrs. Boyd agreed to sell for $150,000 all cash within 30 days. While Mrs. Boyd sat at her desk, penning this agreement to her attorney, RN hovered over her and purposely dropped the $10,000 cashier's check. She picked it up, exclaiming, "What is this?"

Pretending to be flustered, RN explained that he had simply brought the check along as a possible payment on account. He quickly endorsed it to Mrs. Boyd, saying, "when your attorney is ready to approve the sale I will only have to pay him $140,000."

Then he rushed back to San Francisco to see Boyd's attorney and presented him with his *fait accompli*. He followed this *coup d'état* by buying the Blackhawk Ranch, all the land between it and Diablo and up to the top of Mt. Diablo, including the official Mt. Diablo Base Meridian Monument and the right-of-way of Mt. Diablo Scenic Boulevard. Most important, he started the Mt. Diablo Country Club.(4)

BIG NEWS, BIG PLANS, BIG MEN Not only was the purchase of the Oakwood Stock Farm headline news but the news kept coming as RN announced plans to sell Club memberships, market lots for summer homes around the golf course that was to be designed by Jack Nevelle—who later designed the Pebble Beach course—create a half-mile long lake for swimming, fishing and boating, engineer a water system for the area using artesian wells and mountain springs, construct a road to the top of Mt. Diablo for auto racing and build a swank hotel at the top.

RN's ambitious and grandiose plans required big bucks and even bigger publicity. He set his sights on the big man of the times, William Randolph Hearst. RN designed a bold plan to involve the man who controlled the nation's biggest chain of newspapers and magazines. Hearst's chain reached millions daily. With so much at stake, RN plotted judiciously. The year was 1916 and RN was 38 years old. Radio and TV were unknown and a national publicist of Hearst's stature was an invaluable aid.

He went to L.A. where he had learned Hearst was staying and sent him a telegram. He recalled, "I sat up most of the night writing and rewriting the telegram to a man I'd never met. But I knew I had to catch him on the first try." Before noon the following day, Hearst sent RN a wire, "Meet me at 10:30 next Thursday morning." The following Thursday, he went to Hearst's room at the Alexandria Hotel and knocked on the door. Hearst said, "Come in young man and spill it!" RN outlined his plans and dreams for the Oakwood Farm including the Club, the community of Diablo, Mt. Diablo, Blackhawk and the surrounding area. He wrote, "I paced up and down for over an hour in front of this big man I'd never met before. Finally, he said, "Enough for now; I'll meet you next Thursday at 10:00 a.m. at the Ferry Building in San Francisco and we'll take a look at Oakwood. My mother, Phoebe Hearst, has a country home near Pleasanton (now the Castlewood Country Club). From the mountain, you can look right down on her place."

RN met Hearst and his retinue of advisers and lawyers at Oakwood but RN, as usual, was a jump ahead. Prior to their arrival, he had his stablemen herd all the horses but two up the mountain and out of sight so there would be no time for the "hangers-on" to catch up with him and Hearst. He said, "I had an important deal to discuss—the most important of my life—and I didn't want any distractions." They rode together for four hours. At one point Hearst selected a hilltop and said, "Here's where I want to build." Together they worked out plans to build chalet apartments at the Club that could connect over the creek to the clubhouse, develop and sell summer villas around the golf course, construct a road to the summit of Mt. Diablo for auto racing and at the peak erect a castle-like exclusive hotel.

Hearst and Burgess agreed on the terms of a contract that RN called "...the biggest advertising contract ever written." The signing of this momentous document, however, was postponed until the completion of Mt. Diablo Scenic Boulevard. Besides extensive advertising in newspapers and magazines, the contract specified that Hearst purchase 15,000 acres "...reaching from Ygnacio Valley to the top of Mt. Diablo and down its southeast slope to Diablo." The agreed-upon price was $1,000 per acre.

William Randolph Hearst.

Artist's conception of the castle-like hotel Burgess and Hearst planned at the summit.

Laying the tracks at the entrance to Diablo. COURTESY OF WILLIAM FREEMAN.

FOUNDING THE CLUB On August 12, 1912, an article in the *Contra Costa Gazette* stated, "The clubhouse which was built at Oakwood by Seth Cook is being remodeled by Burgess and will soon be in condition for occupancy."(5) This established the Club's founding as the fall of 1912.

By January 15, 1917, the Mt. Diablo Country Club had 106 members including William Randolph Hearst. Initiation fees were $60, dues $20 annually. The Club Board consisted of RN as President along with Directors Henry Mehran, William Letts Oliver, E. L. Cooper and E. B. Bull, Secretary.(6)

RN then established a separate company, Mt. Diablo Villa Homes, to handle promoting and selling lots. Sales opened on May 14, 1916 and "...four special trains brought 600 prospective buyers—with another 600 arriving by automobile."(7) The *San Francisco Examiner* says this about these prospective buyers: "Educated women of the no-place-like-home type sauntered about and made discoveries of advantageous sites that they declared the very thing for up-to-date bungalows costing from a few hundred to a few thousand.

"Busy men of affairs and professions, but with taste in landscape gardening and country architecture, stood about and pointed out locations, here for a Tyrolean chalet or a rambling Italian villa; there for a stately English manor house or a re-tiled casa of early California design."

In 1916, RN built his own home in Diablo, overlooking what is now the 18th fairway at 1817 Calle Arroyo, where he and his family lived for 10 years. Then they built a home at 2323 Mt. Diablo Scenic and lived there until 1969.

With the sale of lots underway, Burgess convinced the Oakland, Antioch and Eastern Railroad to lay tracks from Danville (near the old Charlotte Wood School) to the Mt. Diablo Country Club, using the Farm's original Casino as a clubhouse.(8) Burgess is silent on how he conned the railroad authorities but his business acumen, growing political clout and single-mindedness are well documented. A year after "...just motoring around Danville and Tassajara," RN was the proud owner of 10,000 acres of farm land ripe for development.

In 1917, he built a Swiss Chalet for Club members and their guests. Its opening on July 21 was big news. One paper headlined BIG TIME AT CLUB TODAY, saying, "The biggest event of many a day at the Mt. Diablo Park Club is that, announced for Saturday, July 21st, the dedication of the Club's new Chalet, one of the handsomest Club buildings in the west. It has 39 rooms, including suites, modern in appointment."

ISSUED BY
The San Francisco-Oakland Terminal Railways

SPECIAL EXCURSION TICKET
Good for One Continuous First-Class Passage
SAN FRANCISCO
TO
SUMMIT (Mt. Diablo)
AND RETURN
AS COVERED BY COUPONS ATTACHED

Baggage Checked. Going ★ Trip
Baggage Checked. Return ★ Trip

Void after .... 191...

SUBJECT TO THE FOLLOWING CONTRACT AND CONDITIONS:

1st. Going Trip. Good only on date of sale.
2nd. Return Trip. Must be completed on or before date written above by selling agent.
3rd. Stop-overs. Will not be allowed on either going or return trip.
4th. Non-Transferable. This ticket is not transferable.
5th. Baggage. Will be checked to destination only and liability is limited to wearing apparel not to exceed One Hundred Dollars in value for a whole ticket and Fifty Dollars for a half ticket.
6th. Alterations. This ticket is void if more than one date or destination is shown hereon, or if the coupons are detached from contract, or if any alterations or erasures are made herein.
7th. The San Francisco-Oakland Terminal Railways and the Oakland, Antioch & Eastern Railway only act as agents and do not assume any responsibility beyond their own lines. Passengers routed via stage or auto line will be carried over such stage or auto line at the discretion and at the convenience of the carrier, and are not entitled to any option or preference as to the selection of such vehicle.

Amount Paid, $......

W. R. Alberger
Vice-Pres. and Gen. Mgr.

VIA THE SAN FRANCISCO-OAKLAND TERMINAL RYS.
Good for One Continuous Passage
OAKLAND (40th & Shafter)
TO
SAN FRANCISCO
Subject to conditions named in Contract and void if detached therefrom.
Final Destination—Summit and Ret'n
RETURN
IF FOR HALF ½ PUNCH HERE
Issued by The San Francisco-Oakland Terminal Rys.
Form K 129

VIA OAKLAND, ANTIOCH & EASTERN RAILWAY
Good for One Continuous Passage
SARANAP
TO
OAKLAND (40th & Shafter)
Subject to conditions named in Contract and void if detached therefrom.
Final Destination—Summit and Ret'n
RETURN
Issued by The San Francisco-Oakland Terminal Rys.

VIA OAKLAND, ANTIOCH & EASTERN RAILWAY
Good for One Continuous Passage
DIABLO
TO
SARANAP
Subject to conditions named in Contract and void if detached therefrom.
Final Destination—Summit and Ret'n
RETURN
Issued by The San Francisco-Oakland Terminal Rys.

VIA MT. DIABLO SCENIC BOULEVARD COMPANY
Good for One Continuous Passage
SUMMIT (Mt. Diablo)
TO
DIABLO
Subject to conditions named in Contract and void if detached therefrom.
Final Destination—Summit and Ret'n
RETURN
IF FOR HALF ½ PUNCH HERE
Issued by The San Francisco-Oakland Terminal Rys.
Form K 129

VIA MT. DIABLO SCENIC BOULEVARD COMPANY
Good for One Continuous Passage
DIABLO
TO
SUMMIT (Mt. Diablo)
Subject to conditions named in Contract and void if detached therefrom.
Final Destination—Summit and Ret'n
GOING
IF FOR HALF ½ PUNCH HERE
Issued by The San Francisco-Oakland Terminal Rys.
Form K 129

VIA OAKLAND, ANTIOCH & EASTERN RAILWAY
Good for One Continuous Passage
SARANAP
TO
DIABLO
Subject to conditions named in Contract and void if detached therefrom.
Final Destination—Summit and Ret'n
GOING
IF FOR HALF ½ PUNCH HERE
Issued by The San Francisco-Oakland Terminal Rys.
Form K 129

VIA OAKLAND, ANTIOCH & EASTERN RAILWAY
Good for One Continuous Passage
OAKLAND (40th & Shafter)
TO
SARANAP
Subject to conditions named in Contract and void if detached therefrom.
Final Destination—Summit and Ret'n
GOING
IF FOR HALF ½ PUNCH HERE
Issued by The San Francisco-Oakland Terminal Rys.
Form K 129

VIA THE SAN FRANCISCO-OAKLAND TERMINAL RYS.
Good for One Continuous Passage
SAN FRANCISCO
TO
OAKLAND (40th & Shafter)
Subject to conditions named in Contract and void if detached therefrom.
Final Destination—Summit and Ret'n
GOING
IF FOR HALF ½ PUNCH HERE
Issued by The San Francisco-Oakland Terminal Rys.
Form K 129

Tickets for both the train and the toll road.

Train trestles were built to cross the many creeks between Orinda, Lafayette, Walnut Creek, Danville, and Diablo, at right.

An electric line from Saranap in Walnut Creek where it joined the main line to Diablo in 1913.

Waiting for train that delivered the men back to their offices in San Francisco while families summered in Diablo. Courtesy William Freeman.

Later that same year on November 25, the Red Horse Tavern was opened for "strangers at the gates." In addition to a dining room and parlor, there were suites on the upper floor. *The S.F. Examiner* said, "The completion of the Red Horse Tavern, near the end of the Oakland, Antioch and Eastern electric line, providing accomodations for the public has been another important step in the Burgess development.

"The Tavern is used not only by visitors to Diablo, but by motorists and tourists going to the top of the mountain. A motor stage service is operated from the Tavern."

A POST OFFICE To guarantee that Diablo would forever be recognized as a distinct entity, RN realized he had to have an official U.S. Post Office. All he says about this momentous achievement in his *Memoirs* is, "This did not prove to be too difficult and so Diablo was born."

The application to the Post Master General was dated August 15, 1916, and signed by John Curtiss, a Burgess employee. Curtiss described the proposed location of the post office as "...15 miles southwest of the San Joaquin River and 2-½ miles east of San Ramon Creek." He noted, "the post office building would be on the south side of the Oakland and Antioch Railroad and at a distance of 100 feet from the track."(9) Actually it was located in the Old Horse Barn at the corner of Avenita Nueva and La Cadena. On December 8 the facility was officially established with Curtiss as postmaster.

WORLD WAR I The U.S. declared war on Germany on April 6, 1917, and the nation's interest quickly shifted from home and fireside to the draft, battles and supporting the "war to end all wars." "No one," wrote RN, "was any longer interested in buying villas and seeking a milder climate while their sons were fighting a war."

So, too, the war changed William Randolph Hearst's interests, and the contract with the RN Burgess Company never was signed. All those hopes, dreams, plans and agreements came crashing down.

The war also put a serious crimp on RN's business affairs. He resigned from the Claremont and Mt. Diablo Country Clubs, the Bohemian and Athens clubs and was forced to file for bankruptcy in the summer of 1919. He sold his home overlooking the golf course and bid adieu to Diablo. In RN's comment on the disposition of his property, he added this postscript: "Of the three hundred Hungarian ponies I had purchased from Mr. Foster, President of the Northwestern railroad out of San Rafael, I had kept six good riding ponies, so we were all fixed for riding. We had ample pasture for them as well as for two cows, so we had a good start at life on the farm," referring to the farm in Walnut Creek

The training barn, top, was location of the Post Office (left of entrance).

The Carriage Barn was in front of the Training Barn both located near Avenida Nueva entrance. Photos are circa 1892.

COURTESY OF JAMES AND SHELLY MINOR.

Two of Diablo's more well-known horses, Steinway & Charles Derby, with the crew in front of the training barn.

The Inn, formerly the Oakwood Stock Farm Mansion, and later the clubhouse of the '20s, '30s, and '40s. On its veranda members danced on summer evenings.

COURTESY OF THE STEIN COLLECTION

Sitting on the veranda with the train in the background.

owned by his wife. He began life anew in different climes, prospered again and eventually moved to Santa Barbara, where he died on January 22, 1965, at the age of 87.

Even without RN and Hearst, after the war, the Club prospered. Diablo Villa sales and construction flourished all during "the roaring '20s."

Today 643 members and 405 Diablo families are indebted to RN for his foresight and daring. In his book, RN himself claims another legacy—five children, sixteen grandchildren and their children's children.

While WWI had a devastating effect on RN and his partner William Randolph Hearst, it did not have much impact on life in Diablo or at the Club.

People naturally did their part on the Home Front "...and the Easter Party of 1918 featured an eggless egg hunt." Proceeds of Club activities like golf tournaments went to the Red Cross and "memberships in the Red Cross were awarded instead of trophies." The Diablo Post Office sold War Savings Stamps and men in uniform were given guest memberships in the Club. For Club and Community, "the war in Europe seemed very far away." (10)

After the dust had settled from RN's bankruptcy, the Club was bought by George W. McNear, the wheat king who established the first wheat docks on Carquinez Straits and founded Port Costa.(11) The Club later was sold to the members.

Like everything else after WWI, Club and Community prospered and grew. Everyone looked forward to the '20s with great expectations.

Nancie Burgess Shaw was raised in this Diablo house near the 18th fairway.

Robert Noble Burgess, III, Edward Huie Burgess and Elizabeth Ann Burgess (Cox).

His Children & Grandchildren

Fran Burgess Enright remembered that RN was away from home a lot because he had his fingers in so many pies and because he was such a tough businessman. "He'd learned the hard way—he was a driver, a man's-man, rugged, determined, self-made and proud of it, yet rubbing elbows with the barons of the business world," she said.

She mentioned he was a good father, took the children on many camping trips and that he loved to hunt, fish and ride horses. She thinks he will be remembered as an opportunist, foresighted and daring.

Nancie Burgess Shaw said that she was born in a home near the 18th hole, adding, "I don't know where RN was at the time, but I do know he was an entrepreneur of the first order and hard-headed businessman. He was into lumber, land, ranching and ship building in WWI. He had a big heart but only if you hit him in the right spot. He had many friends but just as many enemies. We loved him for the way he was."

Elizabeth Burgess Cox recalled that she was 12 and living in Diablo when he died. "I remember him as very formal yet very warm," she said. "He was especially fond of me, his favorite granddaughter." She added that, "He was a person who loved challenges and risks and never hesitated to say what he thought, but a caring person with his family and grandchildren."

Edward Huie Burgess remembered best how understanding his grandfather was. He said, "in high school I was having a lot of trouble with my family and my parents decided to separate me from brother Bob. So he got to stay at the San Rafael Military Academy and I was shipped off to the San Diego Military Academy. I hated the place and called my grandfather. He was very understanding of my problem because he'd had similar problems with his parents when he was a teen."

Lee Soulé, RN's son-in-law, remembered him as a "friendly guy" who loved to talk about his exploits and the people involved.

Lee said, "He was an environmentalist although no one used the term—interested in nature, planting trees around the Club and stocking Diablo Lake with fish. He loved quail which he raised and ate as beef-steak." He added, "RN was ambitious and far-sighted—often ahead of his times. Some of his ventures failed because his reach exceeded his grasp. The Club and Diablo are an example."

DIABLO ESTATES DEVELOPMENT

Caroline and Rod Davies met old friends Connie and Larry Ives at a birthday party in mid-1994. Caroline told their friends, "I made the most remarkable discovery in a used-book store in Stockton. I found two brochures written by RN Burgess offering homesites for sale in Diablo in 1916 and 1918." She graciously offered them for exhibit in this volumn.

By coincidence, RN's daughter Nancie Burgess Shaw was at the same party. The occasion was the 80th birthday of John Russell. Although no longer club members or Diablo residents, the Russells insisted on having the party on the vacant lot they've owned on Caballo Ranchero for the past 40 years. John said, "We wanted to be here where we had such wonderful times." A host of old neighbors turned out including Dee & Al Headstrom, Jack & Connie Hagopian, Art & Gloria Jones, Elmer & Kay Batts and Betty & Larry Curtola.

Following are excerpts from the brochures supplied by the Davies:

"Country home life in California is rapidly developing. It is due primarily to the automobile, the improvement of our highways, the extension of train service and the desire of the city dweller to take advantage of the climatic conditions which make it possible to enjoy to the fullest, the outdoor, health-giving freedom of the country.

"In the Mount Diablo Estate the man of moderate means by the purchase of a homesite obtains a proprietary right in a country estate, secures membership in a country club and enjoys all the advantages of city conveniences.

"The natural contour of the Mount Diablo properties is admirably adapted to the building of summer homes. The rugged mountain sides, the wooded ravines, the rocky promontories, the commanding grass-blanketed hills, the oak-dotted level stretches—all afford unusual opportunities to the country home seeker to build according to his fancy.

"With the prices of homesites ranging from $300 an acre according to location; with cost of building consistent with the price of property; with the acquisition of a direct interest in the entire project and with the whole mountain as a playground, the Mount Diablo Estate meets every demand of those who seek health and recreation in the possession of a country home.

"Carrying out the same idea they had in view in providing golf, tennis, boating, swimming, fishing, for the recreation of the grown-ups, the founders of the Estate have arranged fully equipped playgrounds for the children.

"At all times the care and protection of the children has been uppermost in the minds of the founders of the Estate. Careful supervision will be made of the playgrounds while the children in their pilgrimages into the precincts of the mountain will be under the watchful eyes of the rangers.

"CLUB AND INN Social life at Diablo centers about the Mount Diablo Country Club. Membership is acquired by purchase of a home site in the Estate, although a limited number of life and associate memberships are open to outsiders. The Inn, maintained by the Club, is for the convenience of the residents, club members and their guests.

"COMMUNITY FARM A novel feature is the community farm. From the vegetable gardens, model dairy and poultry yards, table delicacies will be furnished the club and the residents of the Estate. Here, too, will be kennels and stables to promote the ownership of fine stock while special care will be given the gardens, orchards and livestock during the absence of the owners.

"BENEFITS OUT OF ALL PROPORTION TO COST The cost of acreage for homesites in the Mount Diablo Estate is small compared with the benefits offered in the Country Club: in the Community Farm; in the children's playgrounds; in the privilege of owning a home where all the advantages of city and country have been brought together for your enjoyment."

MOUNT DIABLO VILLA HOMES ASSOCIATION
For further information call or write:
R. N. Burgess Company, 742 Market Street, San Francisco, Cal.
R. N. Burgess Company, Broadway at Fifteenth Street, Oakland, Cal.
Robert Marsh Company, Marsh-Strong Building, Los Angeles, Cal.

MOUNT DIABLO ESTATE
MAIN OFFICES
1302 FIRST NATIONAL BANK BUILDING
SAN FRANCISCO, CALIFORNIA
THE HOME AND THE CLUB
Miss Rosana Allurio
Box 204
Lake Linden
Houghton Co.
Mich
MOUNT DIABLO ESTATE
CONTRA COSTA COUNTY
CALIFORNIA
A community with an ideal
in the Shadow of the Purple Mountain
MOUNT DIABLO ESTATE
Diablo, California
1302 First National Bank Building, San Francisco
R. N. BURGESS COMPANY
San Francisco
ROBERT MARSH COMPANY
Los Angeles
Mount Diablo Estate

TO PICTURE the signs and symbols of the '20s, start with flappers wearing dresses above their knees, jazz bands, Prohibition, bathtub gin, speak-easys, and a wild dance called the Charleston.

See the cars of the well-to-do: 12-cylinder Packards, Pierce Arrows with headlights on their fenders and electric autos that look like horseless carriages, while Henry Ford makes it possible for the common man to own a 4-cylinder Model T.

Move to bootleg gangsters like Al Capone and Bugs Moran shooting and killing in a war over turf and end with Majong at home and Greta Garbo and John Gilbert at the movies.

Charles Lindbergh, a raw-boned kid known as "the Lone Eagle," spans the Atlantic nonstop from New York to Paris in "The Spirit of St. Louis."

Silent Cal sits in the White House saying, "The business of government is business." Rising prices and a heady prosperity culminate in the stock market crash of October 28, 1929.

In Diablo, committees from the Club govern the little community. The Club provides a dairy, a water system and community gardens. A Club committee supervises road repairs and sanitation.

These are the signs and symbols of the Roaring '20s.

Fred and Alice Thomas. COURTESY PENNY HEARN ADAMS.

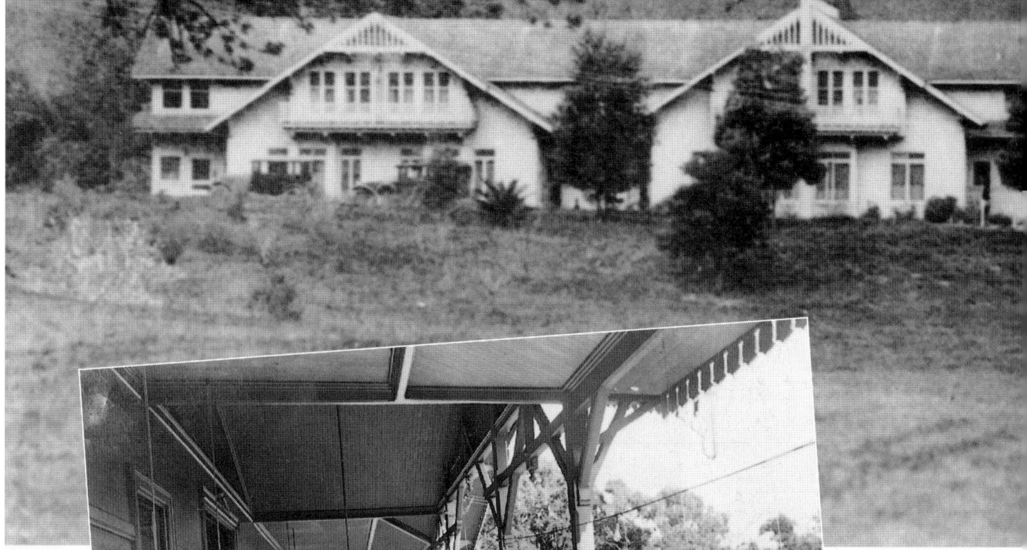

The Chalet, built in 1917.

The Club veranda was a popular spot in the summer.

Chapter III — THE ROARING TWENTIES

Interviews with long-time Diablo residents and Club members have enabled the author to draw word pictures of the '20s. Contributing their fond memories were Beth Thomas Hearn, Elizabeth Wright Freeman and her sons Leigh and Marshall, Myra Mae Hall Stapler, and Bill Thomas.

BETH THOMAS HEARN "The Club was a lively and exciting place, a rendezvous for fun and frolicking." Beth Hearn remembers the Club when she was 11 years old and seeing it for the first time in 1925. During her first Diablo summer vacation, her parents, Fred and Alice Thomas, Beth and brother Bill stayed in the Chalet. The construction of summer villas was just beginning and theirs was not built until 1929. Beth says she walked over the covered passageway from the Chalet to the Clubhouse at 1925 Alameda Diablo. She said, "I remember it was such fun dancing on the veranda. It sloped and we gravitated toward the railing."

Up the hill was the Casino, originally built as a poolhall on the Oakwood Park Stock Farm. The Casino was used as a gambling center, a place to show movies on summer evenings, quarters for staff and changing rooms for the swimmers. The same pool the Club uses today was built in 1922 and last overhauled in the '80s. On the site of the present tennis facility was a playing field for friendly scrimmages and pick-up softball. "It was so exciting," Beth recalls, "Going over the crosswalk to the Club for the wonderful food. Would you believe, breakfast, lunch and dinner was served seven days a week." Travel was long and difficult so the Club was open full time during the summer but only on weekends the rest of the year.

Riding was the favorite summer attraction and the Club maintained a stable of horses at the corner of Avenida Nueva and La Cadena. In that barn also was Diablo's first Post Office. The horses were trained for either Western or English tack and expert instruction was available from Joe Davies, the

***D**iablo's famous lake—scene of summer fun for resident teens.*

The 4th green in the '20s. COURTESY EGON PEDERSEN.

Bill Hale, Sr. plays a round with his sons. COURTESY JOHN HALE.

much loved riding master. Picnic lunches and dinners prepared by the Club chef were a regular feature of the frequent trail rides in and around Diablo or to the top of the mountain.

Beth remarked, "Mostly mothers with tiny tots used the swimming pool. Diablo Lake was the place to be for excitement." It was a man-made lake at the end of Alameda Diablo in an area known as the "160" for the 160 acres of open land owned by the Club.(1) There was a boat dock for canoes and rowboats, a boathouse to store them, a diving platform and a snack shack run by Mrs. Mason. "She was a wonderful person," said Beth, "That's where I learned to drink cokes and still do. When I was a Cal student, we often came out to the Lake for parties and to drink something besides cokes!"

"One of the most daring things we did in our teens was dam running," she said. "We'd 'borrow' our parents' cars for the evening, get a running start up Alameda Diablo and see how close to the dam we could coast. Most made it half way and would then slide back but sometimes one would make it all the way to the top. Once a car made it to the top, slipped over the dam and ended up in the lake."

The golf course was the pride of the Club and a favorite of the men. Women were permitted to play but only with their husbands. Beth recalls, "My father and mother played regularly on Sunday. My father described the course to friends as 'rugged'. Getting and keeping qualified help was difficult and water was always in short supply."

Drought was not the problem, it was the unreliability of the Club's water system which consisted of Mt. Diablo springs and Diablo Lake. "As a matter of fact," Beth said, "besides the Lake, there were several smaller lakes and a couple of storage tanks—enough water in a normal year for the Clubhouse, Chalet, Casino, pool, tees and greens, and summer homes, but not much more.

"The course was mostly new mown hay, and the adobe soil had such wide cracks that whenever a ball landed in one, it was a goner." This was the situation until the Diablo Water Company was annexed to EBMUD in 1958.

The increasing number of summer homes being built was also dependent on the Club's water system and owners were alloted whatever surplus accrued in wet years. A few homes were used year-round and that placed an additional burden on the water system. Beth recalled, "Often, we had summer days with no water. There were two water lines per household: one for inside water—OK to drink but with a sour smell toward the end of summer—and another for outside watering. It was often thick with bugs and leaves, ideal for the garden but not for the lawn."

When Beth's parents' summer home was under construction in 1929 at 2043 Calle Los Calledos, she remembered a group of kids walking to Diablo Lake, saying as they passed, "'The Club is building a new stable; this must be it.' I was so embarrassed!"

Beth recalled the Fourth of July with delight. The celebration was held on the 5th tee where there was space for fireworks. Another big day was Easter Sunday when the egg hunt was held much as it is today but with one major difference. Before the hunt started, 50-100 baby rabbits were turned loose at the top of the hill on the 1st fairway and the children chased them until they were captured.(2) "I always got one," Beth said. Most of the rabbits soon died or disappeared. Beth named one of her catches Penelope and it survived as a treasured pet. The Hearns had a baby girl in 1944 and named her Penelope!

As time went on, the rabbits were replaced by baby ducks until the practice was abandoned in the '50s. Beth recalled that it rained one Easter and the bunny hunt was held in the clubhouse. "There we were, all of us, chasing 50 or so bunnies from room to room. Better they had called it off. That was the last of the bunnies at Easter time."

Beth said she loved Saturdays, particularly the summer parties and dances at the Club, but she really hated Sundays. She said, "My parents always made my brother and me stay home because Sunday was a big party day for the grown-ups and there was a lot of drinking in the privacy of peoples' homes because of Prohibition. Our parents didn't want us to know they drank illegally. The usual adult parties took place at the Club, private and hush-hush again because of Prohibition." Apparently, the Saturday Club parties were such dry affairs, parents couldn't wait for Sunday. "In those days," Beth continues, "my father drove a red Buick touring car. I remember, too, the time my mother got a brand new Hupmobile. She polished and shined it every day."

Beth especially remembered the summer of 1928 because Herbert Hoover, a candidate for President of the United States, came to Diablo. A reception was given for him by the Women's Republican Club at the Dolges' home, 2166 Alameda Diablo. Fred and Alice Thomas attended the afternoon reception accompanied by their high school freshman daughter, Beth. She remembered, "It was very informal, no speeches, just chit-chat with small groups of people asking questions." Beth's younger brother Bill doesn't remember this incident. He said, "I was apolitical at the time—just nine-years old!"

ELIZABETH WRIGHT FREEMAN Her parents, Maynard and Charlotte Wright, joined the Club in 1925 when she was a teen-ager. Elizabeth later became the mother of present residents

John Hale at the Diablo pool as pictured on the cover of the Oakland Tribune's Sunday Supplement. COURTESY JOHN HALE.

William Freeman holds his sons, Leigh (L) and Marshall (R). COURTESY ELIZABETH FREEMAN.

Fred Thomas with his children, Beth and Bill. COURTESY PENNY HEARN ADAMS.

and members Leigh and Marshall Freeman. But in the '20s, the family stayed in the Chalet and traversed the bridge over the creek to the clubhouse for their meals. Elizabeth commented, "The Chalet's rooms were very comfortable but the place was noisy whenever the furnace came on." There was a large steam furnace in the basement which only Cecil Ryder, the Club's maintenance man, knew how to operate.(3)

The dining room was in the center of the Clubhouse overlooking a side garden. The lounge was center front with a large screened porch wrapped around the front of the building. There was a tap room on the ground floor at the back and to the right of the stairs that led to the second floor and the bridge. Elizabeth remembered fondly the spring/summer Saturday night dances. "Bill Freeman would come up from Stanford and we'd dance the night away on the veranda."(4)

When asked about the drive from Piedmont to Diablo, she replied, "It was horrendous. Foremost was getting up to and through the old tunnel.(5) The drive was a tortuous one up high to a dark cavern with water dripping from the roof. Once through it, there was a quick drop into Orinda—just a crossroads really, as were Lafayette, Walnut Creek, and Danville. The road was just wide enough for one car in each direction, and had no shoulders. As we drove into Diablo, there were a half dozen summer homes on the main road, mostly owned by Piedmont people."

Elizabeth also remembered coming to Diablo by train. "That was really fun," she said. We always brought a picnic basket, and with the windows open and the wind in our hair, relaxed on the wicker seats. (The Diablo train began in March, 1914 and operated for the next ten years.)(6) My father and his friends were golfers. Dad played on Saturdays and would return to the Chalet complaining about how many balls he'd lost in the wide chasms on the fairway because the Club was always in a water crisis. My friends and I did a lot of hiking up the mountain. We swam a lot, and rode horses occasionally. The in crowd was at Diablo Lake and drinking was confined to people's homes."

MYRA MAE HALL STAPLER "Mike" as she was called, was six in 1924 when her parents, Herb and Susan Hall began summering in Diablo. Their home started as a garage which belonged to the Club and was on a four-acre plot when they bought it. The garage became their living room and they added a kitchen and a bedroom. There were two couches in the living room where Mike and her brother George slept while their parents had the bedroom. Later they built a tenthouse for Mike. "It was my very own," she remembered fondly. Mike commented, "From then on, every time my parents built a shed to store firewood, it turned into a bedroom. First a second one, then a third, and so, like Topsey, the house grew."

Mike's eyes became misty when she talked about the old clubhouse. "It was a beautiful old ranch-house with a spacious dining room overlooking a beautiful garden. I loved eating in such an atmosphere and I remember attending wonderful parties there. The tap room in the back was paneled in dark polished wood—very British—and had an elegant smell. The whole place was very Victorian. People visited in the tap room. Because of Prohibition they drank in their homes."

In 1926 the Hall's tennis court was built. Herb and Susan loved to play and the court was the center of the family's social life.

Mike's best friend was Shirley Okell. Shirley liked to do the same things Mike liked—all nongirl activities. Their favorite was to take their dogs and tramp the hills looking for dead things. "I know that sounds terrible," said Mike with a chuckle, "but that's the way it was. When we found something dead, and we always did, we'd bury it." Both sets of parents were undone. They wanted their daughters to be nice little girls and do nice little girl things and so invited their Berkeley school chums to visit. Mike said, "Our school mates didn't like to do what Shirley and I did, so we'd go off together and our parents would be stuck entertaining them. We *were* weird."

By 1929 the Club's stables were in their prime and Mike rode and rode and rode. When she wasn't riding, she was grooming, feeding, cleaning, listening to horse talk, and loving every minute of it. Mike wanted a horse but didn't get one until she was in college. By then she was showing horses.

When she was 20, the Abbott family was next door at 1752 Club House Road. They had a son named Sam who rowed for Cal but was out for a while with a collapsed lung and confined to the family summer home in Diablo. Mike's aunt took one look at Sam and decided he was for Mike. But she had to figure out how to bring this about. The World's Fair was at Treasure Island and Mike was entered in the horse show. Her aunt arranged for Sam and his parents to attend. Mike commented, "It was love at first sight. We were married within the year and four children and two Arabian horses later, we moved to Diablo," (1750 Alameda Diablo).

BILL THOMAS He was nine-years old when his family moved into their new summer villa. In previous summers the Thomases had stayed in the Chalet. His father, a San Francisco attorney, rode the train to and from the City. He said, "The 'station' was only a block from our house and it was

"Mike" Hall in a typical clowning pose on the shoulders of fiancee, Sam Abbott.
Courtesy Myra Mae Hall Stapler.

Mike and Sam Abbott engaged to be married.
Courtesy Myra Mae Hall Stapler.

special to watch the train roll in and roll out." But like Beth and Elizabeth, Bill commented, "Even more special than that was the clubhouse."

"The largest room in this beautiful old former farmhouse was the dining room which faced east and a lovely garden," said Bill. There was space for 15-20 tables. At the back of the building, next to the tap room, was a small porch where the Club served snacks throughout the day. "One of my favorite places," he recalled. "Another favorite spot was the wide veranda along the south (front) of the clubhouse and continuing around the west side. It was covered with blue wisteria and had comfortable Victorian wicker furniture. In the heat of the summer it was always shady and cool." Jock Whitney, a Scotsman, taught Bill how to play golf. He took lessons near the 18th hole, carrying his bag of wooden clubs to and from home.

Bill pointed out that swimming pools then didn't have filters as do modern pools. They had to be drained to be kept sanitary. "Every Monday they drained it, scrubbed the sides and bottom with brushes and mops, then refilled it. By Tuesday the water was clear and cold. A week later when it was warm—and smelly—they drained it again."

Gambling was popular for men at the Casino and children weren't allowed there except on Saturday nights for movies. "It started with a Krazy Kat or Bugs Bunny cartoon, followed by the main feature film with stars like Harold Lloyd and Charley Chaplin. While supposedly this was for kids, it attracted enough adults for standing room only," he recalled. "In the daytime, when the men were elsewhere, we kids loved to take a short cut to the pool by racing through the Casino and out the back door, slapping our feet on the wooden floor to make as much noise as possible."

Another fond memory of the '20s for Bill was the summer evening hayrides to Blackhawk. "This was for kids only, seven years up to teens. We boarded the wagon at the old barn when it was still light but beginning to cool down and off we'd go." Two hours later the riders were back at the stables as it began to get dark. The day after this conversation, the author called Bill to check a detail and when Bill was asked, "Anything else?" he said, "No, but I had nightmares all night about Diablo!"

Bill remembered Randy and Teller Weinmann who lived in a two-story home at 2276 Alameda Diablo and the carnivals the boys put on for all the kids. "They'd spend days making fun things for us to do like a sled ride down a grassy hill, and things to hit and targets to throw at, all for a nickle or dime a turn." The Club too had games for the children. Bill particularly remembered a driving contest held on the 5th tee. "I won the Juniors," he said, "with a 205-yard drive. Wish I could do that now!"

Bill continued, "I know everyone's told you about the horseback riding and swimming and partying at the Lake, but did anyone mention the fishing?" "Well," said Bill, "This was truly the greatest for any nine-year old boy. I discovered one place across from the beach and near the boathouse where they stored the canoes and rowboats. It was the best fishing spot and I had a ball catching sunfish. I'd clean them and eat them later." Children, both boys and girls, are still having their "greatest" at Diablo Lake. See page 208.

CLUB ROSTER Look at the 1928 Roster of Members of the Club. It lists the names of 396 men, 48 of whom own Diablo residences and another 16 who own lots. Of the 396, 113 live in Berkeley, 101 Oakland, 73 Piedmont, 31 San Francisco, and the remaining 78 are scattered among the cities of Martinez, Alamo, Los Angeles, Hollywood, Stockton, San Leandro, Antioch, Fresno, Walnut Creek, Hayward, Suisun, Pittsburg, Summit, New Jersey, and Portland, Oregon. Six are listed as permanent residents of Diablo. They are:

William Dolge at 2166 Alameda Diablo

William Hale, Sr. at 1830 Alameda Diablo

Charles Elliot at 1740 Club House Road

George McNear (6 lots on Calle Arroyo facing the 18th fairway)

Dr. Charles Morey at 2139 Alameda Diablo

Bernard Ransome (12 lots on Calle Arroyo facing the 17th fairway)

(See map on inside covers)

Arriving at the club house by train.

Victorian wicker furniture in 1920s Casino.

The Hearns' Hupmobile. COURTESY PENNY HEARN ADAMS.

Car of the day.

COURTESY JOHN HALE.

DIABLO: 1923

The Mount Diablo Country Club with its unrivaled climate and surroundings, has under construction an entirely new 18-hole golf course which is nearing completion under the supervision of William Watson, the famous California architect.

Several of the new greens are now in use and reflect Watson's work at its best. The course will be of championship length but not too strenuous for the average player. The trappings of the greens vary according to the length of the holes, no two of which are alike.

The water problem, which has given the Club management much trouble in the past, is now likely to be solved and green fairways will soon be an accomplished fact. Macadamized roads over the entire route from Oakland have made weekend trips to this ideal country club easy as the journey can be made in less than one hour.

E. L. Cooper as Club Manager has been instrumental in making the Club attractive to members and their families. Claremont and Sequoyah golfers are enthusiastic supporters of the Diablo Club where their families can have unlimited scope to enjoy themselves without restriction. Open-air swimming, pony riding, tennis and croquet are some of the added attractions to the golf course. One is tempted to slice and hook on the 17th fairway as fruit trees with an abundant crop of apples, pears and grapes would otherwise be overlooked.

Frank A. Leach, the famous California naturalist, keeps a strict watch on the movements of the hundreds of rare birds that make for Diablo at certain periods of the year. Frank, now 80 years young, never fails to play at least 9 holes a day. It is no unusual occurrence for three generations of the Leach family to win prizes in the same tournament. Abe Leach, Jr. has a handicap of 12, Abe a 20, while Frank himself can make the game interesting with the assistance of a 27 handicap.(7)

MEMBERS OWNING HOMES AT DIABLO*

George W. Banzhaf	Walter P. Frick	Dr. Charles L. Morey
M. S. Barnett	G. Monroe Greenwood	Henry D. Nichols
W. H. Berg	William M. Hale	Mrs. William Letts Oliver
V. E. Breeden	Herbert E. Hall	Jack Okell
George C. Browne	J. B. Havre	Robert D. Pike
Mrs. W. R. L. Campbell	Stuart S. Hawley	W. W. Potter
Henry C. Carlisle	Herbert Gray Hills	Roy L. Pratt
George R. Chambers	A. F. Hockenbearner	Hubert G. Prost
A. J. Coogan	E. Clarence Holmes	K. B. Putnam
E. L. Cooper	Mrs. George C. Jensen	Mrs. Richard E. Queen
Charles P. Cutten	Mrs. Ernest A. Kahl	Bernard Ransome
W. S. Dinwiddie	J. B. Keister	Ellwood H. Smith
William Dolge	Mrs. C. M. Landers	F. E. Stone
N. B. Douglass	Abe P. Leach	F. F. Thomas, Jr.
A. C. Elkinton	Frank A. Leach, Jr.	Andrew Thorne
Charles Elliott	A. M. Lester	Dr. May E. Walker
Milton T. Farmer	Irving C. Lewis	L. R. Weinmann
Dr. J. R. Fearn	George W. McNear	Fred L. Wolfe

In addition to the foregoing there are ten lot owners contemplating construction of homes.

**A private unincorporated village, located three miles east of Danville, Contra Costa County, California. United States Post Office under the name "Diablo" is maintained. Full telephone, water, gas and electric service.*

John Poulos, Club member since 1978, lent Larry Ives* The Green Book of Golf, *a 1923 publication willed to John by his father-in-law. It contains articles about outstanding golfers and country clubs of California. Herewith is what they said about us in the '20s.

In a 1931 history of the Mt. Diablo Country Club, E.D. Eddy provided a calendar of events for the '20s:

JANUARY A quiet month at Diablo. The Inn remains open, meals are served at regular hours, and all facilities are available to members. Weather permitting, nice days and weekends find many playing the course.

FEBRUARY Invitational Day Sweepstake. Lincoln's Birthday. Valentine Dinner and Dance. Match Play Against Par. Ladies' Invitational Day. Washington's Birthday. 36-Hole Medal Play Sweepstakes. Selective Nine and Low Putts on 18 Holes. Home and Home Tournament.

MARCH Home and Home Tournament. Best Scores for Odd and Even Holes. Best Putting Scores. Ladies' Invitational Day. Home and Home Tournament. St. Patrick's Day Dinner and Dance. Open Day. Medal Play. Monthly Cup Tournament. Open Day. Home and Home Tournament.

APRIL Garden Club Luncheon. Annual Meeting. Dinner Dance. Easter Sunday-Children's Festivities, Rabbit Chase and Easter Egg Hunt. 18-Hole Medal Play Sweepstakes. "Grass Tee and Water" Tournament. Dinner Dance. Women's Medal Play Sweepstakes. Ladies' Open Day-Tournament, Dinner and Bridge. 18-Hole Medal Play Sweepstakes. Invitational Day. Kicker Tournament. Medal Play and Putts. Open Day. Cup Tournament. Home and Home Tournament. Open Day.

MAY Qualifying Round, Club Championship. Medal Play; Gross Score. Mixed Two-Ball Foursome. Club Championship for Women. Tournament and Dinner Dance. First Round, Club Championship. Memorial Day Dinner Dance. Second and Third Rounds, Club Championship. Final Round, Club Championship. Dinner Dance.

JUNE Horses available. 18 Hole Medal Play Sweepstakes. Four Dinner Dances. Six Evenings of Movies for the Children. Qualifying Round, Fourth of July Tournament. Mixed Two-Ball Foursome. First Round, Fourth of July Tournament. Something doing continuously.

JULY Club's Annual Garden Frolic. Four Dinner Dances. Nine Evenings of Movies for the Children. Second Round, Fourth of July Tournament. Fourth of July Celebration: Third and Final Rounds, Fourth of July Tournament; Driving, Approaching and Putting Contests; Swimming Races and Competitive Diving at the Lake; Other Sports. Mixed Two-Ball Foursomes, Rodeo and Horse Show. 18-Hole Match Play Sweepstakes. First Round, Spring-Fall Tournament.

AUGUST Five Dinner Dances. Three Evenings of Movies for the Children. Second and Final Rounds, Spring-Fall Tournament. Qualifying Round, Directors' Cup. Mixed Two-Ball Foursome. First Round, Directors' Cup.

SEPTEMBER Three Dinner Dances. Club Garden Luncheon. La Salle Trophy Tournament. Swimming Events at the Lake. Second Round, Directors' Cup Tournament. Labor Day. Invitational Day. Admission Day. Third and Final Round, Directors' Cup Tournament. Ladies' Invitational. Qualifying Round, Club Championship. 3 Days Match Play. Handicap vs. Par Tournament. Nine "If" Tournament. Second Round, La Salle Trophy.

OCTOBER Invitational Day Sweepstakes. Coon Hunt. Columbus Day. Mixed Two-Ball Foursomes. Women's Golf Tournament (4 days). Hallowe'en Dinner Dance.

NOVEMBER In November the season tapers off as to general club activities, though the week-ends, weather permitting, bring out many members. Armistice Day, Big Game Day with its Dinner Dance, and the famous Diablo Thanksgiving Dinner provide much entertainment.

DECEMBER The holiday spirit burns bright at Diablo during December. A wonderful Christmas Dinner, and a Christmas Tree make December 25th a big day—and the year winds up with a gay and happy New Year's Eve Party.

The proud winner of an Easter bunny.
COURTESY JOHN HALE.

ROSTER OF MEMBERS

Mt. Diablo Country Club

August 30th, 1928

*Lot Owners †Residence

Adams, Arthur C. 634 Oakland Ave., Oakland
Agnew, Albert C. 1106 Bay St., Alameda
Aitken, Alfred C. 53 Domingo Ave., Berkeley
Alexander, Miss M. E. 361 Warwick St., Oakland
Alexander, R. A. 207 Bonita Ave., Piedmont
Anderson, John R. 1550 Oakland Ave., Piedmont
Arnstein, Walter 2211 Washington St., San Francisco
*Ayer, Richard B. (estate) 246 Sea View Ave., Piedmont
Atkinson, Douglass Gordon 76 Eucalyptus Road, Berkeley

Bain, Chas. R. 228 Sea View Ave., Piedmont
Ball, Frank M. 1205 Ashmount Ave., Oakland
*Banzhaf, George W. 213 Hillside Ave., Piedmont
†Barnett, M. S. 658 Colusa Ave., Berkeley
Barry, F. M. 1616 San Antonio Ave., Alameda
Barry, G. C. 815 Paru St., Alameda
Bauer, Lewis F. 319 Blair Ave., Piedmont
Baum, Frank G. 2610 Piedmont Ave., Berkeley
Baumgartner, Mrs. A. C. 280 Lenox Ave., Oakland
Behr, Walter G. L. 506 Park Way Ave., Piedmont
Bennett, J. A. Walnut Creek, California
†Berg, William H. 6225 Harwood Ave., Oakland
Berryhill, James G. 2737 Claremont Blvd., Berkeley
Betts, Mrs. E. E. 182 Alvarado Road, Berkeley
Blackaller, J. T. 68 Lincoln Ave., Piedmont
Borton, E. C. 1007 Morton St., Alameda
Brace, Burton B. 730 Central Ave., Alameda
Brandenburg, Chas. A. 5428 Thomas St., Oakland
Bray, A. F. Martinez, California
†Breeden, V. E. 326 Vernon St., Oakland
Breuner, Louis J. 4 Craig Ave., Piedmont
Bronson, Roy 11 Montecello Ave., Piedmont
Brown, Bradley B. 1112 The Alameda, Berkeley
Brown, Miss Florinne 1889 Jackson St., Oakland
†Browne, George C. Diablo, California
Bruer, Ernest A. 1710 Vallejo St., San Francisco
Bryant, Frank D. 381 Belmont St., Oakland
Buck, Frank H. 85 Second St., San Francisco
Bumsted, E. B. 241 The Uplands, Berkeley
Burnham, Fred K. Spring Hill Farm, Martinez, Calif.
Burns, John D. 5801 Chabot Court, Oakland
Beebe, Ambrose M. 438 Hanover St., Oakland

Cadman, Chas. M. 1315 Dayton Ave., Alameda
Cadwalader, Richard B. 82 Eucalyptus Road, Berkeley
†Campbell, Mrs. W. R. L. 2815 Claremont Blvd., Berkeley
Carlston, Joseph F. Germanium & Redwood Rds., Oakland
†Carlisle, Henry C. 2766 Green St., San Francisco
Carpenter, Dr. Frank L. 1874 Yosemite Road, Berkeley
Carter, Charles W. 767 Calmar Ave., Oakland
Cavalier, William 401 Hampton Road, Piedmont
†Chambers, George R. Hotel Claremont, Berkeley
Clark, Herbert W. 2915 Piedmont Ave., Berkeley
Coates, Alfred H. 31 Alvarado Road, Berkeley
Coit, Roger 1435 Harrison St., Oakland
Colby, William E. 2901 Channing Way, Berkeley
Collbran, A. H. 2904 Avalon Ave., Berkeley
Connolly, R. E. 118 Parkside Drive, Berkeley
Coogan, A. J. 891 Union Ave., Alameda
*Coons, Robert B. 3100 College Ave., Berkeley
†Cooper, Edwin Lee Diablo, California
Corder, Arthur E. 350 Lenox Ave., Oakland
*Corlett, Will G. 754 Mandana Blvd., Oakland
*Cory, Clarence L. 2438 Warring St., Berkeley
Creed, Mrs. W. E. 128 Indian Road, Piedmont
Crellin, Thomas A. Central Savings Bank, Oakland
Cutten, Charles P. 230 Euclid Ave., San Francisco
Cutting, Frederick P. Hotel Oakland, Oakland

*Dargie, Thomas M. 865 Rosemount Road, Oakland
Davis, Roy V. 712 F St., Antioch
Davis, S. A. 2218 Piedmont Ave., Berkeley
DeGolyer, J. B. Hotel Claremont, Berkeley
Dennis, A. R. 175 Commonwealth Ave., San Francisco
Derleth, Prof. Chas. 2834 Webster St., Berkeley
Devlin, Frank R. 2945 Ashby Ave., Berkeley
Dickey, Charles H. Fairmont Hotel, San Francisco
Dieckmann, Miss J. V. 1076 60th St., Oakland
Dinsmore, George B. 312 California St., San Francisco
†Dinwiddie, W. S. 2815 Oak Knoll Ave., Berkeley
Dinwiddie, G. C. 44 Oakvale Ave., Berkeley
Dodge, Chas. S. 2828 Claremont Ave., Berkeley
†Dolge, William Diablo, California
*Donovan, John J. 1166 Clarendon Crescent, Oakland
Dollar, R. Stanley 1099 Ardmore Ave., Oakland
†Douglass, N. B. 28 Domingo Ave., Berkeley
Doyle, Dr. Guy P. 41 El Camino Real, Berkeley
Dugand, J. V. 5 Buena Vista Terrace, San Francisco
Dukes, Dr. Chas. A. 211 The Uplands, Berkeley
Duncan, Robert 159 Hillcrest Road, Berkeley
Durney, Harold J. 1101 Grand St., Alameda

Eby, John D. 259 Perry St., Oakland
Eichelberger, Kirk W. 124 Parkside Drive, Berkeley
†Elkinton, Alfred C. 934 Arlington Ave., Berkeley
†Elliott, Charles Diablo, California

Ellsworth, Oliver	145 Hillside Ave., Piedmont
*Eschen, James N.	1137 Bay St., Alameda
Evans, Perry	2727 Benvenue Ave., Berkeley
Farmer, Milton T.	203 Hillcrest Road, Berkeley
Faye, Hans P.	3122 Claremont Ave., Berkeley
Ferguson, Mrs. Jessie R.	2924 Russell St., Oakland
Field, Edward B.	301 Pala Ave., Piedmont
Fitzgerald, Robert M.	456 Van Buren Ave., Oakland
Fitzpatrick, Dr. E. B.	1504 Pine St., Martinez
Foote, D. H.	Whitcomb Hotel, San Francisco
Force, Harold W.	5902 Taft Ave., Oakland
Freeman, Simeon S.	1049 San Antonio Ave., Alameda
Frisselle, Ralph D.	3036 College Ave., Berkeley
Frost, Francis D. Jr.	101 Plaza Drive, Berkeley
†Frick, Walter P.	Stanford Court Apts., San Francisco
†Fearn, Dr. J. R.	384 Bellevue Ave., Oakland
Gaylord, E.G.	727 The Alameda, Berkeley
Galbraith, Dr. Alexander	781 Highland Ave., Piedmont
Gester, G. C.	2725 Claremont Blvd., Berkeley
Gibson, Miss Maud M.	Route 1, Box 105, Hayward, Calif.
Glenn, R. W.	1658 Grand Ave., Piedmont
Gompertz, Chas. W.	Claremont Manor, Oakland
Greenwood, G. D.	340 Hampton Road, Piedmont
†Greenwood, G. Munroe	1120 Ashmount Ave., Oakland
Griffiths, Farnham P.	1401 LeRoy Ave., Berkeley
Haas, George W.	775 Market St., San Francisco
Hale, Wm. A.	1345 Arch St., Berkeley
†Hale, Wm. M.	Diablo, California
†Hall, Herbert E.	647 King Ave., Piedmont
†Hall, J. C.	6356 Floris Ave., Oakland and Diablo
Hall, James E.	720 Paru St., Alameda
Hamilton, J. Telford	1840 Thousand Oak Blvd., Berkeley
Hammond, F. W.	2030 16th Ave., San Francisco
Handy, Ralph H.	332 Pine St., San Francisco
Higson, J. Wayne	312 Sea View Ave., Piedmont
Harper, Horatio T.	2250 Hyde St., San Francisco
Harrier, Lewis G.	6457 Benvenue Ave., Oakland
Harrington, Frederick L.	108 Hillside Ave., Piedmont
Harris, Thomas W.	2943 Elmwood Court, Berkeley
†Hassler, John F.	Diablo, California
Hasslet, Samuel M. Jr.	171 Santa Rosa Ave., Oakland
Hatch, H. A.	78 Fairview Ave., Piedmont
Havens, Wickham	1236 Ashmount Ave., Oakland
Haviside, John	Concord, California
†Havre, Jean B.	2909 Avalon Road, Berkeley
Havre, Harold J.	100 Woodland Road, Piedmont
Hawley, J. V.	45 Bonita Ave., Piedmont
†Hawley, Stuart S.	244 Derby St., Berkeley
Hays, William C.	2924 Derby St., Berkeley
Heeseman, Charles J.	70 Sea View Ave., Piedmont
Henes, Louis G.	749 Oakland Ave., Oakland
Henshaw, Stuart	149 LaSalle Ave., Piedmont
Henszey, Wm. H.	1012 Bartlett Bldg., 215 W. 7th St., L.A
*Hargear, Frank F.	2928 Derby St., Berkeley
Hills, Herbert Grey	420 Wildwood Ave., Piedmont
Hills, Reuben W. Jr.	90 Sea Cliff, San Francisco
Hindes, Barrett G.	1110 Filbert St., San Francisco
Hiscox, Richard A.	81 Plaza Drive, Berkeley
†Hockenbeamer, A. F.	763 Arlington Ave., Berkeley
Holden, P. T.	1001 Sunnyhills Road, Oakland
Holmes, Halliday B.	1072 Clarendon Crescent, Oakland
Honeywell, Chas. F.	350 Hillside Ave., Piedmount
Honeywell, Frank	2810 Oak Knoll Terrace, Berkeley
Houghton, Edward T.	2801 Claremont Blvd., Berkeley
Hull, Perry M.	Pittsburg, California
Hume, Mrs. S. J.	1849 Arch St., Berkeley
Hunt, H. E.	2 The Uplands, Berkeley
Hutchinson, Chas. T.	Hotel Oakland, Oakland
Hutchinson, Dwight	Alamo, Contra Costa Co., Calif.
*Hutchinson, Ely C.	633 Santa Rey Ave., Oakland
Hutchinson, James S.	1235 Bonita Ave., Piedmont
Hynes, W. H. L.	30 Crocker Ave., Piedmont
Irvine, James	820 Crocker Building, San Francisco
*Jackson, Henry E.	1121 Mandana Blvd., Oakland
*Jackson, Henry K.	King and Hampton Rds., Piedmont
Jackson, Samuel	400 Orange St., Oakland
Jenks, James S.	567 Oakland Ave., Oakland
†Jenzen, Mrs. Geo. C.	37 Bellevue Ave., Oakland
John, Jenkin B.	166 Santa Rosa Ave., Oakland
Johnson, Augustus	1101 Bay View Ave. Oakland
Johnson, Dr. Frank D.	3940 Harrison St., Oakland
Johnston, Erskine B.	84 Eucalyptus Road, Berkeley
Jongeneel, Albert H.	195 The Uplands, Berkeley
Joost, M. W.	Martinez, California
Jorgensen, Christian	444 Mountain Ave., Piedmont
†Kahl, Mrs. E. A.	1275 Caroline St., Alameda
Keane, Augustin C.	1005 Morton St., Alameda
Keeney, Mrs. Florence H.	38 Crocker Ave., Piedmont
Kehrlein, Oliver	431 Wildwood Gardens, Piedmont
†Keister, James B.	929 Arlington Ave., Berkeley
Keller, George P.	1152 Green St., Martinez
Knowles, Harry J.	245 Lee St., Oakland
Knox, Mrs. Charles E.	Cloyne Court, Berkeley
Krom, LeRoy	724 Talbert St., Martinez
Krusi, LeRoy F.	Standard Oil Bldg., Stockton
Kelly, Harold R.	Danville, California
Lamberton, C. H.	433 California St., San Francisco
†Landers, Mrs. Carrie M.	640 Sutter St., San Francisco
†Leach, Abe P.	794 Highland Ave., Piedmont
†Leach, Frank A. Jr.	125 Hillside Ave., Piedmont
Leach, Frank A.	Diablo, California

†Lester, Albert M.	2836 Ashby Ave., Berkeley
†Lewis, Irving C.	313 Henshaw Bldg., Oakland
Lipmann, Frederick L.	Wells Fargo & Union Trust Co., S F
Lochead, James K.	724 Larkspur Road, Oakland
Lohse, Dr. John L.	322 Monte Vista Ave., Oakland
Lombardi, M. E.	18 Roble Court, Berkeley
Longaker, Harold R.	2917 Garber St., Berkeley
Longwill, W. B.	Olympic Club, San Francisco
Loomis, Dr. Frederick L.	1101 Ashmount Ave., Piedmont
Lorber, Hugo M.	186 Hillcrest Road, Berkeley
Lovell, Howell	865 Sunnyhills Road, Oakland
Lundborg, Irving	3837 Harrison St., Oakland
Lyon, Harvery B.	306 Sheridan Ave., Piedmont
Latham, A. C.	6 Sotelo Ave., Piedmont
Latham, Geo. H.	544 Merritt Ave., Oakland
Lion, Edgar H.	810 Paru St., Alameda
†Macaulay, Henry C.	1700 Spruce St., Berkeley
MacConaughey, Harry E.	2015 Central Ave., Alameda
Maltby, Mrs. Eleanor B.	Concord, California
Markell, L. R.	2950 Claremont Blvd., Berkeley
Martin, Kenneth C.	1 Ray Building, Oakland
Mathews, John A.	55 Lincoln Ave., Piedmont
Mattern, George A.	100 Tunnel Road, Berkeley
Matthew, Allan P.	705 The Alameda, Berkeley
Maxfield, Henry U.	204 Perry St., Oakland
*Maxwell, John P.	285 Lee St., Oakland
Meek, Dr. Rodolph W.	436 Bellevue Ave., Oakland
Meese, Constant	240 Stockton St., San Francisco
Mehrmann, Dr. Henry B.	3211 Grove St., Oakland
Melvin, Mrs. Henry A.	2305 Scott St., San Francisco
Mendenhall, Ernest D.	309 Mountain Ave., Piedmont
Merrill, Chas. W.	121 Second St., San Francisco
Merritt, Ralph P.	3815 Huntington Blvd., Fresno, Calif.
Meyer, Geo. H. C.	22 22nd Ave., San Francisco
*Miles, William E.	Box 81, Walnut Creek, California

Miller, Mrs. Elinor C.	28 Hillcrest Road, Berkeley
Milligan, R. S.	304 Pala Ave., Piedmont
Milwain, Wm. E.	1503 Oakland Ave., Piedmont
Moore, A. W.	415 Pacific Ave., Piedmont
*Moore, J. George	405 Montgomery St., San Francisco
Moore, Ralph H.	1800 Arch St., Berkeley
†Morey, Dr. Chas. L.	Diablo, California
Morrison, J. B.	1700 Russ Building, San Francisco
Moseley, Edward L.	132 Hillside Ave., Piedmont
Mosher, Harry A.	421 Staten Ave., Oakland
Muhlner, Frederick P.	3823 Harrison St., Oakland
Murray, William W.	2918 B. Regent St., Berkeley
Musser, Mrs. Francis R.	262 Vernon St., Oakland
Myers, Ralph W.	3215 Claremont Ave., Berkeley
Mattei, A. C.	1233 California St., San Francisco
McCann, Warner	2524 Warring St., Berkeley
*McClure, Malcolm E.	413 Ray Building, Oakland
McDonald, Paul	830 58th St., Oakland
McLaughlin, W. I.	115 Montecello Ave., Piedmont
McLean, A. C. Jr.	1449 Alice St., Oakland
†McNear, George W	Diablo, California
McPherson, J. C.	1514 Alice St., Oakland
†Nichols, Henry Drew	40 Lincoln Ave., Oakland
Nichols, Herman D.	27 King Ave., Piedmont
Noble, Mark	250 LaSalle Ave., Piedmont
Norris, Lucius G.	2023 Oakland Ave., Piedmont
Nourse, B. E.	1100 Paru St., Alameda
Newell, Paul	1110 The Alameda, Berkeley
†O'Connor, Dr. Roderic	Diablo, California
*Okell, Jack	1087 Ashmount Ave., Oakland
Oliver, A. Leslie	268 Vernon St., Oakland
Oliver, Edwin Letts	60 King Ave., Piedmont
Oliver, William H.	417 Madison St., Oakland
†Oliver, Mrs. William Letts	257 Vernon St., Oakland

Olney, Warren Jr.	2737 Belrose Ave., Berkeley
Orrick, Oliver S.	357 Vernon St., Oakland
Osborn, J. Lyle	1124 Clarendon Crescent, Oakland
Otto, Alfred P.	125 Guilford Road, Piedmont
Pangburn, C. W.	Alamo, California
Parrish, Edwin	2842 Ashby Ave., Berkeley
Parrish, Earl T.	1851 Yosemite Road, Berkeley
Parrish, Geo. M.	900 Contra Costa Road, Berkeley
Pattiani, William L.	55 Craig Ave., Piedmont
Pedersen, Mrs. Kate G.	125 Hillcrest Road, Berkeley
Pillsbury, Albert F.	351 California St., San Francisco
Pillsbury, John T.	1775 Broadway, Oakland
Pope, Frank W.	1959 Napa St., Berkeley
Porter, Ernest D.	342 Sheridan Ave., Piedmont
†Potter, W. W.	17 Hillside Ave., Piedmont
Powell, Stanley	3132 Jackson St., San Francisco
†Pratt, Roy L.	2732 Claremont Blvd., Berkeley
Probasco, Ramsey	2728 Haste St., Berkeley
†Prost, Hubert G.	2729 Belrose Ave., Berkeley
Putnam, C. M.	880 Trestle Glenn Road, Oakland
†Putnam, Kingman B.	Diablo, California
Ponting, A. E.	1019 Hubert Road, Oakland
†Queen, Mrs. Richard E.	1980 Washington St., SF
Rand, George H.	3756 Sacramento St., San Francisco
†Ransome, Bernard	Diablo, California
Ransome, Ernest L.	c/o Matson Navigation Co., Oakland
Ransome, Miss Marion	End of Hazel Lane, Piedmont
Ransome, Tallent	Stanford Court Apts., San Francisco
Reed, Ben W.	200 Crocker Ave., Piedmont
Reese, Mrs. Florence G.	20 Oakvale Ave., Berkeley
Reynolds, J. G.	158 Posen Ave., Berkeley
*Rhodin, Carl J.	6168 Benvenue Ave., Oakland
Richards, Dr. Dexter N.	166 Tunnel Road, Berkeley

Richardson, Frederick B.	666 Vernon St., Oakland
Richardson, Girard N.	270 Crocker Ave., Piedmont
Robbins, W. C.	Suisun, California
Robbinson, Harrison S.	2730 Belrose Ave., Berkeley
Rodgers, J. E.	Byron Brown Bldg., Martinez
Rodolph, Chas. T.	276 Adams St., Oakland
Rodolph, George W.	335 Sea View Ave., Piedmont
Reeding, George C. (estate)	16 Terrace Ave., Piedmont
Ross, Hillbert	574 Walla Vista Ave., Oakland
Sample, Samuel M.	420 15th St., Oakland
Schlessinger, Lee	Olds Wortman & King, Portland, Ore.
Schneider, Edward J.	66 Hillcrest Road, Berkeley
Scott, John T.	553 Oakland Ave., Oakland
Shannon, Samuel	2517 Parker St., Berkeley
Sherman, Mrs. Frederick R.	285 Jayne St., Oakland
Sherwin, John W.	185 Hillcrest Road, Berkeley
Sherwood, H. Warner	280 Mountain Ave., Piedmont
Shibley, Ernest H.	637 Vernon St., Oakland
Shilling, Walter W.	5421 Belgrave Place, Oakland
Shuman, J. F.	35 Hillcrest Road, Berkeley
Shurtleff, Roy L.	209 Crocker St., Oakland
*Sims, Richard M.	36 Hillcrest Road, Berkeley
Simkins, William A.	116 Frederick St., San Francisco
†Smith, Carroll W.	331 Bonita Ave., Piedmont
Smith, E. C.	341 El Cerrito Ave., Piedmont
Smith, Melville L.	730 Lakeshore Ave., Oakland
Smith, Wilbur R.	5 Plaza Drive, Berkeley
Snyder, C. H.	2713 Forest Ave., Berkeley
Somers, Frank A.	3636 Clay St., San Francisco
Somerset, Dr. John C.	3100 Lewiston Ave., Berkeley
Spear, Lewis R.	3406 W. Adams St., Los Angeles
Sprott, Albert B.	5440 Arbor Ave., Oakland
Stacy, Charles A.	120 Hillcrest Road, Berkeley
Stearns, Harry B.	98 The Uplands, Berkeley
Steel, Marshall	838 Mendocino Ave., Berkeley
Stephens, Mrs. Augustus	21 Fernwood Rd, Summit, NJ
Stephens, Dr. W. Barclay	1250 Bay St., Alameda
Stevens, Lloyd C.	1021 Sunny Hills Road, Oakland
Stevens, Harry O.	461 Bellevue Ave., Oakland
Stevens, Samuel S.	1071 Ardmore Ave., Oakland
Stevenson, T. D.	54 Sea View Ave., Piedmont
Stolp, Fred A.	103 Montecello Ave., Piedmont
Stone, Frank E.	95 Plaza Drive, Berkeley
Stoner, Reginald C.	2832 Prince St., Berkeley
Striebmann, Dr. Wm. H.	1236 Ashmount Ave., Oakland
Stuard, Harry E.	3 Eaton Court, Berkeley
Stubb, Albert C.	212 Mountain Ave., Piedmont
Sutro, Oscar	2025 Oakland Ave., Piedmont
Sutton, Miss Maud	2301 Prospect St., Berkeley
Swayne, Robert H.	1717 Alameda Ave., Alameda
Sweet, Dr. Clifford	6333 Estutes Drive, Oakland
Sweet, Joe U.	2742 Prince St., Berkeley
Sykes, Dr. A. E.	77 Domingo Ave., Berkeley
Taylor, Churchill	1975 Webster St., Oakland
Taylor, Fred S.	Walnut Creek, California
Taylor Samuel H.	123 Bonita Ave., Piedmont
Terry Samuel W.	Lafayette, California
Thomas, Benj. Frankling	2640 Warring St., Berkeley
†Thomas, F. F. Jr.	683 Santa Barbara Rd., Berkeley
Thomas, Hayward C.	1046 Cragmont Ave., Berkeley
Thomas, Dr. Hayward G.	2940 Summit St., Oakland
Thomas, Reginald	2806 Ashby Ave., Berkeley
Thompson, Mitchell	866 Paloma Ave., Oakland
†Thorne, Andrew	Diablo, California
Thorning, Mrs. Florence	6227 DeLongpre Ave., Hollywood
Tietzen, Paul O.	2840 Claremont Blvd., Berkeley
Tinnemann, Otto	6444 Benvenue Ave., Oakland
Tinning, Mrs. W. S.	706 E. Main St., Martinez
Todd, Jos Zook	130 Woodland Way, Piedmont
Trowbridge, Delger	766 Calmar Ave., Oakland
Turrell, Herbert N.	Syndicate Bldg., Oakland
*Tyson, James	6 Sotelo Ave., Piedmont
Veale, Mortimer B.	Antioch, California
VanNuys, Dr. R. G.	1803 Highland Place, Berkeley
Volkmann, Wm. G.	15 Muir Ave., Piedmont
Wakefield, Dr. Wm. H.	Wakefield Building, Oakland
†Walker, Dr. May E.	236 Hillside Ave., Piedmont
Walker, Randolph C.	214 San Carlos Ave, Piedmont
Warner, Ralph C.	210 Hillside Ave., Piedmont
*Weilbye, Wm. H.	19th and Jackson Sts., Oakland
†Weinmann, L. R.	811 Paru St., Alameda
*Weinmann, William L.	705 Grand St., Alameda
Westcott, George M.	88 York St., Oakland
Whelan, Wm. James	Whitecotton Hotel, Berkeley
Whitton, Frederick	26 El Camino Real, Berkeley
Widenham, A. W.	1112 Ashmount Ave., Piedmont
Wilcox, Charles H.	63 Lincoln Ave., Piedmont
Wilhelm, G. H.	Lake Chabot, San Leandro
Willoughby, H. A.	622 Mills Bldg., San Francisco
Wilson, Francis A.	22 Sea View Ave., Piedmont
Wilson, Miss Mary E.	2538 Channing Way, Berkeley
Witter, Jean C.	116 Parkside Drive, Berkeley
Wolcott, Lee W.	14 The Uplands, Berkeley
†Wolfe, Fred L.	714 Kohl Bldg., San Francisco
Wood, Walter T.	1 Plaza Drive, Berkeley
Wright, Howard E.	2626 Warring St., Berkeley
Wright, Maynard E.	149 Monte Cresta Ave., Oakland
Wright, Robert H	623 Santa Ray Ave., Oakland

One-third of Americans are unemployed; soup kitchens and breadlines feed hundreds while dozens of Federal alphabet soup agencies provide make-work: the NRA, PWA, WPA, NYA, FHA, HOLC.(1) Prohibition is repealed and at the Olympic games Jesse Owens wins four Golds but Hitler snubs the presentation.

Babe Ruth powers the New York Yankees; pro football is born with teams in Pittsburg, Cleveland, Chicago, and Cincinnati. Will Rogers, America's favorite humorist, is killed in an airplane accident. "Gone With the Wind" wins the Pulitzer Prize for Literature and the hunt is on for the woman to play Scarlett O'Hara opposite Clark Gable. The Lambeth Walk is the in dance and Edward VIII becomes King of England but within a year abdicates "...for the woman I love." Congress passes the Social Security Act and everybody turns to radio five nights a week to listen to Amos and Andy. The Lindbergh's baby is kidnapped. Snow White and the Seven Dwarfs make their screen debut. Hitler, Mussolini, and Tojo threaten their neighbors, but Americans do not feel threatened, counting on two oceans to separate them from either menace.

The Club survives but goes through two reorganizations to stem the tide. Pat Patton is the popular Golf Pro. Lots sell for $300 per *acre* in Diablo.

Maynard Wright said, "A real golfer would never join Diablo."

THE DEPRESSION THIRTIES

Chapter IV

Maynard & Charolotte Wright with children.

Let's listen to Elizabeth Freeman, Rose Ferreira, and Cecil Ryder; also seven kids in the '30s—Skip and Marsh Freeman, Tom Edwards, George Hall, Bill Bliss, Bill Thomas and John Hale. Elizabeth is first.

ELIZABETH FREEMAN At the depths of the Depression, Elizabeth Freeman's parents, Maynard and Charlotte Wright, bought a home on five acres in Diablo at 2081 Casa Nuestra. The plot, a high mound overlooking the golf course, was their home for seven summers until Maynard died. He had been an avid golfer who said repeatedly, "A real golfer would never join Diablo with its perennially dry fairways." Elizabeth, husband Bill, and their five sons Leigh, Marshall, Tim, Bill Jr., and Doug spent the summers at their grandparents' home.

Leigh "Skip" remembered the big sand box by the Club pool where he spent most of his time. "I had four brothers to play with and there wasn't much room for anyone else," he commented, then added, "Walking to the Club along Casa Nuestra to El Nido, and past the Chalet was a far cry from what it is today. The road wasn't much more than a gravel path and there were no houses to pass, just open country in every direction. We didn't go to Diablo Lake—too dangerous for us little whipper-snappers."(2)

Marshall too, vividly remembered the pool. "I couldn't wait to get in and I hated it when I had to wait an hour after lunch before Mom would allow us to swim again," Marsh said. He also remembered the Easter *Bunny* hunt (not Easter *egg* hunt). "The bunny hunt dented my life," he recalled. "I caught one by the tail and it pulled off. That was so cruel it's been embedded in my mind ever since."

Tom Edwards, another resident, also remembered Diablo in the '30s. "I took my first step on the porch of the old clubhouse in 1936 when I was a year-and-a-half old," Tom said. He remains the only person to win both the golf and tennis Club Championships (1974).

For the Edwards family, life at the Club began when Tom's parents had their first date—a Cal fraternity dance at the old club (farm) house. "The drive from Berkeley took more than an hour-and-a-half over windy, bumpy, lonely roads. My mother was getting worried. Her anxiety vanished when they arrived in Diablo and she saw rows of candles around the clubhouse porch. They were married within a year," Tom said. Later, the family purchased the MacAuley ranch adjacent to the Magee ranch and Green Valley School on Diablo Road. For them, the Club shifted from a place for summer fun to a year round center of activity.

Bill and Elizabeth Freeman moved to Diablo and joined the Club themselves in 1965. Bill was a member of the Board of Directors and Club Secretary from 1970 to 1973. Elizabeth said, "I've seen pictures in books of the clubhouse and it is referred to as the Inn. The same goes for pictures of the Casino and it's called the clubhouse. Both are incorrect, at least so far as the '20s, '30s, and '40s are concerned. The Casino had a pool table, a bowling alley in the basement, card tables, and gambling machines. It was strictly the men's recreation hall. Women and children at the pool used the changing room in the Casino and help was quartered there on occasion. I remember as a teen racing through the hall where I was not welcome."

Elizabeth took her boys to the pool most days and just stayed there. They got lunch and refreshments at the poolside snack cart. There was a large area of sand back from the pool where the sun worshippers reveled and baked. "Being in Diablo with the Club as the centerpiece was simply the ultimate in living," she said. "Life was so unsophisticated; we were so relaxed. Our biggest problem was watching out for rattle snakes, that and praying the water would last the summer. Diablo is still my ideal of a place to live, a-dream-come-true of fun in the country, and the best possible place to raise a family. One of my warmest memories is of the Halls. Susan was a beauty and a fine person to boot and everyone admired and respected Herb."

CECIL RYDER The Club's "Mr. Fix it" remembered the '30s from another point of reference. In April 1932, at the age of 30, he was hired as the Club's assistant maintenance man. Forty years later he retired, only to be called back time and again during the next five years. "There were no plans or sketches so no one knew where wires and pipes were located. This applied to the waterlines, the sewer pipes, electricity, gas, you name it," said Cecil.

Besides the sewer system—an odd collection of septic tanks and leech lines—there were over

Tom Edwards, at the Diablo Lake above and on the golf course seen below.

Cecil Ryder.

100 miles of water pipes with valves all over the place in no order or by any plan. Cecil said, "When you went to shut off the water, you had to find a valve down from the leak, another valve up from it, and then a third one some other place. If you didn't shut down all three you didn't shut off the water. I was the only one who knew where most of these valves were and I never did find all of them."

In Cecil's first year he worked on the golf course trying to keep the putting greens green and the course playable. The next year, the Club hired Vern Conklin from Stanford where he had been the assistant greenskeeper. He turned Diablo into a first class golf course and taught Cecil how to maintain it. Cecil remarked, "I've talked to the pros who played here and asked them what they thought of the course. Most of them were impressed. Naturally, we never had enough water except in winter. The fairways were as dry as a bone but Diablo's greens were second to none."

Cecil was also the outdoor chef. There were frequent parties at the Lake and lots of weekend horseback rides to Barbecue Terrace in the State Park. A favorite was Sunday brunch when Cecil wore his white hat. Everyone rode up—parents and older kids—and Cecil barbecued the ham, fried the potatoes and the eggs. He also made the Bloody Marys. Cecil said, "I had to watch myself with those Bloody Marys because whenever I'd ask 'When do you want to eat?' People would say 'Wait awhile.' Then, someone would get them singing and those 'whiles' could lead to trouble, especially when the singers had to mount up for the ride back to the Club!"

DEPRESSION EFFECTS The '30s were good times for a few, but hard on many. Elizabeth Freeman said, "We were certainly conscious of the Depression although it didn't seem to affect us particularly. Dad was in diesel engines and somehow the bad times didn't hit him. But I do remember the Club was struggling to keep members and having trouble paying its bills. They came to my father for a loan and he turned them down. As a result there were hard feelings."

Beth Hearn's father agreed to help the Club by purchasing a $1,000 bond and later a second one. When the bonds came due the Club was unable to redeem them. Thomas wanted cash not stock in a new club. For his persistence, he was given property adjacent to his Diablo home. Bill Thomas, a teenager in the '30s, like others interviewed, remarked how fortunate his family was not to be particularly affected by the Depression. He noticed there were fewer people around the Club and adult talk centered around financial troubles because members were dropping out, and no new homes were being built. But other than that, Diablo summers were pretty much as always. Beth's comment was, "You have to realize that no one had much money. We all were in the same boat—just going from day-to-day."

Rose Ferreira also remembered the Depression because the Club had to let half the golf course go unattended. "But our family didn't suffer especially," she said. "We were one of the lucky ones, Joe actually got a raise." Like others, the Ferreiras helped needy families and knew some who were forced to give up their homes because they couldn't pay the rent or make their mortgage payments. Clothes-wise, people made-do with what they had and did a lot of walking to save gas. One of the first things people gave up was their telephone. Just use your neighbor's and give your friends their number!

"There were days in town," said Rose, "when you wouldn't see hardly anyone in the stores, shops, or restaurants, only Elliott's bar was doing any business. Lots of men sat around not doing much of anything—no jobs, no hope. Time was heavy on their hands." Kids helped their parents by combing their neighborhoods selling all manner of gew-gaws and knick-knacks—liquids to brighten old fabrics, rinses to double the life of silk stockings, magazines, candy, toys, *et al.*

The Club was certainly not as active as it had been in the '20s, and less so until the very end of the '30s. Rose Ferreira worked at the Chalet in charge of four other girls and doubled as the Club's hat check girl and waitress at parties and banquets.

Bill Bliss, coauthor of the story of the Bliss family of Glenbrook, Nevada was ten in 1930—his first of six summers in Diablo.(3) He spent his Easter vacations and summers at his grandparents' home—Winifred (Fred) and Grace Potter—which overlooked the 18th fairway. He remembered the Easter Bunny hunts, floating little boats in the creek with his pal next door, Bob Greenwood, and "hunting" together in the hills. He and Bob built forts and ran their Buddy L train on tracks they'd laid on the adjacent property.

Of the Depression, Bill said, "They had to sell the house in the mid '30s because my grandparents couldn't afford it any longer. Grandfather moaned and groaned about the house he'd built on paper profits, money he never had."

Carrol Wilson of Hills Brothers Coffee, now 92, and a life-long friend of Gray (Herb) Hills, became a Club member in 1932.(4) He commented, "The Club launched a program of guest memberships. That's how I got in, no fee, just pay the monthly dues. It was a gimmick to keep the Club afloat. When the Hills traveled as they did every August, we stayed at their villa for several weeks each year until the War."

Diving and swimming in the Club pool. Today the same pool is in use — different kids diving and swimming.

The Lake now is surrounded by private property, but it still is used for fishing. The "Tank" was remodeled in the '80s and now is heated.

William A., William M. & William Hale, Jr., at right. COURTESY JOHN HALE.

Nancy Witter Bates on "Tomboy." Note the Club's horsebarn.

The summer season featured the Children's Rodeo, the Horse Show with its riding, posting, and jumping events, and the gymkhana. There were nine miles of trails within Diablo, plus trails on Mt. Diablo. COURTESY NANCY WITTER BATES.

A '30s CADDY

George Thebolt, who lived in Concord, began caddying at the Mt. Diablo Country Club when he was 15. George hitchhiked to Diablo, went to the caddy area, and waited for "a loop"—a chance to go around the course as a caddy. He earned 75 cents a bag and carried two bags for 18 holes. With good luck in tips he earned $2.00-2.50 per loop.

"This was in the depths of the Depression," he said, "times were tough, and for kids, caddying was good pay. The course seldom was crowded, mostly older men played, and I remember some of them to this day—Stanley Dollar, Gantner-Mattern (of sweater fame), and Dean Witter come to mind. Each hole had a name and we referred to the names of holes, not the numbers, like, "Oh, you're on the Eucalyptus green."

Like most other caddies, George quit after three/four years but to this day he has fond memories of the fellows he worked with and of the good tippers. "We always earned more by cleaning up the mess after the New Years Eve Party on New Years Day," he remembered. "We were extras the club hired because we were cheap, earning 25-35 cents per hour. This was a good perk, as was the chance to play golf for free on Mondays when the Club was closed." (5)

Junior Golfers, L to R: Bob Hale, Peter Farmer, George Parrish, Bill Thomas, unknown, Johnny Ristenpart, John Farmer, unknown, and Henry Carlyle. COURTESY GEORGE PARRISH.

HERB'S SON GEORGE In 1924 Herb and Susan Hall moved into their new summer home overlooking the 2nd fairway. George was six-months old, his sister Myra Mae two-years old and David three. Herb Hall was Club President 1937-41 and again in 1949.

George doesn't remember much about the '20s but he waxed eloquent when asked about the '30s. "It was a youth's paradise. You knew everyone, you did all these fun things together. We developed a camaraderie that has lasted to this day. Whenever I see an old friend from those days, the conversation naturally turns to Diablo Lake and what we all did there. You have to realize that no one *lived* in Diablo—it was a summer vacation fairyland."

When queried about the Depression, George said, "It really didn't touch us. Somehow Dad made it through and life went on pretty much as it always had been. I do remember everything was dirt cheap. You could get help by providing a place to live, three square meals, and a little spending money."

The Club's biggest financial concern according to George's father was the water situation. "If we had a wet winter the Club made it financially, but if the Club had to buy water from the California Water Company, it was sure to end up in the red."

THE CLUB STAYING AFLOAT By the mid '30s Club membership had fallen to 160 and it was offered for sale to the Claremont Country Club "free and clear of encumbrances" for $30,000, an offer that died on the vine.(6) Then, in order to pay its bills, the Club borrowed $115,000 from members by selling them bonds. But soon the bonds were in default. So on September 28, 1936, V.E. Breeden, Herbert E. Hills, Henry D. Nichols, Herbert B. Hall, and A. Leslie Oliver ("the Five Angels") formed Diablo Properties, Inc., and bought the Club lock, stock and barrel.(7) DPI offered those holding bonds a choice, either:

*CASH — $250 FOR EACH $1,000 BOND
(25 CENTS ON THE DOLLAR)

OR

*AN EXCHANGE OF STOCK — FIVE SHARES OF DPI
FOR EACH $1,000 BOND.

Twenty-two percent requested an exchange of stock, seventy-eight percent wanted cash. This was exactly the opposite of what the Five Angels had hoped for. Minutes of November 15, 1936 state, "It was the consensus of Directors that a concerted effort be made to get ... bondholders who were asking for cash to accept stock." The failure of this effort in the hardest of times is not surprising. Eventually $90,000 of DPI's $100,000 capitalization was subscribed. Now the Five Angels had money for much needed repairs, renovation, redecorating, resurfacing roads in Diablo, purchasing a new truck and Toro tractor, *et al.* The end result was that the Angels and the 22-percenters owned all the physical assets of the Club.

In January 1937, DPI spawned a new Club, renamed Diablo Country Club, with Herb Hall as President.(8) It was a non-assessable, non-proprietary organization restricted to 400 members, no initiation fee for the first 200, and dues of $15 per month. As a membership incentive, DPI agreed to pay all operating losses of the new Club from 1937-1940.

By 1940, those losses amounted to $50,000 and DPI borrowed the sum from the Crocker Bank, secured by a note signed by Hall and Hills. Thus, Hall and Hills, pledged their personal fortunes to guarantee the future of the Club. Later the articles of incorporation were revised to permit assessments and in March, 1943 members were assessed $31 each. In his letter of March 15, Hall hastened to reassure them there would be no future assessements beyond the $31 because:

"...110 members agreed to pay $5 per month as a stand-by charge for maintenance of the Club for the duration of the war... (and) that the $5... will be supplemented by rental of the Chalet now being received from Navy and civilian personnel connected to the camp being constructed near Livermore." (Parks and Shoeman)

By means of clever financial maneuvers by a small group of dedicated men, the Club survived the '30s and was given a new life as it moved into the next decade. It's amazing how little of this struggle touched the members generally or their lifestyle, at least in the memory of those interviewed—both Club members and employees. "To many Diablo Country Club was a dream to reach for."(9)

Within several years, the membership was back to 400 and the future looked promising even allowing for the gathering war clouds in Europe and the Pacific.

HOLDERS OF STOCK IN DIABLO PROPERTIES, INC.

(This list was checked with Mr. Hall's on Jan. 14, 1939)

Barnett, M. S.
Berg, Wm.
Breeden, V. E.
Calif. Water Service Co.
Carlisle, H. C.
Dexter, Dudley
Eschen, J. N.
Estate of W. P. Frick
Greenwood, G. M.
Hale, W. A.
Hale, Wm. M.
(On this date stock had not been delivered to him)
Havre, Harold J.
Hawley, Stuart S.
Henshaw, Stuart
Hills, H. G.
Hockenbeamer, Mrs. A. F.
Houdlette, E. S.
Johnson, Walter S.
Kiester, J. B.
Lester, A. M.
Letts Oliver Investment Co.
Levis, J. P.
Lewis, I. C.
Maxwell, Mrs. J. P.
McCann, F. P.
Nichols, Henry D.
Oliver, A. Leslie
Oliver, E. L., Sr.
Parrish, Mrs. Edwin
(Edwin Parrish, deceased)
Pillsbury, A. F.
Potter, W. W.
Prost, H. G.
Ransome, Bernard
Reese, Mrs. Florence
Richards, F. S.
Scanlon, R. H.
Shuman, J. S.
Thomas, F. F., Jr.
Walker, Hubert M.
Willoughby, H. A.
Witter, Jean C.
Wright, M. E.
Klinker, Victor
Pratt, Roy L.

COURTESY OF GEORGE HALL.

STOCK CERTIFICATE

TO WHOM ISSUED	DATE			No. Cert.	No. Shares	AMOUNT	Issued No. Cert.
California Water Service Co	Mch	25	1937	28	60	3000 -	
H. G. Hills	Apr	12	1937	29	190	9500 -	
F. P. McCann	May	4	1937	30	20	1000 -	
Jean C. Witter	"	"	"	31	100	5000 -	
Dudley Dexter	May	15	1937	32	20	1000 -	
A. Leslie Oliver	"	"	"	33	20	1000 -	
Ernest A. Houdlette	May	21	1937	34	20	1000 -	
Griffith Henshaw	"	"	"	35	20	1000 -	
J. Preston Levis	"	"	"	36	100	5000 -	
J. B. Havre	"	"	"	37	20	1000 -	
Victor E. Klinker	"	"	"	38	100	5000 -	
G. M. Greenwood	"	27	"	39	20	1000 -	
H. F. Thomas, Jr.	June	3	"	40	20	1000 -	
					710	35500	

DIRECTOR'S MEETING.

San Francisco, California
October 19, 1936

A regular meeting of the Directors of DIABLO PROPERTIES, INC. was held this 19th day of October, 1936 at the hour of 12 o'clock noon at 901 Crocker Building, San Francisco, California.

There were present at said meeting the following directors:
V. E. Breeden,
Herbert E. Hall,
F. P. McCann,
H. B. Hills, and
A. Leslie Oliver.

President Breeden presided.

The affairs of the corporation were discussed at length. The Treasurer was authorized to pay to Mount Diablo Country Club the sum of Three Thousand Seven Hundred Ninety-three and 15/100 ($3,793.15) Dollars, being the operating losses of that club since August 1, 1936, and to pay to H. G. Hills the sum of Eighty-four and 65/100 ($84.65) Dollars, being his out-of-pocket expense in connection with the organization meeting of the corporation held at the Bohemian Club on June 16th, 1936.

The Secretary reported that only Fifty-three bonds of Mt. Diablo Country Club had been deposited, and that the deposit of Eighty-six would be necessary before the corporation could safely proceed with its plans for the reorganization of Mt. Diablo Country Club. Lists of the non-depositing bond holders were submitted to each of the Directors present with a request that each attempt to contact as many men on the list as possible during the coming week.

Director Hall was requested to contact Mr. Clarence Tantau, the architect, in connection with the improvements contemplated to be made at Mount Diablo Country Club.

There being no further business to come before the meeting, on motion duly made and seconded, the meeting adjourned.

Herbert E. Hall

Secretary.

COURTESY OF GEORGE HALL.

THE CAMELOT YEARS

John, youngest of the three Hale boys, wrote this in February, 1994 about Diablo in the '30s

The 1930s were the Great Depression years, complete with the Veterans' March on Washington, soup lines and massive unemployment. But you would never have known it looking at life around the Diablo Country Club. Sure, there was some belt tightening and some families had to drop their memberships, but for the ones that could afford it, these were the Camelot years.

For the grownups there were dinner-dances, golf, tennis, swimming and horseback riding. Prohibition had ended and Diablo was a wonderful place to get away from it all.

But the children were the ones who really had a place in the sun. For those of us who spent our summers there, it was one long summer camp. The activities started with Easter. Most schools took their Spring break at Easter. Many of the summer homes were opened for that week and it was a grand time to see your friends again. Those of us who were regulars were invited to color Easter eggs several days before Easter. We dyed a whole bunch which were put out on Saturday night by a committee. Most of the eggs were hidden in the rough of the first hole—up to the top of the hill. I think some were left out in the open fairway to make sure that the younger children would find them. A big egg was especially decorated as the "Diablo Egg" and a prize was given to the lucky kid who found it.

The other annual event was the bunny chase. The kids were lined up by age groups, the youngest on up the hill closer to where the bunnies were released. At a signal, the bunnies were released on the first fairway and the kids would all try to catch one. Roy Pratt was a top executive with Del Monte and every year he would supply the cardboard cartons used to take the rabbits home in. Most of them were caught but some always escaped. Their descendants are probably still living around the golf course.

When school let out in June, Diablo would come alive again. I was such a poor car rider that the family only transported me out in June and back to our house in Berkeley in September. This guaranteed I didn't miss a thing in the life at Diablo. Swimming was the main attraction. There was the pool for the younger kids and Diablo Lake for the teens. The water stored there was used by the homeowners and to water the golf course as well as for swimming. In dry years there was always a fight over who got the water. The Lake was a very popular place. It was big enough for boating and fishing, but the main attraction was the swimming. You parked below the dam and then hiked up a trail to the Lake. At the top of the trail was a small building used for registration and a snack shop. Presiding over this was a wonderful woman known as Mrs. Mason. She knew all the children who were members and whether or not we were allowed to charge snacks to our parents' account. She also could spot an uninvited guest from a hundred paces and was quick to exercise her authority. She was always firm but fair. She would put Cokes and candy bars in her freezer for something special. I can still remember getting frozen Snicker bars when I had some money.

The pool and the Lake had lifeguards who were recruited from Cal. They were students who got room and board and an appropriate salary for those Depression years. They usually had a gal at the pool and two guys up at the Lake. Their duties included not only the safety and maintenance of the facilities, but also the operation of a full time baby-sitting operation for the members' children. For every day of the week there were activities planned and supervised by the three lifeguards. These activities were designed for various age groups and centered around the pool and the Lake. But they also included golf lessons, occasional hikes, etc. The evening sessions were usually out on the golf course or around the clubhouse. We'd play kick-the-can and similar games. Every few weeks there was something special. They organized scavenger hunts, water carnivals and a rodeo near the end of the summer. Never a dull moment. Sunday nights we were treated to movies in the Casino. After the films we would stop down at the clubhouse to see if the latest schedule had been printed yet. Monday was a day off for everyone. The lifeguards certainly earned their keep.

The summer of 1942 was the last of the Camelot Years. We were at war, and many youngsters who had once lolled around on the deck at the Lake were heading overseas. Gas rationing shut down the Club. The fun and games were over, never to return.

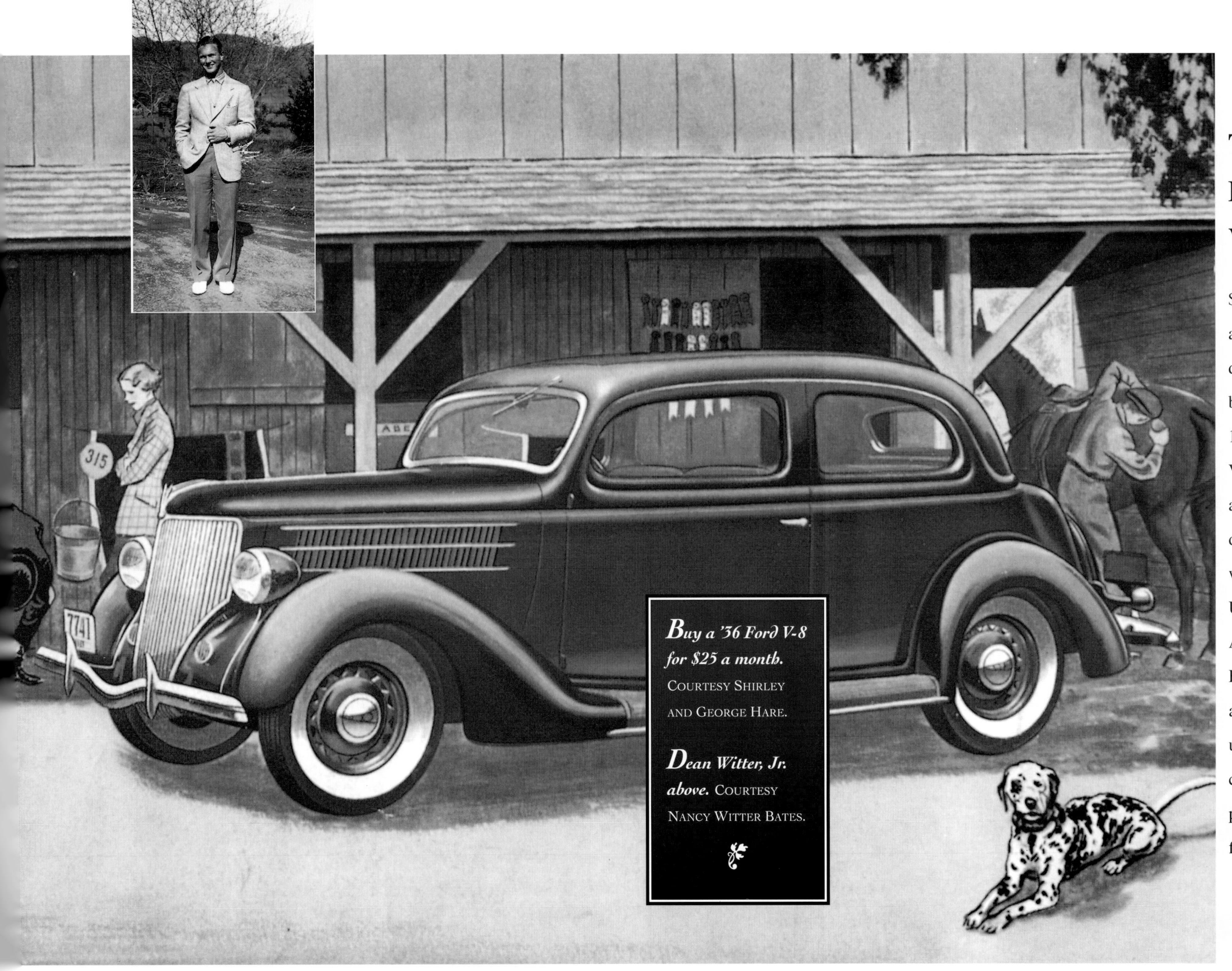

Buy a '36 Ford V-8 for $25 a month. Courtesy Shirley and George Hare.

Dean Witter, Jr. above. Courtesy Nancy Witter Bates.

THE FORD V•8

$25 a month, after usual down-payment, buys any model 1936 FORD V•8 car–from any FORD dealer– anywhere in the United States. Ask your FORD dealer about the new universal credit company ½% per month finance plans.

AUGUST 1, 1936 8e

Walk with Vitality

JANICE

PRISCILLA

MARTILE

CAPRI

AND LIFE WILL WEAR A BRIGHTER FACE

Your face will put its best foot forward when you wear Vitality Shoes. Why? Because you feel most fit when your shoes really fit . . . Vitality Shoes are styled and made to fit your foot as nature demands . . . carefully contoured for true comfort . . . scientifically designed for balanced support and flexibility. And the beauty of their styling will carry you confidently into the forefront of the smart fall fashion picture.

VITALITY SHOE COMPANY • • • ST. LOUIS
Division of International Shoe Company

Your children, too, can walk with vitality in Vitality Shoes with the scientific Vitapoise feature. Vitapoise holds the growing foot in the natural repose position, with a special wedge sole to give support and to assure normal foot alignment.

$6.75 A FEW STYLES $6.00
SOMEWHAT HIGHER IN CANADA

The Charmed Circle of VITALITY Shoes

• Youth and Charm go with you when you *walk with Vitality* in the Charmed Circle of Vitality Shoes.

VITALITY *shoes*

SIZES 2 TO 11 • WIDTHS AAAAA TO EEE

The latest styles of women's shoes for $6.00 a pair. Courtesy Shirley and George Hare.

Check these golf club prices! Courtesy Shirley and George Hare.

Hilda from Cal—the 1936 lifeguard. Courtesy Nancy Witter Bates.

IN THE WORLD'S MOST PERFECTLY MATCHED CLUBS

The Cushion-neck construction comes in Kro-Flite Custom-Built Registered Iron, Kro-Flite Standard Registered Irons, and Kro-Flite Related Irons.

Every club in each set has exactly the same swinging weight as every other club. So, instead of trying to master six or nine different swings, you master just *one.*

Registered Irons are sold in sets only. A complete record of every Registered Club is kept so that any time a club is lost or broken, Spalding can make you up its exact duplicate.

By getting Related clubs of the same index, you can build up a perfectly matched set by buying one or two clubs at a time.

Prices of Kro-Flite Cushion-neck Irons

Custom-Built Registered	*Set of nine*	$90
	Set of six	60
Standard Registered	*Set of nine*	$75
	Set of six	50
Related	*Set of nine*	$54
	Set of six	36
	Each	6

Let your Professional outfit you. Spalding dealers also carry these clubs, as do all Spalding Stores.

© 1930, A. G. S. & B.

Spalding

KRO-FLITE
CUSHION-NECK GOLF CLUBS

GOLF COURSE

Mt. Diablo Country Club

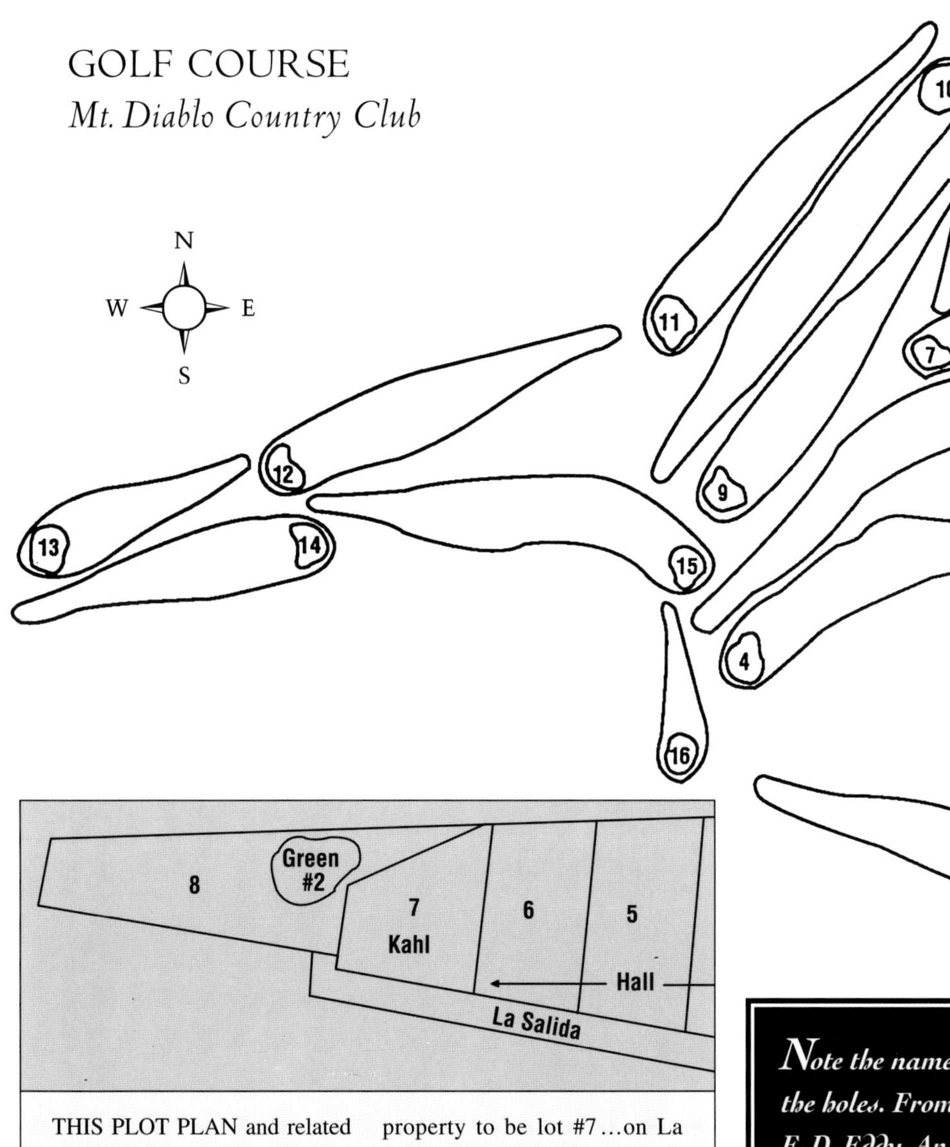

THIS PLOT PLAN and related correspondence, all dated Jan.-July, 1937, was loaned to Larry Ives by Ernest Kahl of Orinda and pertains to his parents' Diablo property. Passages are excerpted: "Our map indicates your property to be lot #7…on La Salida (now Club House Road) …Lot #8 was purchased…by the Club and green #2 was placed on it." Signed Solon Pearce, Manager, Mt. Diablo Country Club, Feb. 22, 1937.

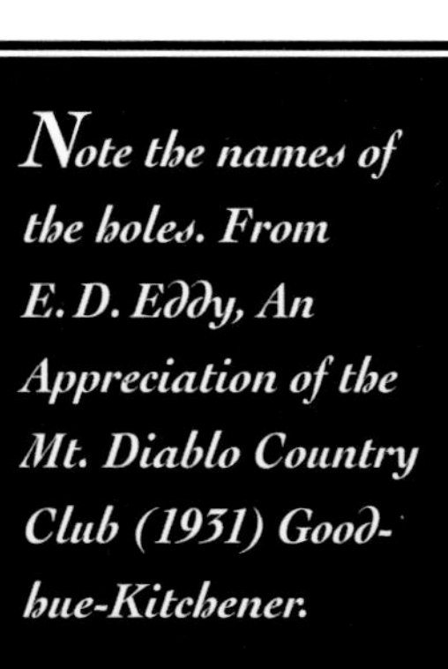

Note the names of the holes. From E. D. Eddy, An Appreciation of the Mt. Diablo Country Club (1931) Goodhue-Kitchener.

Golf balls were cheap, too. COURTESY SHIRLEY AND GEORGE HARE.

NUMBER		YARDS	PAR	STROKES
1	Optimism	400	4	10
2	Creek	374	4	6
3	Snap	167	3	16
4	Outlook	391	4	12
5	Dog Leg	540	5	1
6	Crest	188	3	15
7	Valley	472	5	8
8	Shorty	130	3	18
9	Half Way	403	4	4
	Total Out	3065	35	
10	Monte Vista	505	5	2
11	Shady	481	5	7
12	The Oaks	394	4	11
13	Reservoir	233	3	14
14	Eucalyptus Row	325	4	13
15	Caution	428	4	3
16	Race Track	158	3	17
17	Penalty	364	4	9
18	Home Stretch	473	5	5
	Total In	3361	37	
Total Out		3065	35	
Total		6426	72	

THE CONTRA COSTA COUNTY TELEPHONE DIRECTORY contains numbers, ads, and a yellow page section—all within 35 pages! Fifty-one names are listed in the Diablo section, 222 Danville, 144 Lafayette, 420 Walnut Creek. Alamo is included in Danville. Call the Club. The telephone office is in the clubhouse. The operator, always a female, says, "Number please?" You say, "One, please," and another female voice says, "Mt Diablo Country Club." The Diablo operator knows where everyone is. Typically she'll say, "They're not home now, they're over at—" or "They've gone to Acree's, try around 4." (Acree's was Danville's only grocery, at the corner of Hartz and Prospect.)

A CALL TO BERKELEY IS 20 CENTS, Hawaii, $21.00. Buy the newest "state of the art" in communications—an Atwater-Kent radio—take your choice from the 17 radio stores listed in the yellow pages!

THE GOOD OLD DAYS! A letter addressed to Mrs. E.A. Kahl of Alameda and signed by Solon Pearce, Manager, Mt. Diablo Country Club, states in part: "...The new club is offering non-proprietary, non-assessable memberships for $15 dues... no entrance fee; however, in joining you agree to remain for ...at least one year ...our interior decorator, Winifred Gray Wise, is ...making the old place look beautiful ...our house warming party will be announced soon." Dated January, 1937. COURTESY ERNEST KAHL, ORINDA.

George and Shirley Hare found the telephone book inside a window seat when they were remodeling their home at 1833 Alameda Diablo.

NAMES IN THE 1935 TELEPHONE DIRECTORY

V.E. Breeden
E.L. Cooper (Postmaster)
Dinwiddie
Frick, W.P.
Hale, William M.
Hall, H.E.
Hawley, Stuart S.
Hills, Herbert Gray
Morey, C.L.
Oliver, William Letts
Ransome, Bernard
Thomas F.F.

A view of the Club grounds in the late '40s. Note tennis courts at lower left, driving range at center right; portico between chalet and clubhouse.
Courtesy of Fidelity Roof Company
Ernest M. Upshaw.

FRAMING THE DECADE

Winston Churchill's England—supported by Lend-Lease ships, planes, and armaments—is barely holding its own against Hitler's Luftwaffe. Stalin joins the fray when Hitler launches a second front against the Russian Bear.

On December 7, 1941, the Japanese attack Pearl Harbor "...a date that will live in infamy..." says an angry President. Men 18 and older, are drafted. Women "man" war production factories. "Rosey the Riveter" is their symbol. On the home front, gas, tires, meat, sugar, butter, and shoes are rationed. School children stockpile tin. Radio listeners dote on Eric Severide, H.V. Kaltenborn. William L. Shirer, and Walter Winchell for the latest news from the front, then turn to one of radio's favorite programs, "One Man's Family," for solace. F.D.R. dies at Warm Springs, Georgia and is succeeded by Vice President and former Senator from Missouri, Harry S. Truman.

Ernest Hemingway receives a Pulitzer for his *For Whom the Bell Tolls* and William L. Shirer's *Berlin Diary* is published; McMillan and Seaborg of UC, Berkeley discover plutonium making an atomic bomb possible five years later; penicillin saves lives in WWII.

On May 18, 1945, President Truman authorizes the use of the atomic bomb on Japan and the war ends shortly thereafter. He introduces the Marshall Plan to rebuild war-torn Germany and Japan. The Cold War with Russia begins.

Jitterbugging is the rage as service men and women don civies and one million students overflow America's colleges and universities on the G.I. Bill.

Diablo changes forever from being a place to visit to being a place to live.

THE
DIABLO COURIER
Diablo's Only Home-Owned Newspaper

Volume 1, No. 3 — Saturday, July 12, 1941 — 5 cents a copy

SCAVENGER HUNT SWAMPS CLUB

"Kind Lady" is second play; has crook plot

By Claude Boynton

Six years ago 'Kind Lady" was first presented on the stage of the Booth Theatre in New York City with the well known actress Grace George in the lead role of Mary Herries.

That play was a Broadway success. Director Fred Harris has selected it as the second production for the Diablo summer theatre. Performances will be shown on the nights of July 18, 19, 20, 25, 26, and 27.

"Kind Lady" is an adaptation by Edward Chodorov from a curious short story written by Hugh Walpole. Mary Harris, former teaching assistant in dramatics to Maria Ouspenskaya, is cast in the all-important role of the rich and solitary old lady victimized by a gang of London crooks.

Cast of the English play as announced by Director Harris is as follows:

Mr. Foster, Arthur Waystaff; Mary Herries, Mary Harris; Lucy Weston, Mrs. Clark Anderson; Rose, Harriet Davis;

Four swim records broken in pool races

Junior Diablo club members shattered four pool records and introduced a new comical diving contest at the Fourth of July swimming festivities held Friday at the club pool.

A crowd of 250 club members and guests witnessed the 75 minutes of splashy aquatic competition amid perfect holiday weather.

Following are names of new pool champions and second and third placers, their times, and distances:

Miles Carlisle won the 25 yard free style for boys 10 years and under in 22.4 seconds to smash the old record by one full second. Jane Lowry was second, Kathleen Harrington, third.

Mike Harrington won the 25 yard free style for boys 10 years and under in 18.6 seconds to beat last year's record by 1.6 seconsd. Bob McIvor was second, Pierre Havre, third.

Doreen Aberouette won the 25 yard free style for girls 10 years and under in 20.9 seconds to lower the old mark by 3.1 seconds. Jane Lowry was second, Ann Larkey, third.

Six teams compete for prizes list includes catkins, Adams ale

The 1941 scavenger hunt "fever" broke out all over the Diablo club grounds last Saturday night when Junior club members combined into six teams to ferret out a list of 12 objects.

Participants met at the Casino at 7:15 p. m., chose team captains and received their lists. At 8:45 team members returned to the Casino to check articles and receive prizes.

Articles of the hunt which caused most merriment and interest included: a goober, catkin, calundula, and a bottle of Adams ale.

A taproom order of $1.25 was awarded the winning team consisting of Bette Knox, Bob Ristenpart, Natalie Chambers, Mary Edwards, and Henry Carlisle.

A second prize of a 75 cent taproom order went to the team of Harold Havre, Tommy Witter, Vic Breeden, Bill Agnew, and Pierre Havre.

Candy and horns were given as a third prize to Susan Maxfield, Janet Parker, Susan Brobst, Kathleen Harrington, and Barbara Dunn.

Harriet Culver, Junior activities head, stated that future scavenger hunts will take special measures to reclassify the younger Junior members.

Scavenger Hunt held tonight

Tonight at 7:15 the second in a new series of Scavenger Hunts is scheduled to get under way with a meeting of all participants in front of the Casino.

Following the custom of previous hunts, the teams of five persons will be formed, lists given to team captains, and the contestants started on their way by 7:30.

Deadline for the return and checking in of articles is 8:45, thus giving the teams one hour and a quarter to procure all the varied and numerous items on their lists.

Any means of transportation is permissible.

Sponsors of the hunt guarantee that each article can be found or located on the club grounds.

Only one caution is necessary. Because of the fact that the ninth performance of the Summer Theater will be in progress tonight, contestants are urged not to go near the Red Horse Tavern.

Nine names increase club membership

The Diablo Courier wishes to take this opportunity to welcome to membership in the Diablo Country Club the following new members: Morris B. Carter, Carlisle C. Crosby, (former member), Eugene V. Flood, Creighton S. Gear, Richard L. Hemmingway, Dr. E. B. Leland, Emory M. Marshall, F. J. Moller, and Henry E. North.

Club dance held next Saturday

Another of Diablo's enjoyable Saturday night dances is planned for July 19. Stan Robinson's outstanding music, to which Diablans have danced at previous dances this season, will entertain all those who attend. Dinner will be served as usual from six to nine.

For those who do not wish to have dinner at the club, music will commence at 8:30. All members and invited guests are urged to attend.

Courier Ads Pay

DIABLO COURIER

The Diablo Courier, a weekly journal devoted to the interests of the Diablo Country Club and its members. Edited and published by the junior members of the Diablo Country Club and printed by the Walnut Kernel Press.

Price, five cents a copy, fifty cents a column inch flat rate for advertising. Distributed every Saturday morning.

Editor	*Edgar H. Lion, Jr.*
Bus. Manager.	*Herbert G. Hills, Jr.*
Advisors	*Claude Boynton*
	Harman Jones

Secretary Carol Pratt

Patronize our Advertisers

Rosie the Riveter.

THE WAR–TORN FORTIES

Chapter V

When the 1940s arrived the Club and its small summer community, which survived the Depression, were enjoying a sudden and welcome prosperity. What F.D.R.'s New Deal could not achieve, his policy of being the arsenal of democracy had. With full employment and a full lunch pail at last, "Happy Days were here again!" Unfortunately, the prosperity was short-lived, lasting only through the summer of '42.

Then the full impact of the war hit home and suddenly, Diablo's summer residents and Club members were in uniform, or lacking gas and tires, confined to their homes. The Club stayed open—sort of—until the war ended thanks to a zealous and devoted group of members led by the Herberts, Halls and Hills, plus servicemen who needed wartime housing and a watering hole.

The Club was at its peak in 1941. The roster, a 26-page booklet contained some fascinating information. The total membership was 391. Members were not listed alphabetically but rather by where they lived. The greatest number were from Berkeley (101), followed by Oakland (92), and Piedmont (91). Only members' names were listed, no occupation, addresses, wives' or children's names or telephone numbers were given.

Herbert Hall, a San Francisco attorney was President and H.G. Hills of Hills Brothers Coffee was a member of the Board. These were the men who kept the Club alive during the War and sold it in 1948 to a White Knight when faced with bankruptcy. Another Board member was A. Leslie Oliver who bought four lots at the entrance of Diablo in the early '20s.

William M. Hale, Sr., a long-time resident at 1830 Alameda Diablo was chairman of the Greens Committee and Joe Hendricks was a member of the Grounds Committee. He was later President in

ROSTER

Diablo Country Club

1941

Board of Directors and Officers

Herbert E. Hall, *President*
R. F. Mulvany, *1st Vice Pres.*
V. E. Breeden, *2nd Vice Pres.*
Geo. M. Parrish, *Secretary*
F. P. McCann, *Treasurer*
F. M. Dorward
Robt. H. Eckhoff
H. G. Hills
A. Leslie Oliver
Solon Pearce, *Manager*

Committees

GREENS
Wm. M. Hale, *Chairman*
R. G. Minty
Wm. C. Parker

PUBLICITY
E. I. Harrington
Guy F. Street

ENTERTAINMENT
Robt. F. Mulvany, *Chairman*
E. M. Downer, Jr.
Dr. W. V. Durst
Weldon Emigh
David Gregory
M. Hallmark
Harold Huovinen
R. B. MacFadyen
A. G. McLenagan
W. A. Owsley
C. G. Patch
Guy F. Street
R. C. Van Der Naillen

GROUNDS
Geo. M. Parrish, *Chairman*
Mrs. W. H. Baughman
F. K. Bottomley
J. S. Curran
Stanley F. Davie
Mrs. A. S. Garrisson
Reed Gibson
Mrs. Joseph Hendrick
Mrs. Jefferson Larkey
Mrs. O. H. Lindbloom
Herman Nichols
Percy Wood

GOLF
Weldon Emigh, *Chairman*
A. C. Christiansen
Hugh Ditzler
Clair O. Du Bois
Al. G. Giehl
E. I. Harrington
Stuart Hawley, Jr.
Carlton L. Rank
W. A. Sparling

WOMEN'S GOLF
Mrs. F. M. Dorward, *Captain*
Mrs. V. E. Breeden
Miss Helen Dolge
Mrs. J. E. Durkin
Mrs. E. I. Harrington
Mrs. E. H. Lion
Mrs. Jack Maxfield
Mrs. W. C. Parker
Mrs. C. G. Patch
Mrs. T. C. Wilson
Mrs. R. C. Van Der Naillen

MEMBERSHIP
Morton C. Beebe, *Chairman*
E. F. Becker
F. E. Boyd
John Cooley

LIST OF MEMBERS

Berkeley
Adams, Dr. B. W.
Baird, Lance
Bardet, Geo. V.
Barnett, Jack W.
Barnett, M. S.
Berryhill, J. G.
Blair, W. R.
Blaisdell, J. P.
Boyd, F. E.
Bramming, V. E.
Burgess, C. R.
Burnham, Dr. C. J., Jr.
Buschmann, R. O.
Campbell, Mcculloch
Clark, H. W.
Condliffe, Prof. J. S.
Cooley, John L.
Crum, Bartley C.
Davis, J. J.
Davis, W. N.
Dill, L. H.
Eichelberger, Kirk W.
Ellis, Ralph
Farmer, M. T.
Faye, Miss Isabel B.
Frisselle, R. D.
Garden, Nelson B.
Gibson, Read
Grady, H. W.
Greenlaw, W. W.
Griffith, R. H.
Griffiths, F. P.
Hale, Wm.
Hatfield, J. G.
Hemingway, R. L.
Hills, Dr. C. B.
Hockenbeamer, Mrs. A. F.
Hunter, F. R.
Hutchens, F. C.
Jackson, Edw. W.
Jaeger, W. P.
Janney, F. F.
Johnson, P. W.
Jones, A. G.
Kent, F. A.
Kelner, E. W.
Kiessig, W. F.
Krebs, W. H.
Lamon, Ralph
Legge, Dr. R. F.
Lester, A. M.
Levis, M. M.
Lindblom, O. H.
Linforth, R. H.
Lothrop, Marcus
Lyman, A. L
McLaren, N. Loyall
McLenegan, A. G.
MacFadyen, R. B.
MacGregor, J. R.
MacKay, D. S.
Matthew, A. P.
Minty, R. G.
Moreland, E. S.
Morgan, J. H.
Mulvany, F. A.
Mulvany, H. A.
Neely, G. I.
Norris, H. R.
Olney, Warren Iii
Osborne, J. L.
Parker, Wm. C.
Parrish, George M.
Pillsbury, E. S.
Plehn, Prof. C. C.
Prost, H. G.
Richards, A. C.
Richardson, F. R.
Ristenpart, C. H.
Ristenpart, W. E.
Robinson, Mrs. E. S.
Roesling, R. J.
Scoggins, J. E.
Scott, D. A.
Sims, R. M., Jr.
Smith, T. B.
Stone, Mrs. F. E.
Stone, James E.
Stoner, R. C.
Telfer, Mrs. Emily P.
Thomas, F. F., Jr.
Tyler, J.C.
Ward, G. R.
Watson, Donald
Wernecke, Livingston
Whelden, C. G.
White, C. A.
Whiting, Dr. E. Gale
Wickersham, A. S.
Williams, E. C.
Wright, Mrs. D. H.

Diablo
Cooper, Mrs. E. L.
Corlett, Will G.
Davis, Hamilton C.
Ditzler, H. W.
Dolge, Wm.
Elliot, Charles
Force, R. C.
Hagstrom, Emil
Landers, Mrs. Carrie M.
McGee, Mrs. Wm. J.
North, H. E.
Pike, Mrs. Mamie Pearson
Pillsbury, Capt. A. F.
Queen, Mrs. R. E.
Ransome, Bernard
Stetson, Mrs. Dorothy P.
Thornally, Harry
Tyson, Mrs. Grace H.

Oakland
Alvarado, Robt. P.
Agnew, W. Dean
Anderson, G. R.
Anderson, J. D.
Anderson, J. L.
Banker, B. A.
Beckwith, Palmer
Bender, R. W., Jr.
Biehl, Al G.
Brown, Miss Florinne
Cantrill, S. M.
Clark, A. W., Jr.
Clark, E. H.
Coate, Dr. J. D.
Conwell, G. A.
Cotter, T. A.
Culver, I. S.
Davie, S. F.
Davies, Mrs. D. Wesley
De Velbiss, C. Dudley
Douthit, T. L.
Du Bois, Clair O.
Dunn, Dr. J. E.
Durst, Dr. W. V.
Duveneck, A. C.
Ellis, H. A.
Ferguson, P. Frank
Flood, E. V.
Freeman, Wm. B.
Garrison, A. S.
Geer, C. S.
Gleason, Dr. A. L.
Gregory, David
Gwynn, C. G.
Hall, G. Lyman
Hallmark, M. F.
Harris, Lloyd
Heffernan, C. A.

Jones, W. E., Jr.
Kilgo, W. E.
Knox, John B.
Knox, P. M.
Lang, J. W.
Larkey, Dr. Jefferson
Lawrence, Dr. L. B.
Ledford, Allan L.
Leet, Dr. Norman B.
Leet, Dr. Robert S.
Libby, H. J.
Ling, Lyman
Loe, Dr. Harris D.
Lyon, M. E.
McPherson, S. E.
MacLeod, Clair
Madigan, Walter
Mainwaring, Dr. George F.
Miles, F. L.
Miller, M. F.
Moloney, J. F.
Mordy, W. H.
Nelson, Donald O.
O'Connell, J. L.
Oliver, Edward R.
Oliver, Wm. H.
Ong, R. O.
Ore, C. V.
Owsley, Wm. A.
Patch, C. G.
Petitt, H. E.
Pletcher, R. R.
Price, C. M.
Rank, C. L.
Roberts, James E.
Roberts, J. T.
Rucker, B. W.
Sampson, Lyle
Shafer, John
Shafer, Thomas G.
Sherman, Mrs. F. R.
Sparling, W. A.
Street, Guy F., Jr.
Tantau, C. A.
Terrell, I. S.
Thomas, Geo. W.
Thomas, Dr. W. F.
Trefethen, Van S.
Trowbridge, Delger
Tyson, J. H.
Vance, W. D.
Van De Carr, Dr. F. Rene
Warenskjold, Wm. E.
Wright, Mrs. M. E.

Piedmont

Ackerman, F. W.
Bancroft, J. S.
Baughman, Dr. W. H.
Bechtel, Warren A., Jr.
Becker, E. F., Jr.
Beebe, M. C.
Bliss, W. M.
Brace, B. B.
Brobst, D. W.
Brown, Thomas
Bryan, C. F.
Buckley, Stafford
Carlisle, B. C., Jr.
Carter, M. B.
Chambers, George R., Jr.
Chew, Dr. W. B.
Christiansen, A. C.
Cox, C. G.
Crosby, Carlisle C.
Currier, Farnsworth
Denton, Arthur P.
Dickie, Mrs. G. M.
Dinsmore, Welby
Dorward, F. M.
Draycott, Wm. E.
Dunn, H. I.
Eckhoff, R. H.
Ede, Wm., Jr.
Emigh, Weldon H.
Gibson, M. E.
Gordon, John
Greenwood, G. M.
Gregory, Dr. W. A.
Griffin, Chas. W., Jr.
Hall, Herbert E.
Hall, H. Raymond
Harrington, E. I.
Havre, H. J.
Hawley, Stuart M.
Hendrick, Mrs. Joseph
Henshaw, Mrs. P. A.
Hills, H. G.
Hough, Edward
Howard, J. H.
Huovinen, Harold
Jackson, H. E.
Keyser, M. E.
Kinney, E. L.
Leland, Dr. E. B.
Libbert, C. B.
Lindberg, Mrs. G. H.
Loree, L. Ii
McCann, Frank P.
McIvor, Dr. R.J.
MacLellan, J. A.
Maloney, Dr. H. P.
Maxfield, Jack
Moller, F. D.
Mosher, M. H.
Muhlner, F. P.
Mullings, F. J.
Nichols, Henry D.
Nichols, Herman D.
Noble, Mark
Okell, Jack
Oliver, A. Leslie
Oliver, E. L.
Oliver, Wm. Letts
Otto, A. P.
Perkes, Chas. A.
Pratt, Roy L.
Puch, J. E.
Putnam, C. M.
Pyzel, F. M.
Roeth, Goerge, Jr.
Ross, Donald L.
Schafer, Dr. O. H.
Seeliger, R. J.
Shafft, C. O.
Smith, Dr. Wm. S.
Steel, Earl G.
Symon, D. Russell
Tinning, A. B.
Traverse, C. J.
Williams, Burdick
Wilson, R. H.
Wilson, T. Carroll
Wishon, A. Emory
Witter, Jean C.
Wood, Percy A.

San Francisco

Aydelotte, J. L.
Breeden, V. E.
Carlisle, H. C.
Curran, J. S.
Cutten, C. P.
Durkin, J. E.
Frick, R. V.
Frick, Robert P.
Haight, Stanton
Hill, Dr. H. P.
Hoyt, H. H.
Johnson, W. S.
Klinker, V.
Leeds, C. T., Jr.
Manning, C. H.
Mitchell, E. J.
St. Hill, T. N.
Savage, R. C.
Scott, E. B.
Seeley, Chas.
Seiger, Rudy
Sellman, R. P.
Sellman, W. H.
Sorensen, Dr. Hans W.
Talmage, A. R.
White, Wm. E.
Yater, Geo. J.

Walnut Creek

Aberouette, Felix J.
Biggs, Reg
Dollar, R. Stanley
Gaby, Phil B.
Lochead, James K.
Marshall, Emory M.
Morse, Clarence E.
Mulvany, Robert F.
Newell, Minton H.
Shipp, Kenneth J.
Van Der Naillen, Ralph C.
Wagstaff, Arthur
Willoughby, H. A.

Other Cities And Towns

Andreasen, C. G., Alamo
Ayer, Paul E., Lafayette
Bee, Lonie, Orinda
Beall, R. A., Pleasanton
Blemer, Dr. John, Danville
Bottomley, F. K., Orinda
Cordell, Russell E., Danville
Davi, Vincent A., Pittsburg
Dinwiddie, W. Stewart, Lafayette
Downer, E. M. Jr., Pinole
Edwards, T. O., Jr., Associated
Eschen, J. N., Alameda
Faye, H. P., Honolulu, T. H.
Fox, A. W., Alameda
Fryer, Chas. M., Concord
Gavin, E. B., Port Chicago
Gorman, J. A., Alameda
Hamilton, Lloyd, Vancouver, B. C.
Hannah, Chas. C., Hillsborough
Hannan, J. T., Lafayette
Hickey, James C., S. San Francisco
Hyde, Lee M., El Cerrito
Kahl, Mrs. E. A., Alameda
Kremser, A., Alamo
Krausi, Le Roy N., Alameda
Larson, O., Associated
Lion, Edgar, Danville
McKim, L., Lafayette
Milliken, Wm. J., Danville
Neufeld, Dr. H. D., Concord
Norris, Mrs. Esther S., Danville
Nourse, R. G., Concord
Ocumpaugh, H. E., Alamo
Pearsall, Gilbert H., Los Angeles
Ransome, Tallent, Emeryville
Reed, Ben W., Jr., Danville
Reese, Mrs. F. G., Del Monte
Rheem, D. L., Moraga
Rodman, W. P., Danville
Sampson, P. J., San Leandro
Selby, Milton L., Concord
Sherritt, Maxwell A., Alamo
Timme, E. G., Alamo
Tolles, R. P., Lafayette
Vilas, R. A., Tenafly, N. J.
Webster, F. A., Jr., Richmond
Weeden, Frank, Alameda
West, H. A., Antioch
Wood, J. B., Lafayette

1953. There was a Men's Golf Committee and a Women's Golf Committee. Each had its own chair and there were no overlapping members.

The green fee for guests was $1.00 on week days, $1.50 on Saturdays, $2.00 on Sundays and holidays. The only alternative to carrying your own clubs was to hire a caddy: $.50 per bag for 7 holes, $.75 for 12 holes, $1.00 for 18. There was an additional charge of $.50 per hour if a golfer wanted his caddy to find lost balls—no guarantees! Storing clubs (no carts) at the Club cost $1.00 per month but that "...included cleaning."

Pat Patton was the Golf Pro, later switching to Orinda Country Club. He was also the father of Ron Patton, Diablo's Pro from 1959 to 1965. Pat charged $1.50 for a half-hour lesson. There was also a footnote: "Boys under 16 are not allowed in the locker room." Women didn't have a locker room in 1941.

Members could choose either the pool or the lake for a refreshing swim. In either event, there was a $.50 charge for a guest. Members could buy a swim ticket for $10 that entitled them to 30 swims. Lunch was available at the lake but not at the pool, so "...surrounding the lawn at the pool are wooden tables for those who bring box lunches."

Since only 18 members lived in Diablo, staying at the Chalet was quite popular. Consider these rates: Single, $2.00; Double, $3.00; extra cots, $1.00. Horses were available for rental at the following rates: $1.00 an hour on Saturdays, Sundays and Holidays, weekdays—$1.00 for the first hour, $.50 for succeeding hours. Lessons were $2.00 per hour for one person; $1.50 each for two or more in a class. The instructor would accompany riders at the rate of $1.50 per hour. Should a member become enamored of a particular horse, the animal could be reserved exclusively for that person for $25-35 per month "...depending on the service desired."

With nearly 400 members there was bound to be considerable coming and going all summer long and on weekends in the fall and spring. One could ride the train, of course, but many considered it more fun to drive. The private roads of Diablo posed some problems and the '41 roster addressed them thusly:

"*Traffic*—Roads within the Club grounds are marked with traffic signs indicating which are ONE WAY and the allowable speed limit. All drivers are urged to drive cautiously and to obey these signs. Parking in the intersection between the Chalet and Casino is strictly forbidden. Members could avoid a great deal of annoyance and inconvenience to themselves if they would use the large parking

PLAYING HINTS

The roster also contained information on golf etiquette: "Golfers... for a better game..."

1. Players carrying their own clubs are asked to give way to those with caddies.

2. Golfers playing 7 or 12 holes are requested when 'cutting in' at the 16th tee to give way to golfers who are playing a complete round.

3. When there is a clear hole ahead and your pace is retarding other players, please allow them to go through. This is a 'Three Star' request!

"Note: Caddies have been given armbands with the word, 'Caddy,' printed thereon which they will display when on the highway. Please give them a ride if you have room."

9-year old Bill Thomas displays his latest Lake catch.
COURTESY BETH HEARN.

Preparing for a ride up the Mountain. COURTESY BETH HEARN.

Kady Lou Phillips shown in the late '40s at the last Easter bunny hunt. COURTESY BEE BELL.

THE VALLEY PIONEER

The Only Newspaper Published in and for California's Beautiful San Ramon Valley

Single Copies 10c

Telephone 34

Volume II | Published Weekly at Danville, California | Thursday, June 20, 1946 | Number 21

Fair Bathers Open Season at Diablo Club Pool

Diablo Pool Opens Saturday

The opening of the swimming pool at the Diablo club last Saturday made quite a splash in this exclusive residential community tucked away at the very foot of towering Mt. Diablo. The youngsters wasted no time diving into the cool waters of the newly filled pool while their comely mothers luxuriated in the warm sun of one of the first hot days this season.

Seated at the left are Mrs. Read Gibson, Mrs. Hamilton Davis and Mrs. Bert Henry. On the beach are Mrs. Charles Morey, Mrs. Ralph Phillips, and Pam and Cady Lou Phillips. On the brink of the pool are Louise and Helen Gibson and Nell Davis.

The pool is only one of the many attractive features of the Diablo country club which is being reorganized and will soon have a proprietory membership of about 350 families.

—Valley Pioneer Photo

area to the East of the first fairway." The area east of the first fairway is now parking lot B. This admonition regarding traffic is the only part of the '41 roster that is still relevant 53 years later.

Shortly after Pearl Harbor, Joe and Rose Ferreira rented their Danville home and moved to the Hills' guest quarters at 1833 Alameda Diablo. Joe had been assigned to guard the Club's property, and felt he could do a better job if he were on location. Rose had worked for the Hills as a maid for seven years previously and now also was employed by the Club. They had two sons, Larry, 10, and Bob "Fritz," age 8.

A group of Seabees stationed at Rock City rented the Ferreiras' Danville home.(1) Commented Rose, "We couldn't keep track of who was where or when—they came and went—but there was always a check at the end of the month."

One day Rose was told to serve meals to five men who were staying at the Chalet. She alone was to serve them and no one was to come near them in the Club dining room. Rose watched them carefully—just out of ear shot. They were intent in their conversation, stopping often to draw diagrams on the tablecloth. "The drawings looked like the design you see on a soccerball," said Rose. After four days the men left and she learned that three of them were Oppenheimer, Lawrence, and Teller, the fathers of the atomic bomb.

COLOR TV The author called Ed Teller and Teller told him he was not "in the loop" in those early years. The author also talked to Glenn Seaborg about Rose's story. After a careful review of his journals, he couldn't supply the names of the missing men.(2) He did, however, relate another fascinating war story.

In 1950, the Atomic Energy Commission began a hush-hush project at Livermore called "MTA" an acronymn for Materials Testing Accelerator. It was, in fact, a quicker method of producing plutonium. Ernest G. Lawrence for whom the lab was named was in charge of MTA and he rented a house at 2222 Alameda Diablo for several months. "I remember coming out to confer with Ernest and playing golf at the Club," said Glenn. Then he related this astounding tidbit, "It was while Lawrence was living in Diablo that he conceived the idea of color TV!"

HOME FRONT SACRIFICES Navy officers renting the summer homes in Diablo far away from their permanent residences, felt the burden of sacrifice being required on the home front. At Christmas, for example, they realized that more than "Lucky Strike green had gone to war;"(3) so had

Rose and Jose raised the chickens and then served them in the Club dining room. COURTESY ROSE FERREIRA.

Rose Ferreira.

ornaments, tinsel, and electric lights for Christmas trees. In their place, children gathered pine cones on Mt. Diablo and Navy moms and dads sprayed them with white and red paint, then hung them on their trees, which had also been harvested from the mountain. Fathers made toys of wood because metals were needed by the war effort. "Even the Armed Services found themselves short of metal before the war was over."(4) Where formerly moms shopped and bought, now they mended and baked. But more often than not, the baking was done minus sugar which was one of the first commodities to be rationed, followed by candy and preserves.

The $.05 candy bar was almost impossible to buy. Even at military stores, they were gone the moment they arrived. Beginning in November, 1942, coffee was rationed, followed by butter, canned goods, cheese, and of course meat which required coupons. Worst of all, perhaps, considering the tension and fear from the daily radio bulletins, whiskey was in short supply. Home fronters as well as the Navy officers living in Diablo learned to drink "strange" liquors like rum and tequila. These "local beverages" didn't require trans-Atlantic passage as did Scotch whiskey. Cigarettes were scarce. At military installations world-wide soldiers and sailors lined up to get their share at the PX or Commissary. Many smokers began to roll their own or buy a wooden cigarette rolling machine.

By the time the war ended "...all foods were rationed except fruits and vegetables, and many supplied these from their own gardens."(5) The government mounted a big push for everyone to have Victory Gardens. Diablo's summer residents had started theirs in the summer of '42 and they were quickly taken over by the Navy renters.

If driving a car was not essential to the war effort, an "A" gas coupon was all one could get. This provided enough gas, for example, to travel once a week from a summer house in Diablo to Acrees Grocery in Danville and to a doctor's office if he hadn't been called into service. Getting from Berkeley or Piedmont to stay for the summer represented a major commitment of a scarce resource.

Tom Edwards, whose family lived on their ranch near Green Valley School remembered when his father found an alternative to gasoline. "Dad had to drive to Pittsburg six days a week. He rigged up a device to get the car started on gas, then he would switch to kerosene, then back to gas as he got to the defense plant so there was enough gas in the carburetor to start the engine when he left for home."

Most tried to solve the gas rationing problem by car pooling. But often that wasn't a very satisfactory solution because new tires were not available. When a 1941 car konked out in 1945, it stayed

Jim Stone, 1943 at far left, "on maneuvers."

Daring new style swimsuits shown in the August 15, 1936 issue of Vogue Magazine.

FATHER AND SON, among the first to initiate the club's golf course since reorganization, are Edwin Letts Oliver, junior and senior. Reconditioning of fairways is now on.

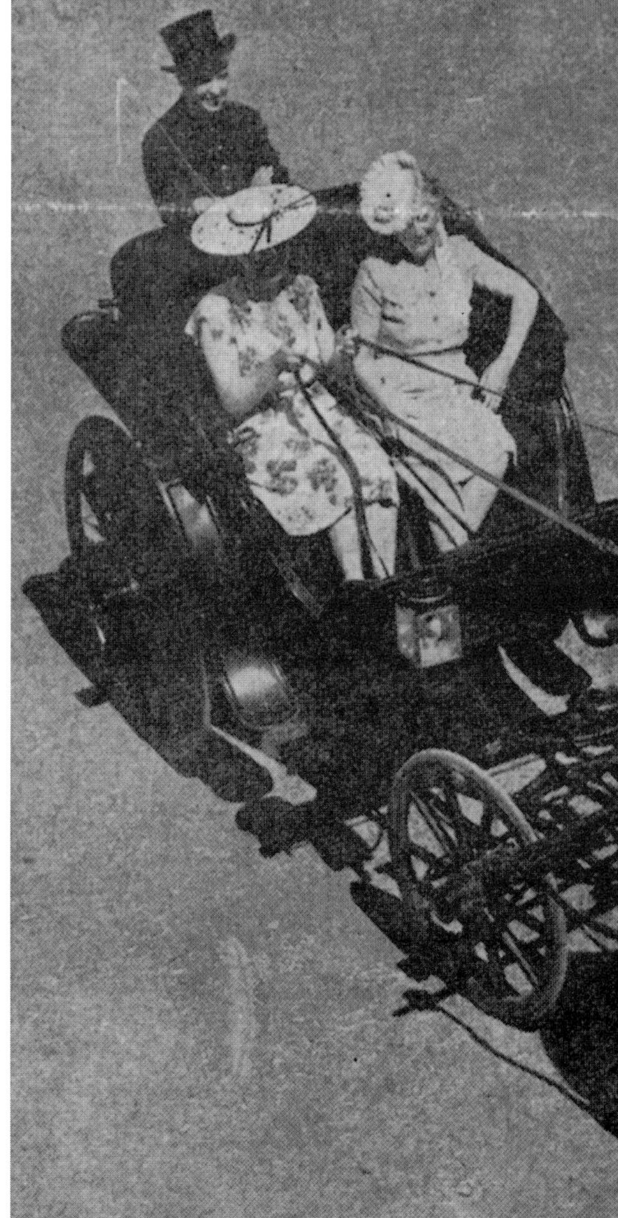

Society . . Club's
Oakland Tribune
ASSOCIATED PRESS . WIREPHOTO . WIDE WORLD . UNITED PRESS
VOL. CXLIV OAKLAND, CALIFORNIA, SUNDAY, JULY 14, 1946 NO. 1

LAST RIDE TOGETHER for Mrs. Emil A. Hagstrom, at the reins, and her passenger, Mrs. Robert Petersen, around the Diablo arena. Mrs. Hagstrom and her sister, Mrs. Paul Neilsen of Frederikshaven (in the role of groom) sail this month from New York for Denmark.

that way. So one had to settle for someone else's old klunk. Auto mechanics and repair parts were hard to find. Detroit was making tanks and bombers; mechanics were repairing ships and planes. The most car owners could do was to have their worn-out tires re-capped—a band aid operation which worked only as long as the cap held.

Fritz Ferreira was eight when his family moved to Diablo, fourteen when they left. During those six years he got to know the Seabees. They were in and around Diablo enroute from Camp Parks to Rock City where the Navy had established a base to train recruits in mountain warfare, road and bridge construction, repair and maintenance.

An apocryphal story is told about the Mt. Diablo-based Seabees. When new recruits were given guard duty, they were carefully instructed to check the locks on the bunkers that housed guns and ammunition in case of an air raid. One bunker in particular was pointed out for special care and attention—it housed the booze supply for the base!

FROM PEACE TO WAR Fritz said, "The first two years, say '41—'42, things were humming. Besides the Seabees, the summer crowd was in full force and the Club was busy, folks golfing and playing tennis, little children and young moms at the pool, everyone on horses and/or at the Lake.

"My friends and I simulated the war by fixing up rowboats and rafts as battleships fighting German subs or Japanese Kamikazes.(6) In the evenings it was off to the Red Horse Tavern where plays and skits were the fashion."

Then all of a sudden the war hit home—the men were gone and women and children were without wheels. The Navy discovered Diablo's vacant summer homes and moved in as year-round renters, beginning first with the smaller houses behind the Red Horse Tavern. Then by December 31, 1944 they were all gone. By war's end the Chalet, clubhouse, and Red Horse Tavern were falling apart from neglect. The Lake was deserted, the horses sold, and the golf course turned to milkweed. Fritz commented, "The milkweed grew to 4-5 feet on the fairways. Owls, racoons, and stray cats made the vacant buildings their home and ran in and out with abandon. The wind blew through open doors and cracked windows, the roofs leaked. It was a sad sight. A few good men tried to keep things going but in the end the Club was all but shut down."

Before the war Fritz remembered Diablo as a very special place, a country enclave with a friendly and compatible group of people. Of the Hills, he said, "Mr. Hills had a 16-cylinder Cadillac and chauffeur. But right after Pearl Harbor he sold it and bought a new four cylinder Willys-Knight, the car that became WWII's famous Jeep."

The Club was desperate for members. Survival was at stake. The Board Minutes of June 24, 1942 state: "There is always the possibility that some agency of the United States Government will purchase the premises or lease them for the duration of the war... If, during these endeavors (to find a use for the Club by government agencies) a sale price was necessary, the same was established at $225,000."

In deep financial trouble, officers Hall and Hills used their personal funds to keep the Club afloat. Temporary support came from the same wartime condition that was responsible for the deterioration of the Club: Navy officers facing a housing shortage; Club members with summer homes to rent. Living in Diablo, some distance from their duty stations, they needed a local pub. The Club supplied it, not at the old club-farm-house where the manager was living, but "up the hill" in the Pool Hall/Gambling Casino which had slot machines. Most of these officers didn't have golf clubs or tennis racquets with them. Just as well because in time the weeds on the golf course were man-high and only 9 holes were playable because of a lack of greenskeepers. The two tennis nets were nothing more than a length of rotted rope.

"1942 was the last good summer at the Club," echoed George Hall. "After that, very few could get there because of gas rationing." He was in the Army from 1942-46 but when he came home on furlough several times, he scrounged enough gas to come to Diablo. "I was impressed by the number of Navy officers in and around the Club," said George. "There was a group billeted in the Chalet and they ate and drank at the clubhouse." George was told that some who had their families with them were renting Diablo houses.

Cecil Ryder remembered the Navy too. "The Seabees from Rock City were all over the place, along with the girls from the telephone company who were housed in the Chalet. The officers and their families who rented homes used the Club as their social center. We installed a juke box and the Seabees danced and courted the telephone gals. It was a great set-up for them."

ELIZABETH ("BEE") BELL Bee lived at 2060 Alameda Diablo during WWII and was active in this tiny enclave. She became good friends with four Navy families who were renting houses on Alameda Diablo. Two of the Navy officers were M.D.s, one was actress Gene Tierney's brother, and all were stationed at Camp Parks, 1942-44. They were from Oyster Bay, New York; Indianapolis, Indi-

Joe Ferreira and one of Herb Hills' sons.
COURTESY ROSE FERREIRA.

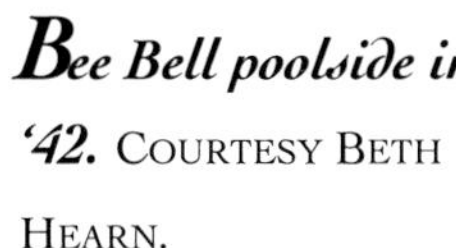

Bee Bell poolside in '42. COURTESY BETH HEARN.

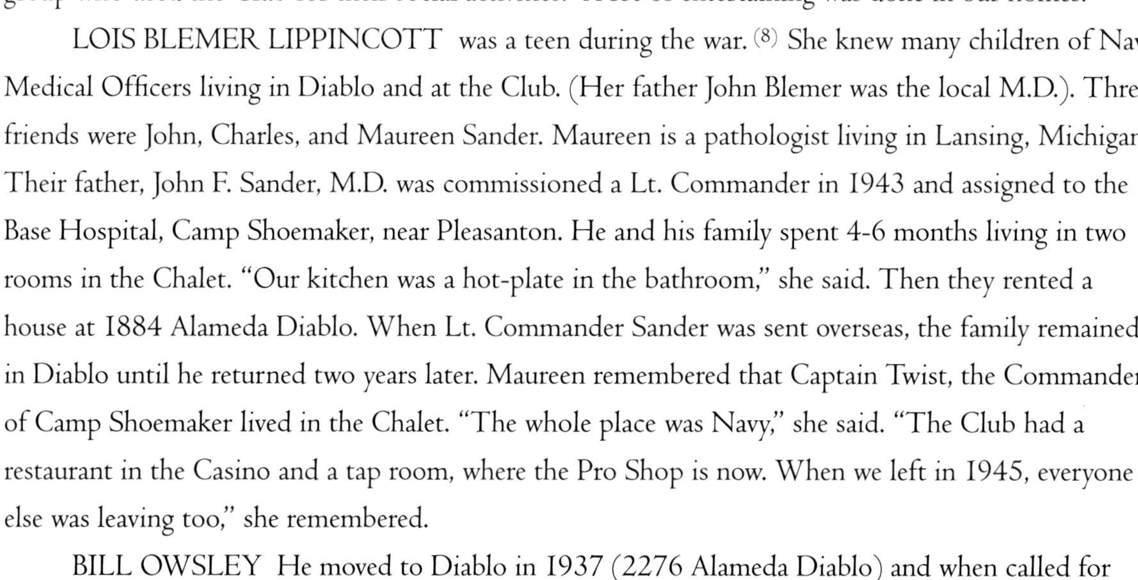

ana; Worchester, Massachusetts; and Charlotte, North Carolina.(7) Bee said, "They were a fun-loving group who used the Club for their social activities. A lot of entertaining was done in our homes."

LOIS BLEMER LIPPINCOTT was a teen during the war.(8) She knew many children of Navy Medical Officers living in Diablo and at the Club. (Her father John Blemer was the local M.D.). Three friends were John, Charles, and Maureen Sander. Maureen is a pathologist living in Lansing, Michigan. Their father, John F. Sander, M.D. was commissioned a Lt. Commander in 1943 and assigned to the Base Hospital, Camp Shoemaker, near Pleasanton. He and his family spent 4-6 months living in two rooms in the Chalet. "Our kitchen was a hot-plate in the bathroom," she said. Then they rented a house at 1884 Alameda Diablo. When Lt. Commander Sander was sent overseas, the family remained in Diablo until he returned two years later. Maureen remembered that Captain Twist, the Commander of Camp Shoemaker lived in the Chalet. "The whole place was Navy," she said. "The Club had a restaurant in the Casino and a tap room, where the Pro Shop is now. When we left in 1945, everyone else was leaving too," she remembered.

BILL OWSLEY He moved to Diablo in 1937 (2276 Alameda Diablo) and when called for Navy duty, continued to pay his Club dues. His first station was Reno, in 1942, and he remembered returning home every chance he got to go to Navy Club parties. He mused, "The Chalet was loaded with 75-100 officers who were billeted there and at the Red Horse Tavern because the BOQ (Bachelor Officer's Quarters) at Parks were full. They ate in the clubhouse and also held orientation classes there." With a smile a mile wide, Bill related, "A covey of nurse Lieutenants were billeted in the Chalet too. Need I say more why I came home every chance I got!"(9)

DOROTHY PETERSEN She was aware of the Navy's presence in Diablo during WWII through her son Steve and his friend Sandy Ferrell. They found a Navy pontoon near Diablo Lake. They hauled it to the Petersons' back yard, added mast and sails, and eventually sailed it down the Sacramento River from Red Bluff.

Thinking about her years in Diablo Dorothy said, "Take a look at the large building on the corner of Avenita Nueva and El Centro. This was famous as the Red Horse Tavern, built to accomodate visitors to Diablo and motorists going to the top of Mt. Diablo. Originally, this lovely old building had a charming veranda across the entire front. There were original Gibson Girls painted on the walls of the tack room." In 1948 it became the Red Horse Apartments.

JAPANESE-AMERICANS Hugh Ditzler, who played an exhibition match with Cliff Mayne at the opening of the new tennis facility in September, 1961, lived in Diablo 1940-42, when he was nine years old. On a Sunday afternoon in early December, 1941, he and his grandfather were playing in their fishing pond when his mother came running out of the house very agitated and excited to tell them the Japanese had bombed Pearl Harbor. Hugh said, "I really didn't understand then but the next day when I went to school I did. There were several Japanese kids in my fifth grade class and all of a sudden the other kids were mistreating them for no reason at all. I was really upset. These were nice farm kids and whatever happened on the radio wasn't their fault."

Sometime later Hugh realized the Japanese kids weren't at school anymore. They just disappeared and he didn't know why. His family put up blackout curtains on all their windows and they practiced huddling in the hall away from them. He said, "My mother told us not to tinker with the curtains or try to raise them." His father was somewhat of a thespian and active in the plays and skits performed at the Red Horse Tavern. Hugh commented, "I'd ride my bike to see the show and put clothespins on my wheels to make it sound like a motorcycle." When Hugh was eleven he used to go to the Casino to help put out the Club newsletter. He remembers making gelatin dittoes and delivering newsletters on his bike.

By the end of the summer of '42, all the maintenance staff had left for war duty or war work and soon Cecil Ryder was the only one left. He didn't leave because Hall and Hills, who were fast becoming owners of the Club, were successful in obtaining a draft deferment for Cecil because working for the Club was "...indispensable to the war effort."

"The Chalet was a busy place," said Cecil. "First, it housed the McNeil men who were building Camp Parks and Camp Shoemaker. Then came the telephone girls. In the early days of the war, there were 185 telephone girls at the camps and housing was next to nil, so the Chalet became their home." Helen Bliss was among those telephone girls housed in the Chalet and taken by van to and from the camps. That's how she and Cecil met and were married in 1945.

By the mid '40s some members wanted to take over the Club themselves— make it their very own—but they couldn't raise the money. Others complained about "those rich guys who want to steal the Club from us." Gradually the Hall/Hills group took over. Their attitude was, "We'll keep the Club together and give it back to the members for what it cost us to maintain it."

The Phillips Family, next door neighbors of the Hearns and still close friends.

Marian Waldo and daughters in the '40s.
COURTESY BEE BELL.

Beth Hearn with Mike and Penny.
COURTESY PENNY HEARN ADAMS.

Colonel Norman J. (Buzz) Hearn with fellow officer Major Ault, Wiesbaden, Germany, 1945.
COURTESY PENNY HEARN ADAMS.

After the summer of 1942, Club participation consisted mostly of mothers with children whose husbands were flying, soldiering or ploughing the high seas. Mothers congregated around the pool. The once popular Diablo Lake was still there, but used less and less as the war continued.

BETH HEARN SAID: "My life was child-centered. I took Mike and Penny to the pool every day. There wasn't a kiddy pool like there is today so we had to keep a careful eye on our children when they were in the shallow end. Other mothers with their kids were there too. We talked about our children, the war, and the whereabouts of our husbands. Many, like Buzz, were somewhere in Germany, some in England, Anzio, North Africa, others flying fighters and bombers over Germany, still others were in places in the Pacific we had never heard of before. We were frightened and lonesome. Talking about it made our lives bearable."

As the war was winding down and victory in Europe was expected to be announced (August, 1945) Rose Ferreira was serving dinner at the Hills'. It was a victory celebration party. Among the guests were the William Hales (1830 Alameda Diablo) whose son Bob was returning from the European front. During the dinner, William Hale, Sr. was called to the telephone and told the ship carrying Bob had been torpedoed and all aboard lost. Bill Hale, Jr., who survived his wartime service, married Barbara Hale, his brother's widow, built a house on Diablo Road and raised Bob and Barbara's daughter, Judy, as his own.

Rose remembered taking care of Jim Breeden's children who lived on Alameda Diablo. Jim had been in a German POW camp and had managed to escape with 27 other GIs. Rose also talked about the shortage of hay and how after a day's work at the Club, Joe would take his Fordson tractor, put a scythe on it and cut hay on the 16th, 17th, and 18th fairways. He did this for a number of people, including himself. "He did it for the war effort," said Rose.(10)

For a few, life went on untouched by the war, especially children and young teens like Tom Edwards. Tom remembered finding his grandfather's old hickory clubs in the attic. Johnny Juris, the Club Pro, sawed them off to the right length for a 12-year old and regripped them. Tom recalled, "I had a 3 wood, a 5 iron and a putter which I carried whenever we played." Today, Tom owns a full set of the finest clubs, "But then," he says, "those three clubs were all I had and I played better than I do now."

Like many other early residents, Tom's fondest memories were of Diablo Lake. It boasted a 30-foot slide, high and low diving boards and a rope swing that carried kids half way across. There were flood lights for night parties. Big kids and teens alike came early and stayed late. "The greatest fun," Tom says, "was playing tag. We played all day hiding under the raft or a float or best of all, in the big hollow oak tree. If the player was good at holding his breath, he could swim under water into the hollow of the tree to hide and never be tagged!"

There was also a lot to do in the horseback riding department. The year's biggest event was the summer rodeo. Young calves were brought in and the kids rode them till they fell or were bumped off. Everyone won a prize. Tom summed up his youth in these words: "Despite the war, for us kids, Diablo was the greatest. It was as if you'd died and gone to kiddy heaven."

By 1945, most of the military presence in Diablo was long gone. Cecil remembered it this way, "My draft deferment was to keep up the Club. That proved to be an almost impossible job with building materials in short supply. We fixed up the first nine holes, but the Club's revival didn't take."

HOUSING TRACT PLANNED By 1946 WWII was finished and so was the Club. The war years had taken their toll. The Club was in debt, membership was nil, the facilities dilapidated. Herbert Hills and Herbert Hall were desperate. To stave off the inevitable, they sold considerable Club property at $300 an acre to a few who had cash including the Petersons, Mills and Helfrich brothers. After another failing year, in March, 1948, they put the Club and all its physical assets up for sale. Myra Mae Hall Stapler recalled, "My father said it was the saddest day of his life. He said he felt like a GI who had been mortally wounded."

Ed McGaw, a well-known Contra Costa builder bought the property and was making plans to build several hundred GI homes that would be sold for $10,000 each. The deal was in escrow. The Diablo Country Club was about to become an historical footnote.

Larry Curtola, who had run the largest ship repair facility for the Navy on the West Coast, was in the market for land on which to build "better" ($12,000-$14,000) GI homes. He saw the Club in a real estate listing, and, remembering it fondly from his caddy days, traveled to Diablo and met Hall and Hills. "After I showed some interest in keeping the Club while also building houses on part of the property, Herb Hall said, 'Where do you bank?' I said, 'Bank of America, San Francisco.' He said, 'Who do you know?' I said, 'Fred Ferroggiaro' who was the Executive Vice President.

"The questions stopped. We continued to negotiate and I continued to examine the buildings and grounds. Later, I learned that Hall and Ferroggiaro belonged to the Claremont Country Club and

DIRECTOR'S MEETING.

San Francisco, California
December 4th, 1942

A special meeting of the Directors of DIABLO PROPERTIES, INC. was held this 4th day of December, 1942, at the hour of 3:30 o'clock P.M., at the office of the corporation, #910 Crocker Building, San Francisco, California.

There were present at said meeting

Directors	Frank P. McCann,
	A. Leslie Oliver,
	V. E. Breeden,
	Herbert E. Hall.
Absent:	Director H. G. Hills

President V. E. Breeden presided.

Mr. Breeden stated that the meeting had been called for the purpose of discussing the financial condition of Diablo Country Club and its effect upon Diablo Properties, Inc. He pointed out that the Properties company had been assuming the Club's deficits since the organization of the Club and that presently there were no funds of the Properties company available to meet the present deficit of the Club, which amounted to approximately $8,000. He further pointed out that the Properties Company had borrowed from Directors H. G. Hills and Herbert E. Hall in the amount of approximately $51,300, evidenced by a promissory note, which note was secured by a pledge of all of the bonds of Mt. Diablo Country Club, and that if Messrs. Hills and Hall were obliged to advance funds for the present indebtedness of the Club, the note would be in default, and that Messrs. Hills and Hall would then be in a position to foreclose on the pledge....

A special meeting of the Board of Directors of Diablo Properties, Inc.
COURTESY GEORGE HALL.

Barbara and Bill Hale. at right.

Casino becomes new clubhouse, below.

Susan and Herb Hall, age 56 and 57 in 1950. COURTESY GEORGE HALL.

that when Herb asked Fred about me, Fred said, 'Larry Curtola can do anything he says he'll do.'" In point of fact, the purchaser of record ($445,000 for 115 acres) was Diablo Properties, Inc., Larry Curtola, President, Joe Alioto, Secretary (later Mayor of San Francisco).(11) Larry said, "There was no written contract, our handshake was our bond. Joe and I each put up half the money. A year later, I bought out Joe's half but he remained my attorney and friend."

Saying that Curtola "purchased the Club," is not quite correct. What he did was buy the stock of Diablo Properties, Inc. That raised an interesting question: how can the company that owned it still be the owner after selling it? According to minutes of DPI, April, 29, 1948, upon Curtola's agreement to purchase at $445,000, Herb Hall as President of DPI and Herb Hall as Secretary resigned. At the same time they appointed Laurence Curtola, President of DPI and his partner and legal advisor Joseph L. Alioto, Secretary. So by an exchange of officers, the same company was both the former and new owner.(12) Now it's clear, isn't it?

By April, 1948, the agreement was operational. Larry would provide the money and the manpower to rebuild the Club, the Chalet, the golf course and the system which supplied water to the Club and community of Diablo. The management of the Club, Larry insisted, must remain the responsibility of an elected Board of Directors. As Larry put it: "I'd never been around a country club except as a caddy, the likes of Hills and Hall had been around them all of their lives. I knew construction, they knew how to run a club. The Club was broke, I was solvent from wartime cost-plus operations." It was a fortuitous partnership. Larry got 160 acres for his own use plus some lots on the edge of the golf course which he later sold for $5,000 each. Larry also acquired the 17 acre knoll, now the El Nido area.

One day Herb Hall said to Larry, "My wife and I love the view of the knoll from our patio (1778 Club House Road) and we never want to see it changed. Can I have it?" "Sure," said Larry, "I'll let you have it for $17,000." And so it was agreed. After the Halls died, the knoll was sold in 1973 to Bob Mainhardt for development. Ironically, "Fritz" Ferreira was the contractor!

Larry commented, "I understand why Herb Hall felt the way he did. He loved what he saw and didn't want it to change. I liked the Club for a different reason. To me it was authentic, historic and symbolic of the good life."

CASINO BECOMES CLUBHOUSE Making the broken down Casino into a modern clubhouse, Cecil remembered, was a big challenge. Curtola tore down the old horse barn across from the

Red Horse Tavern "...before it fell down..." and used some of the timber to build the new clubhouse, including the columns adorning the front entrance. Cecil said, "Working for a single owner was different from working for Club officers who were only around on weekends. It took getting used to."

One day shortly after Larry Curtola bought the Club he told Cecil he was going to lick the water problem by bringing water over the mountains. He said with enthusiasm, "I just bought the ranch at Pine Canyon on the Walnut Creek side of Mt. Diablo where there is an abundance of water." Cecil responded, "Owning the land has little to do with it. You have to own the water rights, too." But Larry went ahead and bought pipe. Now that he owned the land and had the pipe, all he had to do was put Cecil to work. But nothing happened because Cecil had been right about water rights. Curtola had to make alternative plans.

In 1949 the Ryders started building their house in Danville. When Larry heard about it, he said, "Cecil, if you move down to Diablo Road, you're fired. I won't have my maintenance man living off the premises." Cecil replied, "Well, Mr. Curtola, in that case I'm fired." A couple of days later Larry came to him and said, "Cecil, you're not married to this place, you're married to Helen, so forget what I said about being fired." Cecil recalled, "That was typical of Larry Curtola. When he found he was wrong, he was willing to admit it. Not many people can do that."

A gala opening of the Club took place on September 12, 1948 with over 500 in attendance. The old club-farm-house had been remade into a residence which Larry and Betty occupied for 26 years (1949-1975) raising three daughters, Corrine, Christine and Constance. The new clubhouse (our present facility) featured an enormous ballroom that was an immediate hit. Henry Gallagher's 12-piece orchestra played for the opening.

When the social season in the East Bay began in 1948, Diablo was the center of it. The *San Francisco Examiner* gave the event a double spread. For the next dozen years, no social event of significance was held other than at the Diablo Country Club. "We had space, a place where people could be comfortable, we had prestige. It was a beautiful place," said Larry, "and it was the perennial favorite with the UC fraternity and sorority crowd."

People often asked Larry why he built such a large ballroom. He replied, "The County needed a place big enough for more than 100 people and sufficiently prestigeous to bring people in at night. After all, they couldn't play golf after sundown."

A PLAN FOR THE REESTABLISHMENT OF THE DIABLO COUNTRY CLUB

The undersigned, admittedly ardent Diablans, (sic) have undertaken the task of reviving Diablo Country Club which was forced by the exigencies of the war to cease operations in May 1943.

This achievement could not be accomplished except for the very generous offer of Diablo Properties, Inc., which owns the properties formerly used by the Club, to sell the properties to the Club, at its out of pocket cost which presently amounts to approximately $90,000. Diablo Properties, Inc. is asking for no profit on its investment or even interest on its money, though it is manifest to anyone who is acquainted with the real estate market that land values at Diablo have appreciated materially during the last three years. However, it does insist that the new Club be on a proprietary basis and that memberships be sold for an amount sufficient in the aggregate to reconstruct a 9 hole golf course, to put buildings, grounds and equipment in first class condition and to have sufficient working capital to assure its financial integrity.

After a careful survey we believe that between $225,000 and $230,000 will be needed to purchase the property and to meet the requirements of Diablo Properties, Inc. We therefore propose to solicit 350 proprietary memberships at $650 a piece, plus $130 federal tax, or a total of $780. Such a program would produce $227,500 after tax and permit: (1) The reconstruction of a nine hole golf course; (2) The erection of a modern stable for the boarding of horses; (3) Renovation of the Chalet, men's locker room, women's cottage, main Club House; (4) Rebuilding men's and repairing women's dressing rooms at the lake; (5) Repairs to the swimming pool and tennis courts; (6) The restoration of the gardens; (7) The purchase of the Club's properties which are worth $250,000; and (8) An initial working capital of approximately $25,000.

It may develop that a nine hole course will not adequately take care of our needs, but we believe it sound to proceed in this manner. A well-balanced course of this length may be established, using nine holes of the former course, which will permit us to develop the additional nine over a period of time if play warrants. By using the old layout with green locations already graded and the entire course piped by watering, we will be able to keep our costs of rehabilitation to the minimum.

Our new stables and fine trails leading through the Mt. Diablo State Park should make this one of the best riding units in the Bay Area. Once Diablo Country Club is reopened it should not be long before it again holds its old position of the finest family Country Club in Northern California.

All applications for membership must be passed upon by the Committee on Admissions. Checks in the amount of $780 as they are received will be escrowed until May 1, 1946. If by that time the full sum of $227,500 has not been raised the money will be returned. Naturally the sooner our goal has been reached the sooner we can start the work of rehabilitation.

It is our intention to have a Club which in quality of membership will be unexcelled. Your name has been suggested as a prospective member and an application is enclosed.

EXHIBIT A
PROMISSORY NOTE

$230,000 Oakland, California, April 30, 1948

In installments as herein stated, for value received, we, LAURENCE CURTOLA, as maker, and DIABLO PROPERTIES, INC., a California corporation, as accommodation maker, jointly and severally promise to pay to the order of H. G. HILLS and HERBERT E. HALL, at the office of Herbert E. Hall, 910 Crocker Building, San Francisco, California, the sum of Two Hundred Thirty Thousand Dollars ($230,000), with interest from the date hereof on the unpaid principal at the rate of three per cent (3%) per annum.

We jointly and severally further promise to pay said principal sum and interest as aforesaid in installments as follows, to wit:

Thirty Thousand Dollars ($30,000) of principal, plus interest as aforesaid, on or before May 31, 1948;

Seventy-five Thousand Dollars ($75,000) or more of principal, plus interest as aforesaid, on January 15, 1949;

Fifty Thousand Dollars ($50,000) or more of principal, plus interest as aforesaid, on or before June 15, 1949; and

The balance of said principal, plus interest as aforesaid, on or before January 15, 1950, on which date the entire unpaid balance of said principal sum, with interest as aforesaid, shall become due and payable.

Should default be made in the payment of any installment of principal or interest when due, the whole sum of principal and interest shall become immediately due and payable, at the option of the holder of this note.

Principal and interest are payable in lawful money of the United States of America.

If action be instituted on this note, we jointly and severally promise to pay such sum as the court may fix as attorneys' fees.

This note is secured by a deed of trust of even date herewith to Title Insurance and Guaranty Company, San Francisco, California, from Diablo Properties, Inc., a corporation.

DIABLO PROPERTIES, INC., a corporation
By LAURENCE CURTOLA
President
By JOSEPH L. ALIOTO

The Diablo Country Club
Formal Opening and Dinner Dance
on Wednesday, the eighth of September
Nineteen hundred and forty-eight

Cocktails 6 p.m.
Dinner at 8 p.m.

$7.50 per person
Informal

Exhibit A. Promissory Note, DPI, above.
COURTESY GEORGE HALL.

Larry stated, "I mostly kept my distance from the Club's operation. But when we started up in 1948, I did insist that the $300 initiation fee (dues were $17 a month) be put into a separate account so that anytime a member was dissatisfied he could get back his original investment. If they weren't happy I didn't want them around." Larry also saw that the assessment was limited to $100 per year. Later, when the membership suddenly dropped from 400 to 200 Larry got the Board to drop the initiation fee for the first year of each new membership. Within weeks the Club had its full quota of 400 members. He said, "I'm glad I was able to help when I could."

Larry Curtola did more than help. He saved the Club from developers, preserving it for the benefit of the members and the community.

LOIS BLEMER LIPPINCOTT'S OLD TIMER MEMORY

I lived the first 3 years of my life at Diablo in my grandparents' summer home, "Old Faithful," on the right side of Alameda Diablo behind a huge oleander hedge. I remember morning bird songs mixed with the skritch, skritch, skritch of the gardener's rake on the pebbled paths around the house. The house had a walled patio with a huge fireplace and all the rooms had double doors opening onto it. We employed a Filipino couple, Leo and Lillian, in the kitchen; Ruth, my nurse; and Tom Flores, the gardener who went with us to Green Valley Farm when my parents built it in 1937.

I remember Diablo as a world of endless summers of tireswings, Easter bunnies, rodeos and water everywhere. We little ones escaped the heat in the safety of patio play pools and lawn sprinklers or the Club's elegant children's pool with its wondrous sand beach. In stern contrast, the Lake was a huge, mysterious, dark body of forbidden water with ducks feeding on its steep banks and turtles plopping off half submerged logs. Only 'grown-ups' swam there!

Piedmont cousins were everywhere, plus a score of pseudo 'aunts' and 'uncles.' We would all gather and caravan up Mt. Diablo to picnic on warm summer evenings. Noisy and carefree, spread out on blankets, playing ukuleles and feasting on huge slices of watermelon for dessert...life was good!

A note written to the author in May, 1994.

THE NIFTY FIFTIES

Chapter VI

ALL IN THE FAMILY Diablo in the Nifty '50s was best characterized by Betty Curtola when she said, "It was a time of family, a feeling that Club and community were one—interdependent—sharing the good life and our growing children." Diablo was a small, homogeneous town of like-minded people. Everyone knew everyone, their children, even their horses, dogs and cars. And nearly everyone swam at the Club because there were no air-conditioned homes and few home pools. Most children had a horse or access to one. The Club was more like a community center than a country club.

Activities abounded for children, teens, and adults. Golf included a junior program; there was an organized swim team, and horseback riding. An instructional equestrian program and drill team, the Double D's, was under the direction of Bettye Johanson. The Club maintained a stable of horses for hire at the upper end of Alameda Diablo. There were many overnight rides to Barbecue Terrace in the Park. "Because we were family, I think this had a positive effect on children's behavior," Betty Curtola concluded.

Ben Reed and his wife Susan moved to Alamo in 1938. Then he left for WWII duty with the OSS, the forerunner of the CIA. Robin was born in 1940, followed by Bambi in '43 and Daphne in '46. Within a few years, everyone was talking about the Reed sisters. "They took to water like ducks," recalled Ben proudly, and dominated the swimming at Diablo for a decade.

ROBIN From the mid '50s, Robin was the head lifeguard and swim coach, admired and loved by young and old. Now Robin Prouty, an 8 handicapper at the Silverado Country Club and mother of two boys, wrote:

Betty Curtola with Larry.

Chris Ives, President of The Double D's.

The Double D (Danville-Diablo) Junior Horsemen began in 1954 with headquarters at the Humphrey Arena on Stone Valley Road. The Arena is on a six-acre plot given to the community for its use by Dave and Marge Humphrey.

Double D's win at the Cow Palace. L to R, Pat Welch, Patty Ford, Kathy Morrison and Bren Giffin. COURTESY ROBERTA SEABURY.

Dave took the measurements of the Contra Costa County Fair horse arena in Antioch and planned the Humphrey Arena as an exact duplicate.

DEAR JIM:

It was fun talking to you yesterday. Dad told me you might be calling. You were some organizer—supporting the swim program in those "good ol' days" when the pool wasn't heated, we had no team suits or sweats, had to supply our own food and drinks for our splash parties, and raise money for our end-of-the summer bash to Santa Cruz.

As you might have guessed, I have very fond memories of the Diablo Country Club as a young person. It was a special place for kids and the pool area was where most of them congregated. I called them "the Diablo Gang" which ranged in age from 10-18. Some of their names were: Gary and Candy Hendricks, Nibs White, Pete Dozier, Mike and Penny Hearn, Bambi and Daphne Reed, the Rossi brothers, Ashley, Ann and Brett Stone. One of my favorite lifeguards was Don Anderson.

The swim team was what brought us all together. Our biggest rival was Orinda Park Pool. Our own Fourth of July races were very popular with the children and teen-agers. Bill Owsley added his special touch as the MC.

Another very special person was Dave Hakman. In 1957, we shared lifeguard duties and coaching the swim team. Dave was a student at Cal from southern California. He introduced all of us to skateboarding, which was the highlight of that summer. All of us built skateboards with 2 x 4s and attached steel roller skates to them, a far cry from the skateboards and roller blades of today.

One of our favorite outings was to skate down Mt. Diablo at night with the headlights from the Volkswagons illuminating the way. It was crazy, but great fun!

Another adventure was sliding down the 15th fairway on blocks of ice until the golf course superintendent "discouraged" us.

Several times after lifeguarding in the evening, a gang of us would play golf as an eightsome in our bathing suits and bare feet with the Hendricks' dog tagging along!

In the '50s, the Club was a special place where kids of all ages had a wonderful time as a group. It was a real family Club, and sadly, those days are gone forever.

These are just some of my favorite experiences. It would be fun to have a reunion with the "Old Diablo Gang." If you publish anything about Diablo, I would love to know about it so I can get a copy.

Fondly,

THE CONTEXT The Eisenhower years—a time when the economy is adjusting from wartime to peacetime and the Cold War has just begun.

Earl Warren and an economic boom dominate the California scene fueled by an explosive birth rate of WWII baby boomers and an unprecedented immigration from the midwest and south. There is a shortage of housing, and shopping malls—an innovation—are springing up in suburbia.

Schools are double-sessioned, teachers in short supply. Moms wear dresses, at just below the knee, with gloves and hats. Nylons have replaced silk stockings. Dads too wear hats, use tie clasps and wear handkerchiefs in their breast pockets.

Kids *dress-up* for school—boys in slacks and shirts; girls in skirts, sweaters, bobby sox and saddle shoes. The big bands of swing are in sway. Herman Wouk's *The Caine Mutiny* gets the Pulitzer for novels.

Everyone looks for shade and pools in summer because air conditioning is for office buildings. The New York Giants move to San Francisco, the Brooklyn Dodgers to Los Angeles. Radio is everywhere with the favorites Jack Benny, Fred Allen, Bob Hope, Ozzie and Harriet and Groucho Marx. With the war over and gas plentiful, Americans return to their first love—their cars—and drive-in theatres and restaurants are popular.

Houses cost $10 per square foot, and five cents buys a pack of Wrigley's Spearmint Gum, and everyone's favorite, Juicy Fruit.

Sunday dinners at the Club are $2 and a new generation is moving into Diablo.

See how many Diablo youngsters turned out for the ever popular Easter egg hunt in the '50s.

Back row L to R, Daniel, Samuel, George, and Herbert Hall. Front row L to R, Suzette Abbott, Judy, Suzette Hall, Susan Hall, Myra Mae Abbott, David Hall, Windy Hall, Betty Hall, Cynthia Abbott. COURTESY MYRA MAE HALL STAPLER.

A 1954 swim meet. L to R, Joe Hendricks, Club President; Johnnie Juris, Golf Pro; Jay Hendricks, Josh Owsley.
COURTESY BILL OWSLEY.

Daphne Reed tees off with the Junior Golf League.

SWIMMING Diablo's swim team, with Robin in charge, had a modest schedule of several meets with other clubs. This was before swim clubs in organized leagues became popular. At the end of each meet the results were posted. Here is an example from the September, 1957 *Inferno:*

DIABLO JUNIOR SWIMMING RESULTS

LIVERMORE AQUAROD Daphne Reed-2nd Freestyle; Ann Stone-5th Butterfly;

LAFAYETTE JUNIOR OLYMPICS Mike Hearn-lst Diving;1st Butterfly;

Ann Stone-1st Freestyle;-2nd Butterfly; Daphne Reed-1st Diving;-2nd Freestyle;

Bambi Reed-1st Diving; Penny Riser-1st Backstroke;-4th Freestyle;

Pam Owsley-2nd Freestyle; Barry Eschen-2nd Freestyle;

Bill Humphrey-2nd Diving; Nancy Bogue-2nd Diving;-3rd Freestyle; Karen Eschen-4th Butterfly

COMING MEET Sequoyah Country Club at Diablo, September 8, 1:00 p.m.

JUNIOR GOLF was popular in the '50s and even became famous. Youngsters, aged 6-18, played in weekly tournaments both with their parents and by age groups. They competed in Hayward, Sacramento, Fresno, San Francisco and at the Claremont and Del Rio Country Clubs. Perennial sponsors were Joe and Benjie Hendricks, Bill and Fran Owsley, Bill Warren and Russ Knowland. Bill Owsley also MC'd the events and "kids" of the '50s fondly remember him, mike in one hand, glass in the other, the flow of contagious laughter and good-natured repartee. The policy was that every player got a prize and the sponsors saw to it that they did with proper ceremony on the patio at the end of play.

A very popular half-hour children's program on the newly emerging TV was Walt Disney's Mickey Mouse Club. It had pictures of all sorts of children doing all kinds of activities, a Club song, an intriguing serial, "The Adventures of Spin and Marty," and featured current events. Diablo fell into this latter category with this announcement in the February, 1956 *Inferno*:

LATE FLASH: Monday, February 6, 5:00-5:15 p.m. News Reel scenes of Diablo's Jr. Invitational Golf Tournament will be shown on the Mickey Mouse Club Show. (TV)

Notice that the announcement specified TV, because otherwise everyone would have turned on the radio!

Somehow, Walt Disney had heard about the Club's Junior Golf Program and a TV crew had spent a day filming the Juniors in the summer of '55. The filming ended with an awards ceremony on the patio. Later the Juniors were invited to visit the Disney Studios and meet the Mouseketeers. What a thrill! Bill Owsley remembered, "I saw it on TV twice. The kids saw it at least three times. I think this is the only time the Diablo Country Club has been on national TV."

By now, everyone is aware that the Club was well-known for its Easter Sunday morning Egg Hunt. Dyeing eggs the night before Easter was an *event* too, but just for adults. The committee assembled Saturday night in the men's locker room. There were 500 eggs to be dyed. The committee, augmented considerably by their friends, learned that the chef and the manager had had a shouting match, the manager had lost his cool and summarily fired the chef. Realizing the Easter brunch was the next day, he then swallowed his pride and talked the chef into staying just for the brunch.

On this particular Easter in 1955, following tradition, Joe Hendricks and Bill Owsley hid the eggs around the first tee on Easter morning. The children arrived, dressed in their Easter finery, and the hunt began. When the children picked up their eggs, they squashed! Yellow yolks ran all over their Easter best. "The fairway looked like an omelet," Bill said. Inspired by vengeance, the chef had soft-boiled the eggs. The manager joined the departing chef!

Children's Christmas parties were even more popular than Easter. The 1957 party was typical.(1) It started at 3:00 p.m. with Christmas carols and entertainment. Santa arrived at 4:00 and gave presents to children between the ages of two and ten. Each family brought a gift or gifts, value not to exceed $1 each, depending upon the number of children in the family. Each gift was labeled to indicate age and sex and dropped into a large bag in the Club lobby the day prior to the party. There was an early children's dinner with movies following in the downstairs family room. While the kids were thus occupied, the "old folks" sneaked in a little booze, some dancing, and then dining.

Gail Breitwieser wrote, asking: "Do you ever find anything that is very cleverly written in all those old *Infernos?"*

Answer: Yes, at right is an example from a December, 1958 issue. The author, obviously a woman, unfortunately is unknown.

"All male golfers born in 1908 or earlier are invited to join Nifty Fifty for 1958," the January '58 *Inferno* proclaimed, "...at $1 for old members and $2 for new ones." John Blemer, long-time Danville physician, Club member, and inveterate golfer turned 50 in 1958. He organized a special

CAPTAIN FORTUNE AND SANTA ZERO IN ON DIABLO

Between 'Ho-Ho's' and snatches of 'Jingle Bells' Santa has assured the *Inferno* that he will be at the Diablo Children's Christmas Party on schedule. Since no Diablo youngster between the ages of two and a hundred would miss this party anyhow, this message is really addressed to boys and girls who were only one last year and may not have their mothers and fathers properly brainwashed.

KIDS! Bring your parents to the Club at 2:30 p.m., Sunday December 21. Besides you, they should have with them a dollar present for you and one for each of your brothers and sisters who come. Each present should have written on it the age and sex of the child for whom it is intended. If it is the kind of a present where sex does not rear its ugly head like, say, a switchblade that any child could use, the age will be enough.

Captain Fortune of KPIX TV will entertain from 2:30-3:30. If your mother and father don't know Captain Fortune, you have been pretty lax with them on Saturday mornings.

Promptly at 3:30 Santa will arrive to give presents. At 5:00 p.m. a buffet will be served. This will NOT include roast beef or turkey or horrible old steaks with black outsides, but will be food for the most discriminating child: Hot Dogs, Hamburgers, Spaghetti, Jello Salad, Desserts and Favors. If you prefer not to eat your favor, that is of course, up to you, but most red-blooded American children find them delectable. You will have to let your mother or father accompnay you to the buffet table. It pleases the old things to think they have something to say about what you eat—ha-ha and ho-ho, as Santa would say—and besides, you need them to sign the chit!

tournament for himself and others 50 or older. As one of his former golf partners said, "Doc loves to win and figures to for sure with his own tournament!" The tournament continues to this day.

The February, 1959 *Inferno* headlined, *"Ron Patton is our new Pro, and we wish him the best of luck at Diablo.* Ron is 31 and married to Joyce. He has a girl, Stacy, 4-years old, and a boy, Jeffrey, 2-years old. Ron's father is the well-known and well-liked Pro at Orinda Country Club," (and Diablo Pro in the '30s). The same *Inferno* reported that Alex Stewart, Chairman of the Jackie Jensen Charity Pro-Amateur Tournament scheduled for the Club, February 17, 1956 reported the 130-man field—one pro to three amateurs—was filling rapidly. The article continued, "Half the $20 entry fee will go to the Children's Hospital. The remaining $10 covers use of the Club's facilities, entertainment, and a steak dinner at Diablo after the event." Jensen, former UC football All-American was a Boston Red Sox outfielder at the time.

In 1957, the Holyniners started the New Year with the satisfaction of receiving the OUTSTANDING ACHIEVEMENT AWARD of the year from the editor of the *Inferno*. It was a proud moment when the Holyniners were presented with the Helfrich perpetual trophy engraved with their group's name as winner of the "Man of the Year" award for 1956.(2)

Not to be outdone by their nine-hole sisters, the 18-hole women's group penned this special appeal for action in the July '57 *Inferno*:

> *"Vacation is here! Now is the time for all you golfing mothers to park the kids by the pool, then dash to the first tee. Now is the time to let housework go to pot and figure things out the easiest way. With all the planned activities for the youngsters and teen-agers, what better Club is there than Diablo?"*

JUNIOR JIVE

HELLO EVERYBODY, this is ole Pam again. Hope you've all been having a good time this summer. Sure has been a lot of activity. There was a swimming meet Saturday, August 15, with Orinda. Sure was a lot of fun. Some of our people were sick and couldn't enter, but we gave Orinda a good try anyway. Ann Stone, one of our best swimmers, had a cold but swam for us anyhow and won some ribbons. Daphne Reed, Kelly and Sherrie White, Roberta and Lindy Kane, Pete Cronin, Phil Greer, Johnnie Blanco, just to mention a few, but everybody really tried. Diablo cleaned up in freestyle, but in the other strokes they beat us something awful. To make you feel better, Orinda has swum in six other meets this summer and won all. We're the closest anyone has come point-wise to Orinda. Guess we'll have to work harder on the other strokes. We are hoping to have another meet this summer, this time with Sleepy Hollow. I think we all should thank Morey Simmons, who is leaving us soon, for his really good coaching. Hope we see you again.

The weather sure has gotten colder, looks as if Fall is coming early. School is almost here. It sure has been a wonderful summer. I hope I can look forward to seeing lots of the kids during the winter. The last golf tournament for us will be the Father and Daughter, Mother and Son. I'll give the winners in the next issue. Talking about golf, I think the kids should give their thanks to our Pro Ron Patton and his assistant Pro, Will Strong. Thanks.

I want everyone to know that I appreciate the wonderful people that helped with the children's activities and made it possible for us to have had such a wonderful time this summer. And also thanks for reading my article. See you soon. Please call me with any news at VErnon 7-4051.

The juniors had a regular column in the Inferno in order to keep close touch with each other. An example is Pam Owsley at age 15, from the September, 1959 issue.

WOMEN PLAY—Not to be outdone by their golfing husbands who moved into second round competition in the Mapes Partnership best ball golf tournament today, the ladies started competition also in a tournament of their own at the Washoe county links. Left to right, and all from Diablo country club at Oakland are: Mrs. Lloyd Rossi teeing off; Mrs. William Owsley, Mrs. George Shank and Mrs. Larry Curtola. (Chamber of Commerce photo)

This aerial picture of the golf course club grounds, homes on Alameda Diablo and around the golf course features the racetrack (lower left). The track was famous in the days when Diablo was the Oakwood Stock Farm. Trees outlining the track may be seen to this day.

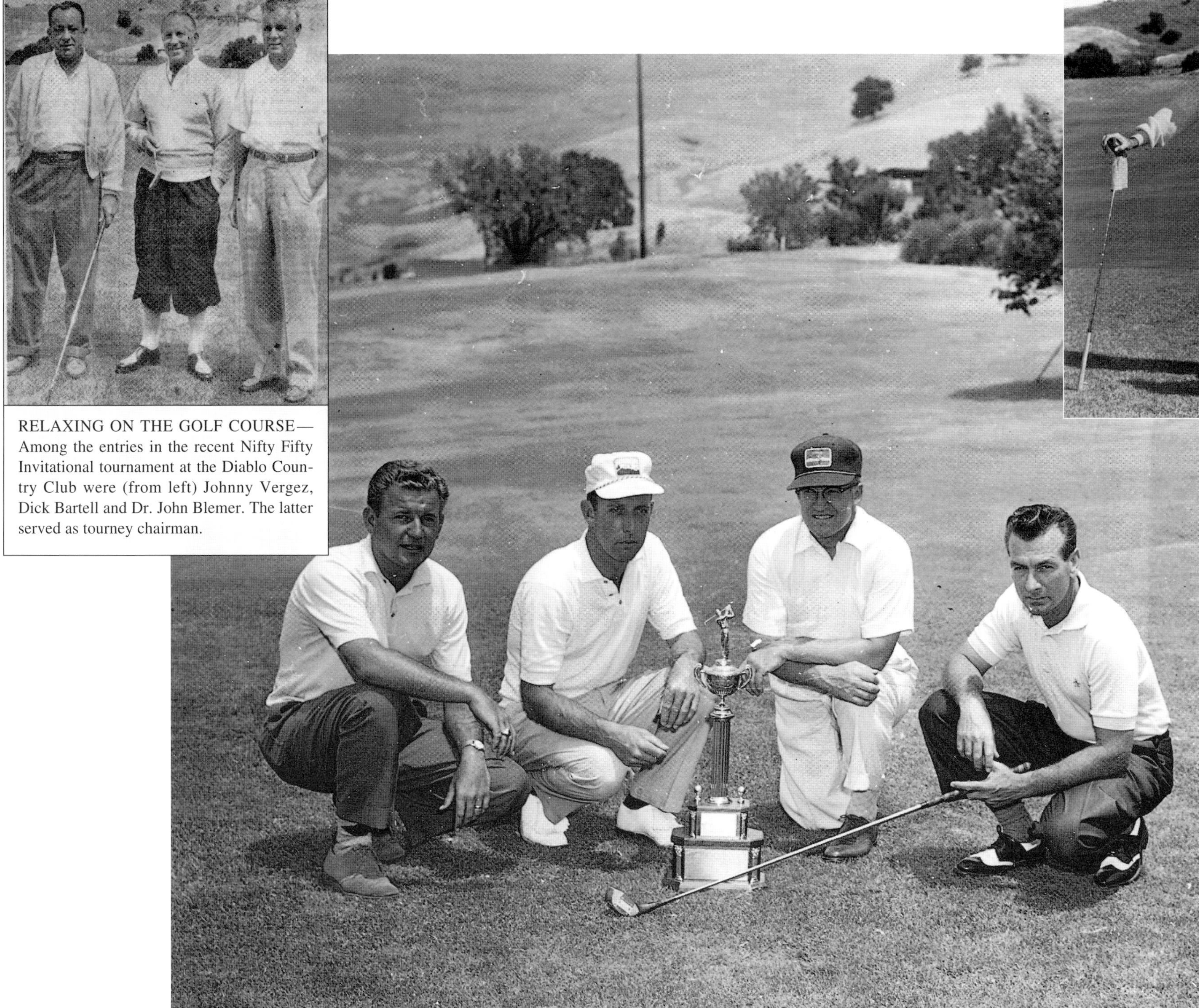

RELAXING ON THE GOLF COURSE—Among the entries in the recent Nifty Fifty Invitational tournament at the Diablo Country Club were (from left) Johnny Vergez, Dick Bartell and Dr. John Blemer. The latter served as tourney chairman.

Doc Blemer and his well-known, ever faithful golfing companion. COURTESY LOIS BLEMER LIPPINCOTT.

Ron Patton (Golf Pro), Bud Shank, DeWitt Krueger, Lloyd Rossi in 1959. Bud Shank's 62 still stands as the Diablo Country Club's all-time course record.

PARTIES Each year the Club chartered buses for the Big Game, played alternately at Palo Alto and Berkeley. The buses featured a complete bar. The game was followed by a dinner dance, featuring "Dr. Don" leading a yell or two, since Don Priewe was Cal's yell leader in 1948. The November, 1957 event is still being talked about. Herewith is an excerpt from the *Inferno*: (3)

BIG GAME

"Oops! My gosh—did we ever goof. Did you read the announcement about the Big Game Party on the 23rd of November? Remember, it said (in the *Inferno*) that you could get transportation, lunch, anti-freeze, dinner, dance, and TICKETS for the game. Well, you can get the first five items plus some surprises—But, the tickets? Oy! What a noodnick. You and I both know full well that I can't get tickets for you for the Cal - Stanford game. *Tickets for Si-wash vs Mud River Flat Aggies on Thanksgiving Day, yes—but Cal - Stanford, NO, NO, NO!* It doesn't take too high a marble count to realize we are telling you that you have to get your own tickets.

Call today for your reservations. Your name will be put on the bus list, the lunch list, the dinner list, and the dance list—any listing from then on will be your own doing.

Remember—we have NO tickets for the Cal - Stanford game. We do have two good seats for the Si-wash - Mud River Flat Aggies biggest of all bowl game!"

According to the *Inferno*, the crowd gathered in the parking lot, to board the buses, "...it looked as if an army was on the move." In good time, and in good spirits, eventually five buses with their 200 passengers pulled out headed for a thrilling game at Berkeley. At the dinner dance that night the gals all sported chrysanthemums and the lads wore beanies, making the Blue/Gold - Red/White decorated ballroom look like a real college post-game dance. "...Way beyond our expectations" was the consensus.

MAD BALL Another popular annual social event was the Mad Hatter's Ball in March. A 1958 *Inferno* said this: (4)

"Circle this date on your calendar, Saturday, March 29, then phone the baby-sitter! This is the party you don't want to miss. It's a wonderful cure for "cabin fever" after the long winter rains.

"Remember last year all the Mad things that went to people's heads, like cakes, chickens, golf club, flowers—drinks? This year should be even greater, because we have a whole new field to work with—Sputniks, Muttniks, and Satellites. (Russia sent off its first Sputnik on October 4, 1957, to the shock of the free world.) Now that should start the wheels running, and put you in orbit for one of the

'LUAU NIGHT' PARTY THEME FOR DIABLO

Sarongs and muu-muus will be the attire of the feminine guests at Diablo Country Club Saturday evening, and the masculine half of the gathering for the club's "Luau Night" will wear aloha shirts.

Chairmen of the event, at which decor and program will be Hawaiian, are Mr. and Mrs. Robert Armstrong. Flower leis will be provided and Hawaiian singers and dancers will entertain at poolside.

Assisting the Armstrongs are Mr. and Mrs. William Warren, Mr. and Mrs. Rig Ballard, the Frank Walkers, the Carl Noeckers, Mr. and Mrs. Jim Prince, Mr. and Mrs. Fred Udall, the Glen Powells, the Robert Seeleys, the Les Fimrites, Mr. and Mrs. William Winslow, Mr. and Mrs. John Barone, the Spencer Archers.

Many of the club's members will be guests at the Chalet over the weekend of the event, among them the Charles Gwynns, the H. I. Martins, Mr. and Mrs. B. O. Kirkland, the Winslows, the Fimrites, the Powells, Mr. and Mrs. Arthur Brunckhorst, Mr. and Mrs. Lawrence L. Moore, Mr. and Mrs. Robert Collins and the Reg Bowmans.

Mrs. Warren plays accompaniment as Diablo Country Club members prepare for Saturday's Luau Night

DIAMOND HORSESHOE is theme for Diablo Country Club's Western Fiesta, set for next Saturday, with true "old West" atmosphere created by props for annual party. Guests will be driven from parking lot in horse-drawn hay wagon, and orchestra for outdoor dancing will hold forth in a corral. Steak barbecue will be the entree. Preparing for the event are Mr. and Mrs. Jim Stone (at left), chairmen, and members including Chester Eschen, (standing, with palomino), Mr. and Mrs. Sam Abbot (at right) and, not in picture, the Ed Connors, William Hales and Tom Suttons. A "talking horse" will present prizes for six best men's and six best women's Western costumes at midnight.

beautiful prizes. But in order to be a part of all this, you must wear a hat. Either that or be a square and *buy* one at the door.

"One thing is sure - it will be the gayest, and it will give you a chance to use your head! Consider this lineup:

Roast Prime Rib of Beef Dinner. 'Dance to the Music of Henry Gallagher.' Wear the Maddest Head Gear, Price - $5 per person - all inclusive. Make your reservation *NOW!*"

MORE PARTIES There were other "traditionals"— the Lou Armstrong Luau in August being the most popular.[5] Throughout the '50s and '60s it was an exceedingly successful event with an Hawaiian floor show piped directly from the islands and outstanding local talent "sandwiched in." The native food was stamped with the "Armstrong" trademark. This was always Lou's show and a tribute to her organizational and hostess talents.

Sam Abbott played Lady Godiva at the Horsemen's Party in 1958. Jim Berryhill owned the horse. Courtesy Myra Mae Hall Stapler.

The '59 Anniversary Party. L to R, Bailey & Marie Justice, Henry Gallagher, band leader, Frank & Mildred Rossi, Buzz Knowlton, Carol Krueger, the R.D. Fishs, Aida & Les Foley, Billie & Bill Van Bokkelen, Benji & Joe Hendricks, Betty Curtola, DeWitt Krueger, Larry Curtola. COURTESY DEWITT KRUEGER.

A '50s Anniversary Party featured the "Andrew Sisters", Bill Owsley, Frank Walker, and W.B. Van Bokkelen.

WATER CRISIS

When Joe Hendricks was President in '53, he insisted on filling the pool for Easter despite the need to conserve water. "Empty pools are unsafe," he insisted, "besides, a filled pool is more fun." After filling the pool, there was a severe water crisis. The Club had no drinkable water! People arrived for Easter brunch and had to settle for soft (?) drinks. Everyone blamed Joe.

Joe was oblivious to the problem because his summer home on Club House Road by the 3rd tee was at the end of the waterline so he had water.

Wanting to be in tune with the Easter spirit, at brunchtime Joe donned an airplane hat that squirted water. He and Benji walked to the Club to join their friends, all of whom were grumbling about the water crisis. As Joe greeted his friends, he squirted them. His hat was in tune but it played a sour note.

1959 Club Board. L to R, (seated): DeWitt Krueger, Bob Seely, Bailey Justice, (standing): John Enright, John Barone, Buzz Knowlton, Frank Rossi and Lou Schrepel.

MANAGEMENT OF THE CLUB Keeping up the membership was the greatest challenge of the '50s. Initiation fees were raised to $800. However, there were other problems besetting the Board. The following *Inferno* excerpts tell the story:

"In August the Club spent $4,955.41 for water and the power to pump it on the golf course. Part of this water came from the Contra Costa Canal and part from EBMUD by way of the Diablo (Curtola) Water Co. This expense did not take into account the labor cost in getting that water on the course. Two men watered at night and drew time and a half after their fifth day on a union contract.(6)

"The use of the golf course increased 25% over last year. Over 100 golfers per day were playing. Maintenance of the course continues to be one of the Club's major problems. There is a serious water shortage as well as increased water costs. The Club hopes the problem will be solved next year when EBMUD comes to Diablo.(7)

Bill Owsley, Van's partner, Bill Van Bokkelen, Gennaro Filice.

"The Club will provide its own access road ...by utilizing the entrance near Hagstrom's (now Mehran's) and the road along the 17th and 18th fairways. It will provide a very scenic entrance to the clubhouse."(8) *(It never happened. Whoever came up with this brilliant idea never checked with Larry Curtola who held the purse strings.)*

Would you like to go to dinner at the Club, served on Fridays, Saturdays, Sundays and holidays? A five-course dinner is served from 7:00-9:00 p.m. for $1.65, children $.75 plus free movies for them and a 10 cent charge for their babysitter.

Stay overnight at the Chalet. Why not? Better take advantage of the present price, the following increase in rates goes into effect January 1, 1956:

> $6.00 for room with bath.
> $5.00 for room with ½ bath.
> Weekly rates 6 days with 7th day free.
> Kitchen $2.50. The new rate represents a 100% increase over the pre-war 1941 rate.(9)

SHOTS FROM THE PRO SHOP Norm Tauscher wrote that "the greatest thrill to the membership and myself was the overwhelming turnout for the father and son tournament held Sunday, the 28th of August, 1955." Sixty fathers and sons attended the 7:00 a.m. breakfast on the patio and 90 played in the tournament.(10)

With the headline, "New Baby: the Holyniners of Diablo," the formation of a new group of women golfers was heralded in the 1955 *Inferno.*

"Because women golfers felt that their inexperience in golfing and their ability to play a full round has prevented them from being active in the Women's Group, and because of limited time due to children, outside activities, many have not been able to participate in the Women's Group." Five women who played nine holes occasionally realized the potential of organizing an active group of like-minded sisters in August, 1955. Thus, the new baby was born.(11)

MISCELLANEA To improve service and reduce operating expenses, an *Inferno* article reported that "consideration is being given to relocating the Men's Grill, now in the basement under the Club offices, and building a family dining room overlooking the practice fairway. A survey is underway as to the cost of these alterations."(12) (*It was 30 years before the family dining room overlooking the practice fairway came about—in the 1986 restoration of the clubhouse.*)

By February, 1956 the Club's roster was nearing its "...closing point for the first time since the reorganization of the Club after it was purchased in 1948 by Larry Curtola. A pipeline running from the Concord Canal to Diablo Lake has been built at a cost of $170,000. Diablo Lake has been enlarged and an additional lake is under construction that will have twice the storage of our existing lake. In all, we will have three lakes to collect water for storage so our fairways will look like putting greens in the very near future."

Horse activities peaked in the '50s. Some of the action brought reaction, as witness:

"Considerable damage has occurred to our greens and fairways from horses breaking out of their stables and corrals. Children have been negligent in observing the bridle paths around the golf course that were designed for horseback riding. Your Board of Directors is requesting parents to outline to their children the bridle paths that are to be used by the horses and the dangers of being hit by a golf ball."(13)

Yes, the '50s really were nifty—an interlude of tranquility, congeniality, and family between the war-torn '40s and the protesting, chanting and screaming '60s.

Bailey Justice. Anniversary Party as President.

Seated left to right, Bailey Justice, Marie Justice, Larry Curtola, Mary Fish, Les Foley, Benjie Hendricks, Joe Hendricks, Aida Foley, Betty Curtola, William Van Bokkelen, Billie Van Bokkelen, and R.D. Fish.

Bailey Justice (below, left) received the first Helfrich Award from Bill Helfrich in 1956.
COURTESY GERI HELFRICH.

MEMORABLE MEMBER: BAILEY JUSTICE

Bailey Justice, oldest living Club President (1958) became a member in 1949. It was a "gift" from Larry Curtola. Bailey was in the landscape business and had planted 1,000 trees in Sun Valley Estates, a development in Lafayette owned by Curtola. Larry sold it still owing Bailey $350. As it happened, right after the sale, the buyer died and the development bogged down in litigation. Larry went to Bailey and said, "I own a golf club, you're a golfer, why don't I give you a membership for what I owe you?" And so it was done. "Plus," Bailey added, "he threw in a case of Scotch."

Bailey and Marie began playing golf regularly in the early '50s. Bailey found the tees were in bad shape. When the job of Chairman of the Greens Committee opened in 1954, the Board said, "You're a landscaper, let's see what you can do." Bailey devoted himself to relandscaping the course.

He extended the sprinkler system "...there never was enough water..." to ensure that the tees were watered regularly. He relocated and completely rebuilt the 1st tee, then upgraded the 3rd, 4th, 6th, 7th, 10th, and 11th tees. He completely redid the 9th fairway because every winter it got so water-logged it couldn't drain. He tilled the entire fairway, brought in tons of dirt, and changed the tilt so it would drain properly.

"You see," Bailey said, "being in the business, I had all the equipment plus the know-how. When I had the course almost completed, Joe Hendricks, the President, came to me. 'Bailey,' he said, 'we don't have the money to pay you." Bailey replied, "Well, that's okay for me, but you must pay the equipment operators the $1,000 they've earned." That arrangement resulted in the Club getting a $10,000 job for $1,000. "Revamping the course was my enduring contribution to Diablo," Bailey remarked.

When Dorothy Stone learned that Bailey was a skilled horseman, she invited him to go riding with her. She had heard grumblings from golfers about horses being on the bridal paths and service roads surrounding the golf course while they were playing. She and Bailey rode on Sunday morning with the Club President tipping his hat and waving to his golfing friends as he cantered by. "That was the end of the complaints," said Bailey, "but my buddies sure gave me a bad time."

"I have the warmest spot in my heart for the Club," Bailey said. Among his fondest memories are his children growing up at Diablo, hosting his parents' 60th wedding anniversary at the Club and the weddings of three of their granddaughters.

MEMORABLE MEMBER: DEWITT KRUEGER

"I've always been good with numbers," said DeWitt Krueger, "so when I joined Diablo in 1950, I soon was Chairman of the Finance Committee."

This was a post De held for the next 10 years, except when he was President in 1959. In the '50s the Club led a hand-to-mouth financial existence. The Club didn't have a regular bartender or chef. Parties were BYOB and food was served only on Sundays.

De struggled to keep the Club in the black. In those years the president's most important job was stretching the Club's credit to cover its debts. "The two big bills were booze and meat and they came due and payable on the 15th," said De. Members' dues, Diablo's primary source of income, didn't arrive until the end of the month. So De had to play the rubber game with the Bank of California, getting them to stretch the Club's credit for those crucial two weeks.

The Club was also trying to pay off Larry Curtola. Often he had to play the same rubber game with him. But this was easier because Larry wanted the Club to succeed.

Among the Club's presidents there has been a tradition that each does something special—usually some improvement—as his contribution to the members. "I stewed a good deal about what mine might be," recalled De, "because money was so tight." Then laughing heartily, he told of his decision. "The men's toilet at the Snack Shack was on the fritz. I had it fixed and added one for the ladies. I'm sure other presidents have done more remarkable things." Perhaps so, but none so basic.

The biggest night of those years was Casino Night. The Club rented all the necessary gambling equipment and members took charge of the various tables and stations. One particular Casino Night was a real winner—big turn out, lots of hilarity, crowds of active players—truly a memorable event.

As midnight approached, it became even more memorable. The District Attorney of Contra Costa County walked in with two of his deputies. Everyone headed for the exits. The Club was caught red handed and Frank MacHugh, the manager, was arrested and taken to jail in Martinez. The Club bailed him out the next morning for $25 just in time for him to read these headlines in the S.F./Oakland papers:

"DEN OF INIQUITY IN DIABLO"

"SWANKY CLUB RAIDED"

"COUNTRY CLUB'S MEMBERS CAUGHT GAMBLING"

Shown at the 1959 Anniversary Party, L to R, DeWitt & Carol Krueger, Doris & John Price, John & Fran Enright, Bea & Harry Ahoe.
COURTESY CAROL KRUEGER.

Sometime in the mid-'50s, there was a big, important golf luncheon and the Club was short of waitresses. Cecil said to the manager, "My wife could help by pouring coffee. I'll call her." Helen rushed over to the clubhouse and promptly learned that pouring coffee wasn't a one-time only job. She retired 18 years later. During that time she served in the dining room, breakfast room (the room with a fireplace that is now the Men's Room off the bar), the Snack Shack, the men's locker room and at all the big parties. She said, "The Saturday night and holiday dances were fun to serve and I loved the big band music."

PREDICTION As De left office, he wrote this to the members: "As 1959 draws to a close, there are certain reflections I have with respect to the year's administration of the Club's affairs. Our goal has been to advance the Club's financial position a step upward on the ladder to our ultimate goal of complete ownership by the members. This will take time and patience, but I am convinced that this will be attained in the near future." (De was right in his prediction. See page 92.)

Men's Locker Room in high gear.

THE LARGER SCENE At Cal, Berkeley, students protest the banning of Communist speakers on campus. The Free Speech Movement is born and joined by students and non-students protesting the Vietnam War.

Almost overnight a nationwide social and sexual revolution is underway. Draft-age men burn their cards and emigrate to Canada. Women throw their bras away and join communes. Thousands gather at Woodstock, New York, to sing and scream. Jack and Bobby Kennedy and Martin Luther King are assasinated. Unmarried couples are living together. Now anything goes and few look askance.

The U.S. economy is growing at a little less than 6% a year. Carbon paper, mimeograph machines and flashbulbs are passé. Jet airliners, interstate highways, direct long-distance dialing, and Polaroid cameras are speeding up people and their lives; at beaches and pools, young women show off their bikinis.

Marijuana, rock music, the Twist, Elvis Presley and the Beatles are all hot properties. The '60s launch a revolution affecting everyone and everybody *then* and *since.*

A one-acre lot on Calle Arroyo sells for $15,000—an unheard-of high price.

People driving to Diablo learn new words on their car radios such as zip codes, Weight Watchers, Valium, transistors, computers, lasers, the pill, and LSD.

Larry Curtola.

Bill Houston, 1961 Club President. He held the office again in '62, '79 and '80.

The Strident Sixties

Chapter VII

"Buzz" Knowlton, Brigadier General, USAF, Retired.

MEMBERS BUY THE CLUB By 1961 the 13 years of Larry Curtola's stewardship came to an end. The Club was reestablished, reorganized and prospering. Larry said, "It was time to move on, time for members to take over so they could be a part of it, and have a say in its operation without feeling that someone was looking over their shoulders. I was glad I was able to help when I could." He had done more than help; he had saved the Club—the third time in its 49 year history.

Sometime in January, 1961, Bill Houston, Club President and Larry began meeting for breakfast to discuss the sale. An important part of the Club's operation had been the Curtola Water Co. which provided water for the Club and community. Bill said, "The members didn't want it. We figured EBMUD would soon annex the area. All we wanted was the Club's 115 acres." Larry estimated his water company was worth $130,000, the Club $500,000. Bill thought otherwise and had found a bank willing to lend perhaps as much as a half-million (including money for improvements after purchase) for a first deed of trust on the property. By March, Larry agreed to forego the water system, but stood fast on the half-million. Bill commented, "I knew what the bank would lend and that it was a half million just for the property." Negotiations were at a stand still.

In April, Bill and Larry agreed to break the stalemate by playing the napkin game. Each wrote a number on his napkin and exchanged them. Larry wrote $465,000, Bill $425,000. They looked at their napkins and Bill said, "Larry, it's do-able if we can split the difference." Larry responded, "Then the sale price stands at $445,000. I really want the members to own the Club." Bill recalled, "Larry was a fine person to deal with. He really wanted Diablo to fly." Larry recalled, "Bill was responsible for a smooth transition from me to the members."

The problem with the sale was that the Club had no money. But it did have Al Layton on its Board of Directors and Al also happened to be a Director of the Bank of California. Houston had conferred with him while negotiating with Curtola and had won Al's backing for a half-million dollar loan. But now Al said, "Bill, I'll support the loan application on one condition. Diablo needs a first class tennis facility. In order to get the money, you have to agree to set aside $25,000 for a new tennis complex."

Bill figured that with $445,000 to Larry, he'd have $55,000 for improvements, including a tennis center. As it turned out, it was a sweetheart of a deal—115 acres at $3,870 per. At today's prices it would be $200,000 or more per acre. A facetious wag might even say it ranked with Seward's purchase of Alaska or Jefferson's Louisana Purchase. Later that month, the loan was approved, Curtola paid, and the members took possession on May Day 1961.

LOCATING THE TENNIS COMPLEX Finding a place for the three tennis courts and Pro Shop put Bill Houston and the Board between a rock and a hard place. The only open area with the necessary space was the practice fairway. Bill said, "It was a Catch 22. If I take it for tennis, the golfers will be mad; if I don't follow through on the deal, everyone will be mad. The golfers will have to give ground, literally. The courts will be built on the practice fairway. To this day, my golfing buddies have never forgiven me."

An *Inferno* editorial said, "At the present time our inadequate golf practice area could be better utilized for the building of new tennis courts and eventually a second swimming pool and recreation area. . . . This tennis facility would . . . attract . . . new . . . members without putting any more traffic on our golf course. It would also create more clubhouse activity . . . Construction . . . can be partly financed from the initiation fees of these new members."(1)

In March the program submitted by the Tennis and Recreation Committee was approved by the Board. Bill wrote:(2)

"Contrary to rumors you may have heard, this (the tennis facility) is a 100% self-supporting and self-financed project. Regular members will not in any way be assessed for this much-needed activity at Diablo. Instead, regular members will benefit not only by having the additional recreational facilities for their families, but the net worth of their individual memberships will increase by this newly acquired asset. The Board recognizes the need for a better golf practice facility and plans are already underway. What tennis can accomplish for the Club in additional

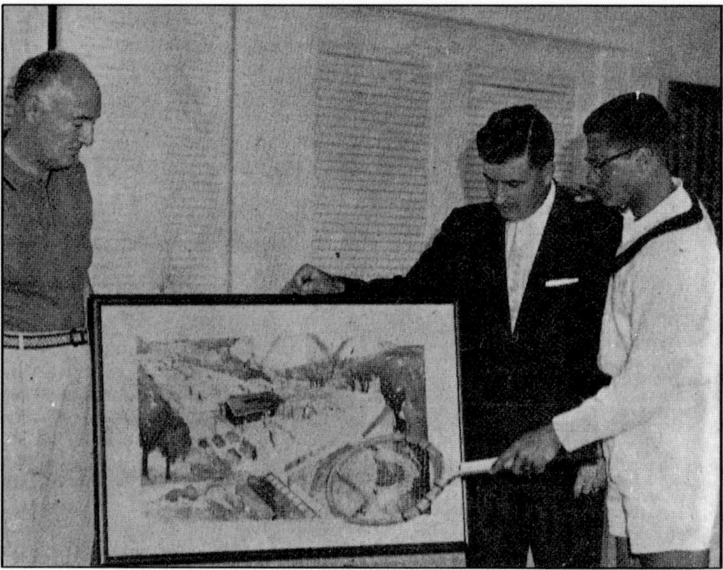

TENNIS PLANS TAKE SHAPE AT DIABLO

CHECKING PLANS — Al Layton, head of the Tennis Committee at the Diablo Country Club watches as pro Dick Overstreet points to the new facility. Looking on is club president Bill Houston, VALLEY PIONEER PHOTO.

Plans have recently been announced by the Diablo Country Club to install new and complete tennis facilities at Diablo. Three new tennis courts are to be constructed this spring with pro-shop, practice and related facilities.

One hundred new, non-assessable and transferrable social memberships are being offered to the many San Ramon Valley residents interested in promoting this new program at Diablo. The new family memberships are designed to appeal to those particularly interested in the tennis, swimming and social affairs at Diablo and include all club privileges except the use of the golf course.

The Diablo tennis program will represent the only first class tennis activity in the San Ramon Valley which is blessed with ideal tennis weather most of the year, and tennis enthusiasts are eagerly looking forward to starting play this summer.

The Diablo Country club has announced the retention of Dick Overstreet as tennis professional. Overstreet, who has developed a number of outstanding young players in recent years in the East Bay, will supervise the recreation program and give tennis instruction.

The announcement comes at a most opportune time, since the Diablo Country Club will soon have a completely remodeled and renovated locker room and men's grill. Future plans include additional tennis courts equipped for night play, special locker facilities, a second large swimming pool, sundeck, snack bar and outdoor barbecue.

members, increased revenue, and general activity far outweigh the temporary inconvenience of losing a portion of the practice area." (3)

All of this came to pass but with it an unexpected side effect: pitting golfers against tennis players, a condition that exists at all clubs that cater to both.

PARTNERS AT WORK Buzz Knowlton, who enjoyed great success as the perennial Membership Chairman, was elected President in 1967. He doubled the tennis membership, added two new courts, and was responsible for substantially increasing the regular membership.

Hal Morgan in his1965 President's message said, "The big news is the tremendous interest we are getting from our membership drive. Buzz and his committee have done and are doing an excellent job . . . We will have a waiting list for the first time in the history of Diablo Country Club." (4)

Millie and Buzz Knowlton in 1967.

Buzz wrote a monthly *Inferno* column called "Buzz-a-Buzzing" which always included a brief sketch of new members. Buzz said, "Yes, it seems I was recruiting members forever. In those days we had to find new ones like crazy just to stay even. I did it because, as a Diablo homeowner, I felt it was important to have a stable and flourishing Club. When everything else is said about the virtues of a country club, the bottom line is that it's good for property values. Besides, Millie and I believe we owe something for being able to live in Diablo and belong to the Club."

Millie, as Buzz's proactive partner, took over the *Inferno.* "It was both a rewarding and demanding job," she said. Like editors before and after her, she concluded, "In time, the job becomes more demanding than rewarding. Editing is both labor and time-intensive. It involves writing, managing, budgeting, taking photos, editing copy, supervising the typesetter and printer, solving problems, and a multitude of related jobs. I'm glad I did it when I did."

Buzz said, "I started saving *Infernos* when I first served on the Board of Directors in 1958 and I've done so ever since." The Club's file of *Infernos* was inadvertently destroyed during the renovation, but thanks to the Knowltons, Phil Kane and numerous others, the Club has a complete file of back issues. A list of *Inferno* editors is in the Appendix.

THE TENNIS SAGA On the Club's original tennis courts, located where the golf carts are now housed, Dick Overstreet, who had been an assistant Pro at Orinda, was giving lessons to a group of kids in 1959. It wasn't easy. The two courts were pot-holed and fragmented. Balls bounced crazily and the children were a mixed bag of age, dress and ability.

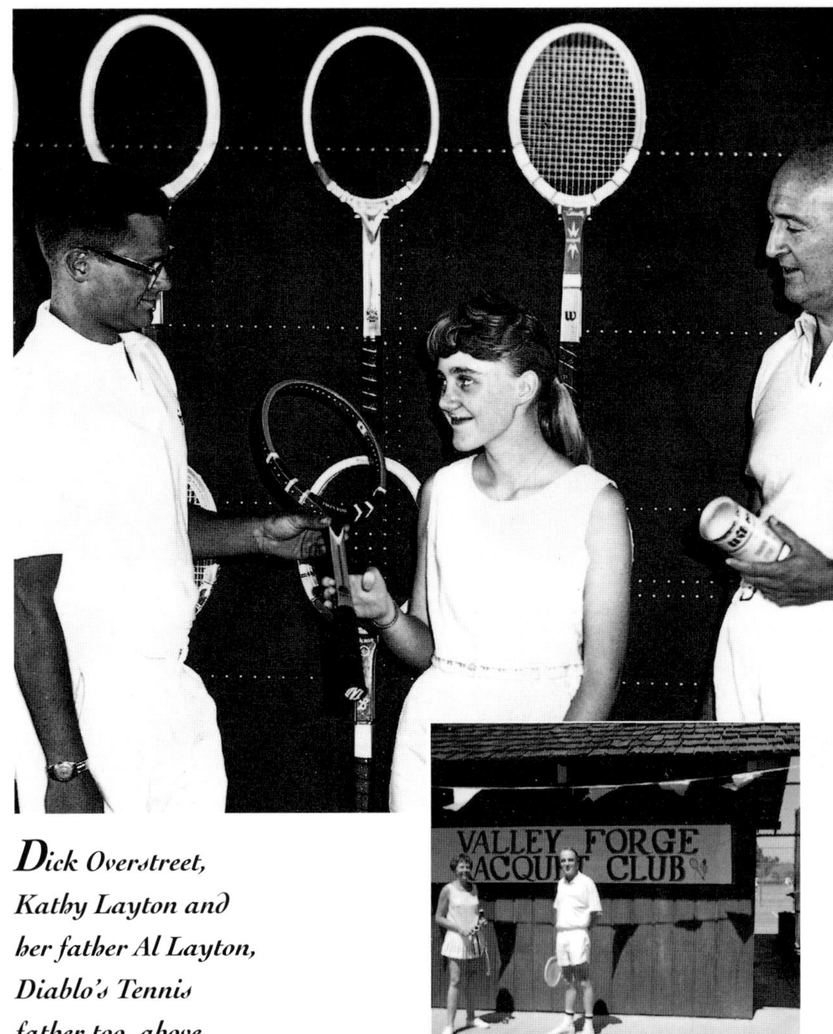

Dick Overstreet, Kathy Layton and her father Al Layton, Diablo's Tennis father too, above.

Ginny and Bill Rei at 4th of July Tennis round-up, inset upper right.

Brett Stone at the net. ALL PHOTOS, COURTESY DICK OVERSTREET.

Tennis everyone. But not quite everyone, only Ward La Cava, Reed Rubey, Ben Hammond, Casey Mehran, Dick, Francie Helfrich, Melissa Toney, and Vince La Cava. COURTESY DICK OVERSTREET.

Al Layton and his son Jim loved to play, but not on those funky courts. Al became the driving force of a movement to get new courts. He spearheaded the construction of three new courts and a Pro Shop in 1960 and the hiring of Dick as the tennis pro.

Thus began Overstreet's reign of 19 years—a time when tennis experienced a spectacular national rise in popularity. Diablo's new program attracted hundreds of new members, many with talented children. Among them:

Kristy Pigeon who played at Wimbledon.

Brett Stone, UC Davis star and sports stores entrepreneur.

Jon Toney who was the Diablo Pro, 1980-87.

Tripp Gordon, Director of Tennis, Hilton Waikoloa Resort, Hawaii.

Devin Sconyers, head Pro at the San Francisco Tennis Club.

Plus others too numerous to mention.

THE PIGEONS Darlene Pigeon remembered clearly the early tennis times. Her fondest memory was the sociability, compatibility and congeniality of the tennis group. "Frank and I loved Twilight Tennis on Thursday nights," she said. "I remember how we all gathered after 5:00 p.m. for a few sets, went to the Club for dinner, all sat at one long table, and had one entree for only $3.95! Sometimes we'd get carried away after dinner and go to someone's Diablo home for more fun and frolic. It was the people who made it such fun—the likes of the Petersons, Edwards, Woods, Clarks, Dittos, Gordons, De Johns, Reis, Osmers, Potters, La Cavas, Moulds, Redmonds, Cuenins, Rubeys, DeChenes, Stones, Sconyers and Priewes. As for Frank, he'd say his fondest memory was Saturday morning tennis and breakfast afterward at the Club to kibitz." Darlene remembered how Dick taught all day, everyday, and saw to it that lots of kids had jobs in and around the Pro Shop. It was a family of young tennis hopefuls, Kristy Pigeon among them.

Kristy didn't begin her career until she was 12—old for a beginner. She played tennis the first time at San Ramon High in between AAU swim events in her black tank suit and bare feet with an old wooden racquet. Someone watching said to Frank, "Buy that kid some shoes and get her some instruction." Several weeks later, the Pigeons joined Diablo (1963) and Dick began giving Kristy lessons. She summarized her accomplishments in a call from Sun Valley, Idaho. "In 1964, two weeks before I turned 14, I qualified for the Nationals at Forest Hills. I felt pretty cocky. I said to myself, 'This is the first step, the rest will follow.' For three years, 1966-68, I was on the team that won the Girls Inter-Sectional Championship. At 17, I won the U.S. Girls Championship singles and doubles. That same year, 1968, I won the Junior Singles Title at Wimbledon but lost in the Seniors round of 16 to Billie Jean King. For six years, I was ranked among the top 10 U.S. women players and in 1970, a member of the Wrightman Cup Team." Kristy retired at 22, hung up her racquet, and hasn't played since. She said, "Tournament Tennis was fun and exciting in the beginning. Then it became practice, work, practice, work, but worth it because I was winning. But when I hit the BIG TIME, and the wins started to be few and far between; I just burned out.

"All in all, however, I benefited. I learned to cope, deal with disappointment and disinterested team-mates, set goals and be persistent. And I learned the importance of fair play, and family and friends who believe in you."

BRETT STONE His fondest memory was playing sun-up to sundown with the other kids in his age group which consisted of Rick and John Alamassy, Vince and Ward La Cava, Gilbert Stockton, Alex Mehran, Mike and Gary Knowlton, and Frances Helfrich and Melissa Tony.

At the time, Rick was the best and this bugged John who was older and more serious. With his red hair and freckled face, he was also more short tempered. Brett said, "Rick was having a slump one summer and we all were suddenly beating him. Everyone that is, except John. In frustration, he threw his racquet over the fence into the La Cava's front yard and ran off to the pool. I learned my tennis and honed it by being with these kids."

At San Ramon High, Brett played #1 and #2 singles and #1 doubles. He lettered four years at UC Davis and was Captain his senior year when the team was fourth in the nationals. His UC coach was Will Lotter, who was at San Ramon High in the '50s. On the team, Brett got tired of going to Sacramento for equipment, so he started a tennis shop and now owns two sports stores, and does workshops for tennis instructors.

JON TONEY REMEMBERS Jon said, "My fondest memories fall into two categories, as a kid growing up and as the Club Pro." Being a little fellow growing up among lots of big ones, he looked up to Kristy, Vince and Ward La Cava and Brett Stone. "Brett was my role model," he said, "I wanted to be like him." He also looked up to the many adults who would hit balls with him. "It was so nice of them and when I got big, I did the same for the juniors."

Kristy shows her early form.
COURTESY DARLENE AND FRANK PIGEON.

Kristy at Wimbledon. "My first crack at Wimbledon and a dream will soon come true as this May (1968) I leave for my first European tour. I realize I represent the youth of America and I will do my very best. Thanks, Diablo." (Inferno, April, 1968)

COURTESY DARLENE AND FRANK PIGEON.

Wednesday, May 8, 1968

KRISTY LEAVES FOR WIMBLEDON

A career that began on the courts of San Ramon Valley High School just six years ago will reach its climax next month when Danville's Kristy Pigeon walks out on the courts of the venerable All England Lawn Tennis and Cricket Club in London — the locale of the historic Wimbledon Tennis Tournament.

Wimbledon, the dream of every female tennis player in the world, has been a sellout for a year and has attracted some 200 of the top players in the world — all by invitation.

The flaxen-haired Kristy leaves in the morning for her historic journey, and could certainly be excused if she slept the entire trip. In addition to playing countless local tournaments, Kristy has been burning the midnight oil in an effort to graduate with the class of '68, a full six weeks ahead of her classmates. A B-plus student, Kristy found it necessary to double up on class assignments to make this trip.

Her coach, Dick Overstreet of Diablo Country Club, who introduced Kristy to the game and has tutored her ever since, feels she has a chance of doing very well in London. "It seems there has always been someone who has knocked Kristy off as she was reaching for the brass ring, but her game is at its zenith now. Hers is a powerful game, that lends itself to grass, and I think since she has started to use the steel racquet, her game is even stronger and faster than before."

As the Pro, 1980-87, men's Saturday morning tennis stands out in Jon's memory. He commented, "It's a time when anyone and everyone comes to the courts, picks up a game with whomever, and plays for the sheer joy of it. At most clubs, play is prearranged. Diablo is an exception. Others should be so lucky. That's the spirit of Diablo."

Jon had two junior teams that won the Northern California title: Girls 18 in 1982 (Heidi and Gretchen Sorensen, Mary and Ann Spicer, Erin Corcoran and Julie Davis); Girls 15 in 1983 (Debbie Edwards, Kristen Hansen, and Monique Barrons).

Jon continues to be a player in demand, winning the Silver Racquet in 1992 with Jerry Udelhoven. "But I didn't defend it very well," he said, "losing it the next year with Kris Surano. But I'll be back!" He was, and won with Jerry in 1994.

FRIDAY NIGHTS Semmes and Peggy Gordon reminisced about Friday nights. Tennis and golf had combined Twilight Play to a single evening and now it was being held on Fridays and has been ever since. What they liked was the informality and relaxation. "It was loose," said Semmes, "everyone, (or most everyone) was there for fun. Few cared who won or lost and we often went to someone's house for a barbecue afterwards."

Of his son, Tripp, Semmes said, "if it hadn't been for the Club, Tripp wouldn't be where he is today—Director of Tennis at the Hilton Waikoloa Resort Hotel on the big island of Hawaii." When he was learing the game at Diablo, there were three work-out teams: the Pushers (beginners), Blisters (mediums), and Aces (best). Tripp quickly advanced to the top.

Peggy said, "Dick was very good with beginners. He gave them a solid grounding in the basics." "But by high school," said Semmes, "Tripp needed something more. He found it in Floyd Baker, the coach at Monte Vista High School. He guided Tripp to the top of the northern California high school ladder and the Oakland City Championship, then counseled him to accept a tennis scholarship at the University of Alabama."

CAROL AND HAL SCONYERS Among the Sconyers' fondest memories were the tournaments and the tennis committee. Carol said, "Everyone joined in. We had mother/daughter, father/daughter, mother/son, father/son, brother/sister, husband/wife tournaments, play-days on July 4th and Labor Day, then the Silver Racquet Invitational."

Hal interrupted, "The Tennis Committee was a workhorse group." Play became so demanding

Francie, later—much later—the letter writer. COURTESY DICK OVERSTREET.

Court spectators, if not players, Semmes Gordon, Jim Stone and Bill Rei.

John Toney at the University of Oregon. COURTESY DICK OVERSTREET.

Tripp Gordon – Pro, below.

that the committee raised $5,000 to match the Club's $10,000 for two new courts which were built in 1967. Then the committee scheduled work-days. All the players, young and old, turned out to pull weeds, plant flowers, and put in a drainage system.

Many who watch matches on courts 1 and 2 and occupy the hillside benches aren't aware that Club members built them. Hal donated railroad ties and on a work-day weekend, members built the grandstand in use today. The crazy brick drinking fountain by court #4 was Bob Cuenin's and Don Priewe's contribution. Hal stated, "All these accomplishments were symbolic of members' interest and support to keep the tennis program on the move, a form of voluntary assessment."

Carol remembered Devin's first big win. It was the Valley Pioneer Junior Tournament in Danville. Devin was 10 and determined. The win wasn't the biggest of his life but certainly he took home the biggest trophy. It was over three feet tall! At Piedmont High School he teamed with Brad Gilbert to be one and two in the Bay Area and played on the UCSB team. Later he became Brad's assistant coach and traveled with him to Paris, Brisbane and Wimbledon. Now he's the head Pro at the San Francisco Tennis Club.

DICK OVERSTREET Arriving for an interview with the author, Dick came with a fertile memory and several boxes of pictures. "I was one of the tennis pioneers in the East Bay. I began teaching in my early 20s in the late 1950s and quit in my early 40s. These were the best years of my life. My career included hundreds of students, kids as well as adults too numerous to mention, all of whom acquired lifelong skills for their leisure hours.

"I specialized in teaching a simplified form of tennis—emphasis on the basics like 'turn, step, swing', so a beginner could get to a playing level as quickly as possible.

"Tennis at Diablo gave me and my family a taste of the good life, lots of fond memories, and lots of good friends. I owe a debt of gratitude to the members for all of this."

Each month Dick wrote a column in the *Inferno*, always about the tennis goings-on. But once he slipped-in this non-tennis item in the June, 1967 issue *"Please don't bring your dogs to the courts; with Hoopy, BoBo, Tucker, Kelly, and Tiger, it's a bit crowded already."*

EDWARD LA CAVA, M.D. Another junior interviewed was Ward La Cava. He said: "My junior high years in Diablo were a quintessential time. Growing up in and around the tennis courts was a respite from the storm. It was a time to learn values, the skills of competition, build character.

Benji Rei, Tripp Gordon, Ricky Overstreet, legs by Les (Hansen), assistant Tennis Pro. COURTESY DICK OVERSTREET.

THE Valley Pioneer

(Feb. 6, 1963)

FOLGER'S COFFEE 2 lb. 99 cents, Best Foods mayonaise 1 qt. 49 cents, Lipton's onion soup 2 pac. 33 cents, Grade A fryers 39 cents lb., 1 qt. vodka $3.49, Denver beef 59 cents lb., hamburger 39 cents lb., ½ gal. ice cream 77 cents, bacon 65 cents lb., 3-5 bedroom homes $35-$40,000

Devin Sconyers.

Corky Mainhardt, assistant Tennis Pro, hand strings a racquet in 1963. Is this a lost art?

Debbie Redmond.

Spinning to serve—Frances Helfrich, Alex Mehran, Melissa Toney and John Taapken. ALL PHOTOS COURTESY DICK OVERSTREET.

Most of Dick's charges played for the sheer joy of it. One was Francie Helfrich (Hauck). She wrote:

Boston, Mass.
March 1, 1994

DEAR JIM,

About Diablo and the Club in the '60s—it was a kid's paradise! The sun was always hot, we checked in at noon, and had to be home by 6:00 p.m. Best of all, we had the Club. It broke down into three factions; golfers, tennis players, and pool rats. For most kids, golf was too slow. It required large blocks of time, concentration, heavy shoes, AND there were lots of adults around. Not a fun combination for most of us.

Tennis á la Overstreet was a far more interesting pursuit. There were lots of great-looking older kids around, clinics, lessons, round-robin events, tournaments and of course, the Tennis Team. It was Dick's idea that there could *only* be tennis—something about swimming "ruining" the leg muscles or some other drivel. It made a lasting impression on few of us. Even the faithful were tempted by the cool blue water. For the rest of us, aspiring to blue-stripped gut racquets and another new pair of Converse tennis shoes was enough. We did it because it was really fun, helping the little kids, making our moms feel old on the court, and my personal favorite, men's tennis on Saturday morning. Playing with dads was the best game around. I got to play flat-out hard, it was a challenge and a compliment to be included.

There was always time for food at the pool snack shack and an occasional trip to the adult world of the Terrace Room for ice tea, fruit salads and better hamburgers! Then it was back to the pool! This was grueling work, but a perfect tan was the order of the day! Hours and hours spent playing in cool water, roasting and basting young skin, checking out the older kids and lusting over the lifeguards! Remember, Ken?—not Barbie doll Ken, well maybe he was, but God, was he cute! He took my younger brother, Gus, fishing. I even considered taking up fishing! There always were really great-looking young people around. Was there a committee that chose the lifeguards? That had to be *really* tough work!

Was there ever a more sophisticated communications network than Diablo's mothers? Mine knew when we messed-up, from at least three sources, before we had even finished committing the crime. It always kept us honest—and safe.

Tell Brett to shape-up or Sally (Stojkovich Dietrich) and I will short-sheet his bed like we used to!

Love to you and Dorothy,

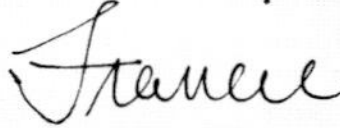

"Dick put up with a lot from us. We put up with a lot from him. In those days, tennis at the Club was evolving. Players were getting better and honing their games. The camaraderie with peers was great, but so was playing with adults—my mom with Brett Stone and his mom with me, Melissa Toney with my brother Vince playing against me and Francie Helfrich; and on and on. All of us, kids and adults, were judged by our tennis skills (or lack of same) rather than who lived where or who traveled when. Tennis was an equalizer."

On a weekend in September '68, 60 tennis players and their children had a work weekend. They built a walk alongside the courts and improved the children's play yard. Club Manager Chuck Thode said, "All Diablo members should take a look at these improvements—this was done by the tennis players themselves. Imagine what this would have cost if we had outside labor? These improvements are a great asset to the Club."(5) A work weekend became an annual event throughout the '60s and '70s.

OTHER BIG TICKET EVENTS The hook-up with EBMUD was completed in '61. President John Enright said, "The cost of bringing the new water into the very elaborate system of valves and connections that Diablo is required to build will be in excess of $7,000. An assessment will be required. By the time the first drop of new water hits our golf course, an amount of $10,000 will have been spent. To install a completely new set of pipes and mains would cost about $100,000."(6)

In September '66, the Board approved $19,000 from its capital improvement fund to pay for the installation of cart paths. Drawings for each hole outlining the direction of the paths were done by Frank Schmitt, Greens Committee Chairman then and President in 1974.

By 1966, memberships were increased to $2,500 and a new Golf Pro Shop was built. Construction was approved by the Board in December 1964. A new Golf Pro Shop, electric cart and bag storage building were erected on the site of the original tennis courts alongside the first fairway. Money for the project was available from the 1964 assessment, "and is presently in the bank."(7)

DIABLO MYSTIQUE Rob Scharnell, now living with his wife Deborah and three children at 2154 Alameda Diablo remembered what Diablo and the Club were like in the '60s when he was eight and attending Green Valley School. He lived in the Diablo Hacienda subdivision just below Diablo which was built on the Oakwood Farm's racetrack. The track is outlined to this day by the eucalyptus trees that surround it. His Diablo friends included John Peds, Baxter Martin, Jill Toney, Ted Friden, and Steve Freeman.

FRONT ROW, Opposite page: (Left to Right) Steve Freeman, Bill Baggett, Susan Sconyers, Liz Moulds, Jill Toney, Al Layton, Jan Cronin, Eric Thomas. **SECOND ROW:** Carol Sconyers, Steffi La Cava, Terry Sconyers, Mary Cuenin, Tim Rei, Kin Gordon, Jon Toney, Mel Toney, Jack Toney, Bill Rei. **THIRD ROW:** Marian McDonald, Hank McDonald, Hal Sconyers, Emily Andrews, Abe Weitzberg, Ann Moulds, Liz De Chene, Stan Thomas. **FOURTH ROW:** Bob Tiernan, Bob Cuenin, John Meyer, Bobbie Meyer, Sally Peterson, Dick Overstreet, Jinny Cuenin, Jackie Redmond, Jean Ditto, Bob De Chene (on tiptoe), Connie La Cava, George Redmond. **BACK ROW:** Sam Ditto, Ginny Rei, Maryam Mehran, Bob Andrews, Billie McKesson, Ken McKesson, Mugs Freeman, Lyn Tiernan, Marsh Freeman (behind shovel award), Frank Pigeon.

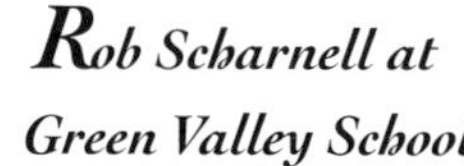

Rob Scharnell at Green Valley School.

Al Layton receives an award from grateful tennis players for their new courts. Note: Someone in back row second from right hiding behind a shovel. Guess who?
COURTESY REED RUBEY.

Ward La Cava, age 13, below.

Ronald Reagan at Diablo reception, below.

Chalet and clubhouse are attached by a portico over Clubhouse Road.

Ladies in summer fashion: Wilhemina Morey, Jane Friden, Barbara Hale, Mike Stapler, and Alice Thomas, at left. COURTESY MYRA MAE HALL STAPLER.

Ladies at the 1967 Anniversary party, below, Jo Anne Lamson, Lilan Kane and Marian Johnson.

DIABLO COUNTRY CLUB

INFERNO

UBLICATION OF DIABLO COUNTRY CLUB — DIABLO, CALIFORNIA — SEPTEMBER, 1964

EXTRA!!

Construction of a new golf shop, electric cart and bag storage building will get under way within a few days. This building will be erected on the site of the old tennis courts.

Your Board of Directors, recognizing the need for these facilities, approved plans and specifications at their last meeting.

Architectural design of the building was done by Arthur Holden and will be in keeping with the present club buildings.

Area will be constructed to store seventy-nine electric golf carts and three hundred golf bags. Display space will be adequate for the golf professional to merchandise his wares properly. A covered porch will overlook the first fairway and teeing area. This should provide *Diablo* will one of the finest golf shops in Northern California.

You will be happy to hear that *most* of the money for this project is available from the 1964 assessment and is presently in the bank.

All of us should be proud of the progress that our club continues to show as time goes on.

Please try to understand our problems during this construction period and we will continue to work in improving *Diablo* for the members.

BOARD OF DIRECTORS
R. Frazer Howard
Chairman Bldg. Comm.

He said, "Diablo had a mystique about it and I decided then I'd like to live there someday. Now I'm lucky to be able to—a dream come true." John Roberts was the principal of Green Valley School, a man Rob admired. He commented, "And here I am living in his house." On hot days in the spring, Rob recalled cutting out of school, hopping on his Schwinn Sting-ray bike, and heading with his friends for Diablo Lake for a cool swim. Ah the '60s!

AS SEEN BY ELIZABETH FREEMAN In 1967, Bill and Elizabeth Freeman returned to Diablo and bought a home. Bill was elected to the Club's Board of Directors in 1970 and served as Secretary from 1970 to 1973.

When asked how the Diablo of the '60s compared with that of the '20s and '30s, Elizabeth replied, "Life in the '60s was more complex and people were more sophisticated than in the '20s and '30s. Diablo was no longer a summer colony with the Club as the hub. Now it was a community of its own with year-round residents—a place to live, not just to visit; a neighborhood, not just a country retreat. Residents now had other centers of interest besides the Club. I think the tunnel and the freeways made the difference."

In many of the summer houses of the '20s and '30s, people walked outside to their sleeping rooms. "When in bed," remembered Elizabeth, "You looked at the stars through the holes in the roof. No one used the place in the winter, so why fix it? That was life in the country. But by the '60s Diablo had become a community with all but two of the summer homes converted to year-round residences, and new ones abuilding."

A HORSEMAN'S PARADISE On Sundays in July, throughout the '60s, the Club sponsored breakfast rides to Barbecue Terrace on Mt. Diablo. Horses departed the Diablo Barn at 10:30, those driving cars left at 11:30. A catered breakfast was served around the campfire about noon. After a jolly time, riders mounted their steeds for the return trip, not realizing they were experiencing the end of a noble tradition.

From the beginning, Diablo had been a horseman's paradise. First as a training, racing, and breeding headquarters, later as THE THING to do. Many moved to Diablo to have pasture for their horses and access to trails on Mt. Diablo. But with the closing of the '60s, interest in horses waned. The Club closed its stables; homeowners began to divide their acreage and sell off lots; barns were converted into homes; country was becoming suburbia.

Tribune photo by John Dengel

9 YEAR OLD GOLF WHIZ

Local Boy Future Star?

BOY GOLF STAR — Johnny Peck, 9, is an 89 shooter at Diablo Country Club. He chats with pro Lyle Wehrman (top) and practices approach shot.

Golf awards given by Ron Patton. Seated are Fred Udall, Bob Cuenin and Rett Turner.

BUD SHANK SETS 72 HOLE RECORD TO BECOME CHAMP

Bud Shank literally burned up 18 of the Diablo Country Club's golf holes recently to become the Club Champion for the 4th time. In gaining the honor, Shank carded a record breaking 269 for 72 holes. He had rounds of 69, 66, 65 and 69. Runner-up Lloyd Rossi, a two-time winner himself, posted rounds of 74, 68, 75, 70 for a 287 total. Third place honors went to Jim Frost, another former title holder who toured the layout in 292.

Larry Hudson, a 5-handicapper garnered low net honors with a 73, 74, 74, 74, for 295.

PHOTO ABOVE— Bud Shank holds the Diablo Club Championship Trophy flanked by Pro Ron Patten, at left, runner-up Lloyd Rossi at Shank's left and DeWitt Krueger, club president.

VALLEY PIONEER PHOTO

With the physical changes came other more significant ones propelled by the '60s social and sexual revolution:

- * from formality to the more casual;
- * from decorum in speech, dress, music, poetry, literature and entertainment to a frankness that sometimes borders on the risqué;
- * from genteel manners and mores to whatever goes.

A new style of life was on the wing as the '70s unfolded.

Jack Lockey, his partner, Bill Owsley and partner Gennaro Filice.

MEMORABLE MEMBER: LOU ARMSTRONG

Do you use the drinking fountain at the first tee? Of course you do. Did you ever notice the plaque? Next time take a look.

So, who was Lou Armstrong? Dozens of old-timers share a unanimous opinion: Lou was a fun-loving, enthusiastic, gregarious, energetic, and caring person who spent the bulk of her time organizing and orchestrating parties and all kinds of other social events in order to make money for the Club.

It's hard today to appreciate how the Club operated on such a shoestring in the '50s and '60s. Eileen Gosslin, member 1950-1977, said, "There were times when the Club didn't have money to pay the monthly liquor bill. We used to bring our own bottles to the Club and pay the bartender each time he made a drink from our own bottle."

By far the best way the Club made money was to get Lou to give a party, which she loved to do. "She was the original party-girl," said Buzz Knowlton, whose wife Millie played golf and bridge with Lou.

The most famous of the Lou Armstrong parties were:

* The Hawaiian Luau, complete with pig roasted in the ground, women in hula skirts and a chorus line of men dressed as Hawaiian native girls.
* Western Frontier Bash, with bales of hay on the patio and guests arriving by horseback and horse-drawn carriage.
* Easter Parties, with everyone dressed up as bunnies.

Her fashion show luncheons were legendary. Lou not only organized these affairs—music, decorations, favors, costumes, entertainment—she also got the troops out with a hot-line of calls. Seldom did one of her parties fall below 500 guests—all benefiting a shaky Club. Betty Curtola added, "It's the women who do the social things that men and women go to and spend money on. Lou knew that and lived by it."

"She really cared about people," said Carol Krueger. "When DeWitt and I joined Diablo in 1950, the first time we came, she was there being the unofficial Club hostess. After introductions she said, 'Let's have a drink' and took us by the hand and introduced us to everyone." She did that for all new members. Jeanne Hague said it this way, "She mothered us all."

Lou's Memorial.

Mary Lynn Peck remembers Lou as a "good neighbor, living just a few doors away on Alameda Diablo. On hot nights in the days when air conditioning was unknown, she'd join the kids and teens to swim at the Club." Lou authored and successfully circulated a petition to get the Board to keep the pool open until 9:00 p.m. on the hottest nights.

Millie Knowlton said, "She wasn't much of a bridgeplayer, but she was always in demand because of her spontaneous wit." "She wasn't the greatest golfer either," said Eileen Gosslin, "about a 125 scorer, but every 18-holer wanted to be in her foursome." Lou was a shallow driver, but she more than made up for it with her chip shots and putter. When her golf cart rolled over on her in a bizarre accident, she was sidelined for six months and walked with a limp thereafter, but it never dampened her spirit and her "joie de vie" even though it ended her golf-playing days. A newspaper report, September 19, 1959 stated, "Mrs. Armstrong was injured when she tried to avoid hitting a dog while going down a steep hill in her golf cart . . ." So like Lou!

Buzz Knowlton summed up Lou saying, "She probably had more to do with the survival of the Club in the '50s and '60s than anyone. She was a hard worker and a very kind person. Although she knew everybody and everything, she never gossiped. The Club was her love. To see it succeed was a major point in her life."

Lou died in 1966 and her many friends wanted her to be remembered by future generations for her unselfish efforts to keep the Club alive while enlivening it. Maude Pratt, a close friend and admirer who lived in the Chalet, chaired a committee to raise money for a fountain memorial.

The December 4, 1968 minutes of the Board of Directors stated, "Upon motion being made, seconded, and passed, the Board ratified the action of the Lou Armstrong Memorial Committee to install a flagstone platform and drinking fountain foundation by the first tee in memory of Lou Armstrong, deceased, a revered and loved member of Diablo Country Club for many, many, years."

The 18- and 9-hole golfers and the Ladies Bridge group contributed $250. The February, 1969 *Inferno* listed the names of 125 other donors. The headline read, "Lucille Armstrong Memorial" and said,

"We wish to thank all members who so generously contributed to the Lucille Armstong Memorial Drinking Fountain on the first tee. This was started by Maude Pratt and thanks to her we now have a fountain to be proud of."

In 1974, Bill started a tree-planting program for the golf course. For $5, anyone could have a Rigney tree planted. In all several hundred were planted. Bill said, "It was a way of saying thanks for all the friends we've made and the wonderful times we've had—something for Paula and me to cherish."

Chub Feeney, (President, National League) Bill, Bing, Tom Dwyer, and Jay Bedsworth.

Bill, Manager of the Minnesota Twins having a word with the home plate umpire.

President Eisenhower and Bill at spring training in Palm Springs, 1962, top.

Leonard Firestone, owner L.A. Angels and Bill, above middle.

Robert Preston, Bill and Nat "King" Cole.

MEMORABLE MEMBER: BILL RIGNEY

Bill was the Manager of the New York Giants from 1955-57, then the team became the S.F. Giants and opened with Bill at the helm the next year in Seals Stadium—the "Stick" didn't exist then. Three years earlier, however, the *Inferno* reported: "New Members: Bill Rigney, Manager, New York Giants, wife Paula and Billy 10, Tom 7, Lynn 5." How come this New Yorker joined Diablo?

The answer is Bill was born in Oakland, attended Oakland High, served in WWII as a Navy preflight instructor at St. Mary's College, married Paula, a UC Berkeley student, and lived in Walnut Creek while he was the New York Giants' Manager. "I'd always heard good things about Diablo, so as soon as we got enough money, we joined. That was in 1955, for $450! It was a decision we never regretted—and it has gotten better every year since," Bill remarked.

In 1971, when Spence Archer was president, Jack Pingree proposed the Club sponsor an invitational on the last Friday in October, to be called the Bill Rigney Invitational. Bill agreed, provided he could designate the charity that would benefit from this first class affair. So a Diablo tradition was born.

The tournament attracted golfers from here and yon, among them Bing Crosby. Bing said to Bill, "You've played in mine at Pebble Beach, so I'll play in yours at Diablo." And he did, in October 1971. He arrived early Friday afternoon and was in the locker room until paged to tee off meeting and signing autographs. Bill said, "Bing Crosby is a memorable guy."

Bill then told about "another memorable guy," Dwight Eisenhower. "He had come to the ballpark as the guest of Leonard Firestone, the Los Angeles Angels owner, and I was just chatting with him as he was about to take a seat in the owner's box." The game was starting and I said, "Mr. President, how'd you like to run the team?" "Oh, I couldn't," said Ike, "I don't know the players or the batting order." Bill replied, "If you can run the country, you sure as hell can run a baseball team." So Ike joined the team on the bench, and for the next three innings managed it like a pro. "The President had a ball," remembered Bill.

Bill has been a major league manager for 18 of his 54 years in the game: 5 Giants, 10 Angels, 3 Twins. He said, "I've saved the best for last—working for the A's, and receiving a World Series ring in 1989." Five years later he was elected to the Bay Area Sports Hall of Fame.

IN OTHER PLACES On July 24, 1969, Edwin (Buzz) Aldrin, Jr. and Neil Armstrong, are the first to walk on the moon "... taking a giant step for mankind," and ushering in the inflated '70s on a high note that soon sours. Richard Nixon disgraces himself and the Presidency in the Watergate scandal and is forced to resign. Sam Ervin, a colorful Senator from North Carolina, chaired the historic hearings and made an indelible impression on millions of TV viewers. Later, everyone speculates about the identity of "Deep Throat," the mysterious source frequently quoted in Bob Woodward's 1974 best seller, *All The President's Men.*

Jimmy Carter's legacy is 19% inflation and a frightening oil and gasoline shortage. He is a one-term President. California passes Proposition 13 limiting property taxes to the existing level. Former Governor Pat Brown's bachelor son, Jerry, is elected Govenor and appoints Rose Bird to the Supreme Court. She is later removed from office by a state-wide referendum.

Elvis "The King" Presley dies suddenly. Patti Hearst, a Cal student and granddaughter of RN Burgess' associate, William Randolph Hearst, is kidnapped by the SLA.(1)

Streaking is the newest fad and the movie "Jaws" makes America paranoid about ocean swimming. Pizza, bagels and pasta appear in abundance on the food counters. Foreign travel is the thing to do as jumbo jets whisk Americans to all parts of the globe.

In Diablo, a one-acre lot on Caballo Ranchero sells for $40,000 and Ken Berhing buys the Blackhawk Ranch.

On March 6, 1974, President Frank Schmitt announced, "We made our final payment on the Club's $444,000 mortgage, assumed in 1971." At the May Fiesta Party, "... the biggest bash of the decade which cost ninety-four people $7.50 each ..." the mortgage was burned at midnight, with all past presidents in attendance.

At the same time members were advised, "We must get our facilities in order as fast as we can," hinting the Board was going into debt in the near future to pay for a much needed automatic sprinkler system that "will give us improved fairways, roughs, greens, and areas around the tennis courts."

Olé shouted for fruitful mortgage-burning party. Charles Hillman wore plaid, his wife a Mexican wedding dress for Diablo party. TRIBUNE PHOTOS BY KENNETH GREEN

Chapter VIII
THE INFLATED SEVENTIES

DIABLO ROAD IMPROVED? Ed Parks remembers the '70s "battle of Diablo Road." With the Blackhawk development underway, most people expected the County to improve the curvy, two-laned road between Diablo Scenic and Alameda Diablo.

The Club Board remained neutral, but not the members. A petition was circulated at Friday night tennis which Ed refused to sign. He said, "I was a developer and familiar with the Blackhawk plan. I couldn't see how it would have much impact on traffic around the east side of Diablo." But Ed's tennis buddies felt otherwise and kept after him—especially at the bar. To keep them quiet, Ed signed. "But I was wrong," he said, "I was right in the first place."

The split in the tennis group was symptomatic of the split throughout Diablo. Those living on the road were adamant—no improvement because a dangerous road is its own best traffic deterrent. Those living elsewhere wanted the road straightened and widened.

Right or wrong, Barbara Hale, long-time Diablo Road resident, persisted and eventually convinced the County planners to take no action and use the money for a bicycle trail from Alameda Diablo to Green Valley School. The trail was built and named in honor of Barbara Hale. To this day the road remains unimproved.

THE GATE QUESTION Ever since the formation of the Diablo Community Service District (DCSD) in 1968, residents and Club members were concerned about the best way to provide security. The initial answer was a private patrol service, and for ten years "rent-a-cops" were used but they proved unsatisfactory.

The District then proposed automated gates at the three entrances to Diablo. The Club Board was not opposed but only mildly enthusiastic because of the added inconvenience to members, two-thirds of whom were not Diablo residents. Also, a small but well organized group of residents opposed gating the community. They resented both giving up free access and the increased cost.

In an effort to arrive at a consensus, the DCSD and DPOA held a series of neighborhood meetings, after which a straw vote was taken. DCSD supplied discussion leaders for the neighborhood groups and the DPOA made the arrangements for the meetings at residents' homes. The DCSD President attended all the discussions in order to capture the flavor of the community.

The straw vote showed two-thirds in favor of gates but one-third opposed. The DCSD Board of Directors voted three to two against gating ". . . at this time."

"At this time" has been extended some 20 years. Meanwhile, a contract with the County Sheriff for a uniformed deputy and an official Diablo car assigned to the area has resolved the problem to everyone's satisfaction. An unforeseen benefit is that the assigned deputies have joined in and become a part of the community, with the Club as their coffee stop.

THE CHALET QUESTION Over the past 25 years, the Chalet had been on a gradual decline, both in use and maintenance. At various times it had been used as a Post Office, Pro Shop, quarters for party revelers and weekenders, the permanent residence of selected members, and finally quarters for Club employees. Matters came to a head in the mid-'70s when the Fire Department pointed out that it was a fire hazard and should be modernized or demolished.

Unfortunately the Club had neither the will nor the way to rebuild or restore it. The Club had used the Chalet as a resource, but never spent a dime to improve it. Now D Day was approaching and the question of what to do went on for several years as witnessed by articles in the *Inferno* and minutes of the Board.

President Cliff Gant wrote in the August 1976 *Inferno*, "Paul Cortese, Long Range Planning Committee Chairman, has been working on ways to modernize the Chalet units . . . The Board is advised that it is feasible to turn a growing liability into a productive asset by converting the Chalet into several spacious and luxurious living units. How this can best be done has to be worked out."

Gant then presented to the membership an outline of a proposal from Paul Cortese for renovating and managing the Chalet. The proposal contained several alternates each of which was discussed. "Paul's proposal was based on an evaluation report of the Chalet prepared by outside experts. The proposal and the evaluation report are available for members to review," wrote Gant. Several detailed

Ed and Doris Parks.

Diablo Country Club

MEMBERSHIP INFORMATION

REGULAR MEMBERSHIP		
Initiation Fee	$8,000.00	
Equity	60%	1 Vote
Monthly Dues	125.00	
Quarterly Minimum	120.00	

REGULAR MEMBERSHIP—WAITING LIST		
Initiation Fee	$8,000.00	
Equity	60%	No Vote
Monthly Dues (75%)	93.75	
Quarterly Minimum	120.00	

While on the *waiting list* status, golf privileges are restricted to: After 1:00 pm on Saturdays and between 7:00 and 9:30 am on Sundays. No holiday or tournament play, except as the guest of another member. Golf on weekdays is unlimited with no payment of green fees.

TENNIS		
Initiation fee	$4,000.00	
Equity	60%	1/2 Vote
Monthly dues	62.50	
Quarterly Minimum	120.00	

JR. EXECUTIVE*		
Initiation Fee	$4,800.00	
Monthly dues	125.00	
Quarterly Minimum	120.00	

*Applicant must be between the ages of 21 and 36 yrs., annual payments of $750 are made until the age of 36 when the full fee is due. Equity is still 60%.

ASSOCIATE		
Initiation Fee	$1,600.00	
Monthly Dues	62.50	No Vote
Quarterly Minimum	120.00	No Equity

SOCIAL		
Initiation Fee	$266.50	
Monthly Dues	31.25	

When prices increased by 50% or more during the inflated '70s, many assumed they would drop back to "normal." But normal turned out to be the new level. Worse yet, the new 1979 prices became a platform for gradual increases during the '80s. In Diablo a $200,000 house rose to $500,000. A new price age dawned as the '80s began.

questions were raised by members. President Gant advised that Paul's proposal was being revised to include a basement area and an area behind the Chalet for parking.

Gant continued, "Since a new offer will be developed by Cortese, I agree to advise the general membership before the Board of Directors reaches a definite decision to accept an offer."

Gant said he ". . . invited and welcomed proposals from other members." He suggested such proposals should be submitted at an early date since the Club had less than sixty days to reply to the present offer. (*Inferno*, February, 1977)

According to then-President Fred Bennett, "At the February meeting of the Board, the latest offer of Paul Cortese was carefully considered . . . The Board unanimously agreed to continue negotiations with him . . . In order to avoid any possible criticism of self-dealing or conflict of interest, Cortese has always excused himself from the Board meeting when discussion of the Chalet was next on the agenda.

"It is hoped that your Board will have a recommendation to make to the members at an early date. If this is the case, you will receive a letter outlining the recommendation and a ballot for you to indicate your preference regarding the offer."(2)

Later, President Jack Hughes said, "A drawing was held to determine the priority list for participation in the Chalet Renovation Program." (Selection of a unit.) . . . Construction will begin around year end." (July '77)

In February 1978, President Jim Hague reported, "The Chalet Lease Project is progressing but not as rapidly as we had hoped . . . The necessary subdivision map has been filed . . . We can see no problems at this time . . ." (Feb.78)

Later Hague said, "As of this date (May 20, 1978), the subdivision map has been approved . . . There have been a series of details that were not anticipated by the Partnership or by the Club and these have been handled as they developed. At this time we see nothing that may cause further delay."

But there were further delays. Construction didn't begin until 1980. Thus rests the "Chalet sale" as reconstructed by the written record. A more personal version is told in Chapter II. It is necessary to read between the lines to realize that the Club sold the building and *not* the land. Bob De John, on the Board at the time, said, "Legal counsel determined the Board had authority to make the decision and member approval was unnecessary. To this day, I'm convinced it was a good deal for the Club and a good deal for Cortese."

Jack Hughes, Club President in 1977, with one of his buddies, Bill Peck.

THE DIABLO COUNTRY CLUB INFERNO

***Inferno mastheads:* As the publication evolved to its present format, seen above.**

Monna Olson, and Audrey Barrie shared the Helfrich Award as Inferno Editors. Monna served an unprecedented 14 years.

In 1976 the Club obtained a $500,000 loan for a sprinkler system, two additional tennis courts, and redecorating of the clubhouse. Memberships were raised to $4,000 and dues to $72 per month. Later, the Board authorized a lake between the 4th and 5th holes and lights on the tennis courts. Amid these physical improvements was an emotional outpouring at the 20th anniversary of the *Inferno*.

THE INFERNO The 1955 beginning of the Club organ was front page news in a 1975 *Inferno.*

"Thinking back a score of years ago to March 1955, when a group of us (were) assembled together . . . seems only yesterday . . . We decided we were spending too much money on postage (a stamp cost $.03) to inform members about Club events. Finally, a bright smiling young dentist . . . came up with an idea . . . 'Why not send out a news bulletin each month to save on postage as well as time,' said Bill Helfrich. So a monthly newspaper was born."

"We must name our new baby," said Bill, and a contest was held. Bill selected *Inferno,* submitted by Mervin Lingle, a member in the printing business. The name rang true since the Club rested in the shadow of Devil Mountain and at one time the Club's property and Mt. Diablo were one and the same. Walt Mullaly designed the red devil as the *Inferno's* logo and Bill became the first editor.

The 1975 Sunday 20th-Year celebration—cocktails and dinner sponsored by the Board—included past presidents, past editors and past recipients of the Helfrich Award which was awarded by the *Inferno* Editor ". . . To the member whose unselfish contributions have made Diablo Country Club a better place for all to enjoy." The Award Trophy, with names of winners inscribed on it . . . "rested on a brass tray surrounded by a mound of camellias, and next to it, a vase held a dozen red roses serving as the center of attraction on the speaker's table."(3)

The real attraction, however, was Bill Helfrich, who was the MC. Honored were past editors Walt Mullaly, Spence Archer, Bob Barry, Millie Knowlton, Evelyn Jackson, Adaline Schmitt, Peggy Baender, and Mona Olson. Mona eventually served as co-editor for a record 14 years. Bill Freeman who published the *Inferno* and Irene Smiley, *Inferno* reporter, also were at the head table. The '75 Helfrich Award recipient was presented to Bob Wall and John Price. A special guest was Majorie Daggett, founder of the Holyniners and a former Helfrich Award recipient.

Letters to *Inferno* editors generally are few and far between. Editors wonder if anybody cares. On July 19, 1972, they discovered *somebody* cares. A statement in the *Inferno* read:

"Yes, nine assorted male golfers care, (proving) . . . chauvinism is not dead." Please write us, said the Editor, "And somewhere in an ensuing issue your answers will be, either profound or devious. But there."

THE CALLER HUNG UP

Buzz Knowlton tells this story about Billie Martin, the former New York Yankee Manager when Martin was named Oakland A's Manager in 1979.

On Billie's behalf, Buzz received a telephone call from a prominent East Bay businessman who wanted to talk to Knowlton as Chairman of the Membership Committee. The businessman told Buzz how much Billie loved to play golf and how pleased he would be to have a membership at Diablo, complimentary, of course.

Patiently Buzz explained the procedure: an application including fee, endorsement by two members, the two-three week posting period, Committee recommendation, and approval by the Board. The caller said, "Then you're saying that the Diablo Country Club does not wish to give Billie Martin, the A's new Manager, a free membership?"

Buzz replied, "Well, you see we have Bill Rigney, the San Francisco Giant's Manager who is a regular dues-paying member here in Diablo. Rigney has been with us since 1955 when the Giants transferred from New York. I don't think he would be pleased if Billie Martin were to be give . . ."

The caller hung up!

BEST OF DOUBLE D.

The winners, back row from left, Lorna Galvin, 14-17; Cathy Burns, 13 and under; Sandy Van Voorhis, Pony Division; front row,from left, Beth Noyes, Chris Ives, tie for Sportsmanship Award; Jenni Cross, Horsemanship Award.

BEST OF HUNTER-JUMPER

Lowrey Jones of Farfetched Farm on Caballo Ranchero started teaching two eight-year olds in 1974 who wanted to learn how to ride. She wound up training 37 young equestrians—mostly Diablo children—over a span of a dozen years. The advanced group was known as the Farfetched Farm Fillies, nine of her protégés who rode off with hundreds of ribbons and trophies at Hunter–Jumper Shows throughout California.

GEORGE WINN
Jerry Barber Protege

DIABLO NAMES NEW PRO

Diablo County Club yesterday picked a new head golf professional, 28-year-old George Winn from Borrego Springs, near San Diego.

Winn, head pro at the De Anza Desert Country Club since September, 1967, was chosen out of a list of 36 applicants to fill the job vacated by Lyle Wehrman's move to Sunol Valley.

Spencer Archer, chairman of the selection committee, said the new pro will be on the job June 1, 1971.

Winn turned pro in 1963 after leaving San Jose State and gained much of his experience under Jerry Barber at the Wilshire Country Club in Los Angeles. Winn also was a teaching pro at the Palos Verdes Golf Club.

He returned to Wilshire to rejoin Barber in 1965 and remained there until he became head pro at DeAnza Desert Country Club.

By ED SCHOENFELD
Tribune Sports Writer

Tournament Chairman Jim Hague presents trophy to Club Champion Art Johnson at the Presidents' Ball. Note cups in background, which were later presented to winners of other tournaments. (Circa '70s) COURTESY JIM HAGUE.

THE TEXT The letter, signed by "Nine Assorted Male Golfers" follows.

"Anyone looking at the last few issues of this publication—would get the impression that the Diablo Country Club was strictly a women's social and tennis racquet club.

Look at the May issue. There are pictures of 30 women and three men; and, most of the articles are about women, tennis, and swimming. Take the June issue. There are pictures of 19 women and three men; and, again, most of the articles are on women and tennis again.

You seem to forget that the men golfers are the backbone of this Club. They are the ones that financially contribute by far the most to the Club. To men golfers, the Club championship is the most important tournament of the year. Many practice and point toward this all year. And what happens? A measley seven lines is given in the June issue about the tournament. Besides the championship flight, there were nine other flights.—Who in hell were the winners?—It has never been announced in the Inferno! Besides a picture of the club champion, there should have been one of the nine flight champions and a story on the tournament.

We think you'd better get with it and support the men who support the Club. -(signed) The Men Golfers."

GOLF Among the golf highlights of the '70s were George Winn's appointment as the Golf Pro, Bud Shank's Championship play, the planting of several hundred trees on the golf course, the Junior Golf team, and of all things, a letter to the *Inferno* editor protesting . . . well, you've just read it!

George Winn was described in the *Inferno* as a . . . "young affable golf Pro." He was hired as the decade opened, fresh from improving the swings, if not the scores, of the "rich and famous." Among his former pupils were Pat Boone, Glen Campbell, Andy Williams, Fred MacMurray, Jerry West of the Los Angeles Lakers, and Roman Gabriel of the Los Angeles Rams. Now he has ". . . just Diablons," and his prices were: one-half hour lesson $9.00, 9-hole playing lesson $20.

The December '70 *Inferno* heralded Bud Shank's triumph over Dave Lamson in the September Championship. It happened again the next year. Bud had a 72-hole total of 289. Runners-up were Dick Graham with 295, and Lloyd Rossi with 297.

A picture of George Foreman adorned the cover of the March '71 *Inferno* . . . not George Foreman the boxer but one of Diablo's greenskeepers. He is pictured planting the first of several hundred trees. The tree planting was spearheaded by Bill Rigney who challenged members to invest in their fairways at the rate of $5 per tree. Two years later, Greens Chairman Jim Hague said, "A fine committee has successfully accomplished the master plan."

1978 was a good year for the junior golfers. Mainstays of the team were Paul Leonard, Ben Rei, Mark Osmer, Tom Shipley, Todd Lindsey, Josh Swenson, Liz Redfearne, Jeff Meyer and Bob Hirsch. Up and coming youngsters included Tim Corcoran, Jerry and Joel Slavonia, John Pianalto and Todd Olson. They were coached by Larry Lindsay, Ken Rader and Tom Corcoran.

SWIMMING As Tim White, the new swimming coach, began the '71 season, his second as the coach, he announced a new schedule of events and revised prices.

The cost of being a member of the team was $10 per family; private lessons $3.75 per half-hour; semiprivate, two to four persons, $24 for eight half-hour lessons; group, five to eight persons, $20 for eight half-hour lessons; competitive stroke, six persons, $15 for eight half-hour lessons.

Most successful was the '76 team. More than 65 families participated, doubling the '75 roster and adding 27 new families. Swim meets ran smoothly with the experienced help of Bill Cronin, Announcer; Gil Fryer, Starter; John Meyer, Timer and Judge; Shirley Osmer, League Representative; Nancy Rubey, Scorer's Table; and Karen Johnson, Refreshments.

Rick and Diane Ernst, 1978 Swim Co-Chairmen, submitted a list of proposed improvements to the Board of Directors. Among the five pages of recommendations were: Eliminate cooking in the pool Snack Shack and convert it to a pool operations center. Provide vending machines for beverages and nutritional snacks. Make food and beverage service available from the Club kitchen. Replace and upgrade lawn furniture and poolside equipment. Maintain pool and surrounding area in as comfortable and well-equipped manner as possible.

The Board acted favorably on these suggestions, so the pool/patio area was made more functional, attractive and a more controlled operation as the swim program moved into the '80s.

PARTIES The annual Anniversary party, Luau, St. Patrick's Day dinner dance, Valentine's dinner, Crab Feed, Tennis Ball, Christmas/Easter parties, and Mother's Day brunch continued to be popular. But the hits of the '70s were the Mexican Fiesta and Italians Against the World events.

The July '76 "Fiesta Fabulosa," as President George Padis labeled it, ". . . was the gayest party of the year. John and Nancy went 'all out.' Viva Oliverios!"

Italians Against the World featured lunch, golf, dinner, and professional entertainment, augmented by Diablo Italians. They called themselves "professionals," but of what, was never clear!

An unusual event was the Junior League's Project "A Day in Diablo" in June, '76. This "most suc-

DIABLO SWIMMERS PREP FOR NEXT YEAR

Although the official swimming season has ended, the Diablo Country Club Swim Team continues to splash in hopes of bettering their second place finish in next year's league action.

Fleet Mark Osmer was named the biggest point-getter on the season followed by Mark Blumhardt, Sue Baggett and Diana Marks. Most Improved swimmer was Heidi Sorenson followed by Brian Smiley, Judy Nageotte and Kirsten Elgaan.

Miss Marks was also named the most valuable swimmer with Missy Thomas the runner-up in that category.

Before capping the season, Sue Baggett informed Coach Tim White that she planned to swim Crater Lake next summer. "There's no way," he told the young aquatic star, "you can't tread water for three hours." "I can too," she retorted and bet her coach a steak dinner that she could do it. For five hours, Miss Baggett worked arms and legs in the club pool while her surprised coach made proper arrangements with the kitchen for a luscious steak dinner.

Junior League teen models: Mary Jane Gordon and Brooke Jones, (not pictured are) Steffi La Cava, Lisa Jones, and Karin Erickson.

cessful" event was a money raiser and featured tours of homes, a fashion show and luncheon. Teen-age clothes were modeled by Lisa and Brooke Jones, Mary Jane Gordon, Stefanie La Cava and Karin Erickson.(4) Diablo "taxis" moved the guests from place to place.

TENNIS Marsh Freeman's first annual Calcutta Tennis Classic was held in July, 1976. The evening before the tournament, everyone met in the clubhouse for an auction conducted by Semmes Gordon. Players who had signed up for the mixed doubles tournament were grouped into syndicates, willy-nilly, by those placing their bets. Eventually, Dan Lubbock and Jane Landry, owned by the syndicate of Tiernan and La Cava, took first place in the amount of money bet over John Osmer and Lynn Nilssen. Dave Edwards and Greta Sorensen emerged as winners on the consolation side over Marian McDonald and Bob Sorensen. After the Saturday/Sunday play, some syndicates won their bets, others lost, amid some despair and much cheering. The tournament was capped by a dinner party.

Sam Ditto, "Dean of Diablo Tennis," dedicated courts six and seven in August '76. The *Inferno* said ". . . with a gala and moderately refined group in attendance." Dave Kipp, the *Tennis Times* correspondent wrote, "Sam was at no loss for words, and although I was forced to miss it, reportedly established his oratorical talents."

Speaking of Diablo's still-crowded courts, in May, 1977, Dick Overstreet (often called Overcoat!) wrote in the *Inferno* that ". . . the wait is not too long." He said this was because of Diablo's system of taking turns by hanging racquets on the fence of court five and giving up the court after one set of singles or two of doubles.

Inflation finally caught up with tennis. In March 77, Dick Overstreet "reluctantly" announced increases in the price of lessons, but interest and participation remained at record levels despite the cost.

The March, 1978 *Inferno* reported, "Tennis at Diablo continues to grow. There are more members and more families playing than ever before."(5) A major reason for the growth was the camaraderie of competition as illustrated in the story that follows.

Patty wants practice to end!

Tennis Awards Dinner Cups to the winners. Kathy Elgaaen, Marsh & Mugs Freeman, Charlie & Pat Moye, Shirley & John Osmer.

Jinny Cuenin, at top. Followed by Bob Cuenin, Peggy Gordon "the Spirit of Diablo", and Semmes Gordon. COURTESY OF DICK OVERSTREET.

MEMORABLE MEMBER: MARSH FREEMAN

Marsh Freeman's backhand (6) was a thing of beauty—graceful, powerful, accurate. When he hit it with a back spin, the result was devastating. It was his most lethal weapon. "Not so," interrupted Mugs, "when Marsh and I played mixed doubles the women would all comment about what a really nice guy he was—until he served, that is. He had an overspin serve that made the ball bounce crazily and diabolically, spinning up and over opponents' heads. It was awesome."

Asked to recall their most memorable experience, both Mugs and Marsh exclaimed at the same instant, "The greeting committee." That was in 1966 when they moved to Diablo. Driving by the courts on a Sunday afternoon to their new home at 36 Campo Pelota overlooking the courts, a group of players was gathered by court three drinking Bloody Marys. When they saw the Freemans, they rushed up to welcome them, offering to share their drinks. Marsh said, "We got Patty's playpen out of the car, put her in it, and rushed to join the group." It included the Cuenins, Gordons, Priewes, and Stones. Mugs said, "We thought 'wow,' what a welcome wagon, and they play tennis too! It was our first taste of the Diablo spirit."

Mugs said she remembered another incident that bespeaks the Diablo spirit. "I thought how wonderful it was to be living in such a quiet, peaceful community—except on Thursdays. We were regularly awakened at 7:00 a.m. by a loud tennis foursome of Bob Cuenin and Jim Stone playing against Bill Rei and Semmes Gordon. It was a Decibel Tournament with Semmes the clear winner."

For ten years, Marsh and Mugs played tennis nearly everyday. As soon as Marsh got home from work, they'd take Patty in her playpen to the courts and practice, play and practice some more.

From 1966-76 Marsh was the all-around best, winning more than his share of men's singles, men's doubles, mixed doubles, and men's invitationals. He or Bob Tiernan were the perennial men's singles champion or runner up. "Bob was my nemesis," said Marshall. "The first couple of years, no matter how hard I tried, I couldn't beat the bastard and you can quote me." (7) Marsh was the champ in '72, '74, and '76. "The irony of Marsh's desire to beat Bob," said Mugs, "is that the first time he did beat him, in the semi-finals in 1973, he lost in the finals to Don Kinkel! Guess it just wasn't meant to be, at least not that year."

Jim Mandley's Skybolt, left, and Marsh Freeman's "Crate 38."

Tennis and airplane buddies Marsh, left, and Jim, below.

Marsh's homebuilt Skybolt, 1977.

Patty, Kim and Steve Freeman can't wait for Dad to finish his airplane, 1975, top.

SKYBOLT PROJECT

Marsh Freeman, proprietor

Jim Mandley, Technical Advisor
Paul Switzer, Original Instigator
Peter McCoy, Welding Equipment

Mail to:
Box 645, Diablo, Ca. 94528
Tel: (415) 837-4563

Package Delivery:
M.W. Freeman
Miller Freeman Publications
500 Howard Street
San Francisco, Ca. 94105
Tel: (415) 397-1881

Site:
36 Camp Pelota
Diablo, California

YOU'RE INVITED TO AN

OPEN AIRPLANE

Cocktails & "Nuts"

COME SEE HOW SHE LOOKS BEFORE BEING COVERED !

6:00 PM - 9:00 PM

FRIDAY AUGUST 6

 See Skybolt N38MF completely assembled in Mugs' garden!

 See if you can figure out how to get it out of there!

See and hear the mighty engine start up about 8:30! (Maybe)

COME AS YOU ARE - BEFORE, DURING, OR AFTER TENNIS OR ANYTHING ELSE.

Marsh and Mugs Freeman

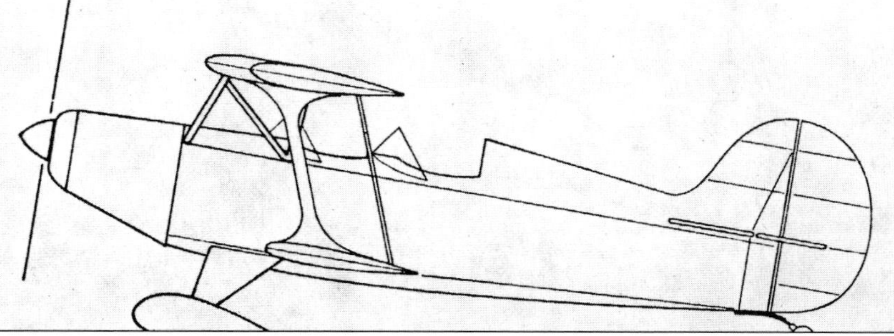

The Freemans started the first Men's Invitational in the early '70s and hosted it at their home. It was held early in the fall, following the golfers' well-established Gold Putter Tournament. So the Freemans named the tennis award, "Golden Balls."

Marsh's last Men's Championship was 1976. Then he had surgery on both knees and was advised to take up flying as had Jim Mandley with his good knees. In the *Inferno* of November, 1976, Dick Overstreet wrote, "Where else can you play tennis on a Saturday morning and have Jim Mandley doing aerobatics overhead while you're trying to serve or a helicopter lifting Marsh Freeman's new toy (a Skybolt biplane which he built) out of his backyard as you try an overhead smash?"

In this, his last year of tennis, Marsh won men's singles and men's doubles but lost to Bob and Lyn Tiernan in mixed doubles. "Otherwise," said Mugs, "he would have had a clean sweep and gone out in a blaze of glory."

Later in a note Mugs added this:

"I have one more vivid memory I forgot to mention earlier. Connie La Cava used to take her girls, Steffi and Nikki, down to the field (which is now courts four and five) every afternoon and train them in their dressage workouts on horseback. It was quite an event to watch—petite Connie calling out instructions like a drill sergeant as Steffi and Nikki deftly performed the maneuvers. It all seemed wonderfully professional to me."

When the new courts opened there was no walkway along the side of the courts, no stairs up the hill to the restroom behind the swimming pool, and no pathway up the hill to Campo Pelota. Marsh and Mugs organized a tennis-player work force—adults and kids. Everyone pitched in. Under Marsh's supervision, a concrete walk was laid from the Tennis Pro Shop to court three, a stairway built up the hill to the restroom, and a pathway to Campo Pelota. "That was the Diablo spirit in action," said Marsh.

The Diablo spirit in action runs both ways. No one is so missed and remembered on the courts more fondly by Diablo tennis buffs than Mugs and *Mr. Backhand.*

Perennial court opponents—Marsh Freeman (L) & Bob Tiernan. COURTESY MARSH FREEMAN.

Steffi and Nikki La Cava at Pony Club barbecue.

Rett and Lou Turner, above.

MEMORABLE MEMBER: RETT TURNER

Rett came to the Club presidency from service as Chairman of the House Committee for three years, beginning in 1963. Prior to his committee tenure, the swim program had been treated like a poor relation, "because it didn't generate income for the Club like golf, tennis, and outside parties did," said Rett.(8)

Believing that swimming should be a valuable Club perk, Rett had a better idea: double the investment and quadruple the results! Instead of hiring one coach each year, he decided to hire two, one with experience, one inexperienced, and then move the younger one to the lead slot the second year, thus providing continuity. With Jim Stone who chaired the swim program, they went to the U.C. Placement Office where Lou, Rett's bride-to-be, lined-up Cal's swim greats for interviews.

The result was a succession of outstanding coaches and winning swim teams. Most memorable of the brightest and best was an Aussie, Dave Parsons, the "Crocodile Dundee" of his day. Marsh Freeman says of Dave, "He was one of the most engaging personalities I've ever known. Our kids still talk about him."

As President, Rett used his business acumen to install these controls:

1) A numbered chit system so all chits were accounted for;
2) Kitchen scales so the meat was weighed at the Club, thus paying the *delivered*, not the purchased weight;
3) An inventory system so each bottle of liquor and wine was accounted for;
4) Golf and tennis pros reporting to the manager;
5) Job descriptions for all personnel;
6) A system of monthly minimums for all members.

The minimum question was hotly debated. One side was convinced the Club would lose members if they were required to spend $25 a month. The other side countered the Club couldn't survive without a guaranteed monthly income.

Rett made a bet with the Directors. He wagered, "We won't lose one single member." The board adopted the minimum, but during the first month, one member resigned in protest. Rett said, "I lost the battle but I won the war."

Don Kinkel supervises tennis players building new paths.

Tennis was the game of the '70s throughout the world. The word wasn't "Tennis Anyone," it was "Tennis Everyone." Courts and clubs sprang up like mushrooms. Competition for members was keen and Diablo was losing out because it had only three courts. "The natives were getting restless," said Rett.

He met with the tennis group and said, "Get twenty new members and you'll get two new courts." The group agreed and went to work. "That turned out to be a piece of cake," said Rett. "You see, I'd done a survey of how members spent their money at the Club. It proved tennis players spent more than anyone."

Rett recalled one member whose business went belly-up. The Feds seized his assets, including his membership valued at $2,000 and announced a Saturday morning public auction to sell it. Rett went, but no one else was there. He bid $1.00 and bought the membership for the Club. Diablo's profits: $1,999.

Rett is proud he kept the Club afloat through tight-money times. He said, "I feel so proud seeing what the Club is today. It's come a long way in the past twenty years and I'm glad to still be a part of it."

MEMORABLE MEMBER: SPENCE ARCHER

According to Spence Archer, President 1971-72, and a former *Inferno* editor, Bill Helfrich originally planned that the *Inferno* editor should select the person to receive the Helfrich Award that bears his name. "I agreed with Bill because the editor was the one person most in the know." (9)

Expounding on that theory, Spence explained, "The editor's most important job was to recruit a qualified staff of reporters. Some are 'givens' such as the Club Manager and Golf and Tennis Pros. It's part of their jobs to write a monthly column. The others are volunteers, willing to serve . . ."

Once an able group of volunteers was recruited, it was the editor's job to ride herd on them and enforce copy deadline. "In my day," Spence said, "quality control, which editors typically exercised by heavy-handed cutting and rewriting, was minimal. We had quality control through the caliber of our reporters. What I most remember from my eight years as editor are the people who worked with me. They were willing, able and dedicated. Millie Knowlton was one who always went the extra mile."

Spence Archer, Club President 1971-72 and Inferno editor for 8 years.

Spence continued, "Simply by the nature of the job, the editor got to know all segments and aspects of the Club and who were the people making it go." Today's editors do not participate in the selection of Helfrich Award recipients. The '90s are an age of specialization. Editors edit and boards make decisions.

Spence was responsible for persuading the Club's finance committee, chaired by De Witt Krueger, to allocate $5,000 to remodel and refurbish the main entrance and foyer and still operate in the black in 1971-72. He also originated the system of selling Club memberships in a manner that allowed the Club a profit.

Spence had the advantage during his stewardship of profiting from earlier experience as Club Secretary in 1960-62. It was he, on June 7, 1961, who co-signed with Bill Houston the Bank of California's $445,000 deed of trust to buy the Club from Curtola. He concluded, "It's people you get to know by working with them to make Diablo click that makes it all worthwhile. It's people to people with a common goal—that's Diablo."

President Bill Houston.

MEMORABLE MEMBER: BILL HOUSTON

Bill helped the Club through the first years of the '60s and pushed it profitably into the '80s. He negotiated the sale of the Club from Larry Curtola in 1961 (page 91), played a role in the installation of a new tennis center (page 92), enlarged the men's locker room, and was there when the Club created "profit centers." (10)

Bill remembered when the Board decided to enlarge the men's locker room. "I got ahold of Lloyd Rossi who figured the space could be doubled by digging out the ground from under the Club offices. He brought in a cat and a scraper and the removal began. The dirt had to be trundled from the basement and members took turns running the system. The new ceiling then had to be braced but at what points Rossi wasn't sure. So he got his golf buddies to jump up and down in the Club office. Stationed in the basement, Rossi could then spot where the ceiling moved the most and place his posts accordingly. That's how the locker room was enlarged."

As part of the trundle system, an underground entrance was built with boards and dirt. It went from the golf shop to the men's locker room and was quickly dubbed, "Houston's Folly." Today, it's the hallway, adorned with members' pictures, that goes from the golf Pro Shop to the Men's Grill.

In 1979, Bill decided to throw his hat into the presidency again. He also decided the Club needed "profit centers"—on-going sources of income so it wasn't dependent solely on the members' pocket books and outside parties.

By the mid-'70s, the golf Pro Shop beyond the first tee had become a lemon. It was too far away from the action so it was moved to the clubhouse basement. With the help of Steve Jones, President of the Diablo Property Owners Association, Bob Wall and Harold Smith, negotiations began with federal representatives to rent the abandoned golf Pro Shop to the Post Office. This was the first profit center and brings in $6,000 annually.

By this time, the Chalet was uninhabited except for the two end apartments occupied by the Bailey Justices and Maude Pratt. Paul Cortese proposed leasing the land and converting the Chalet into eight condos. Negotiations were begun under Cliff Gant's presidency, and continued through Fred Bennett's, Jack Hughes', Jim Hague's, and came to rest with Bill. This second profit center brings in $30,000 annually.

"Country clubs are among the worst run businesses," admonished Bill. "Smart businessmen often don't make smart weekend caretakers." He believes private clubs need profit centers, and that, except for food and the swimming pool, each major activity should pay for itself. "That's the ticket for fiscal solvency," he said. "The challenge of all proprietary clubs is to create sources of income other than dues paid by members."

Terrace Room as it was before the '80s restoration.

Men's Bar as it was before the '80s restoration.

Dorothy Petersen's home pictured in Diablo's only snow storm, March 1975.
PHOTO BY WILL ASHFORD

THE ENTERPRISING EIGHTIES

Chapter IX

ARNIE BLACKMUR'S BOOK, *In Old Diablo*, made its debut at a reception at the Deckers' (Minors') home, 1925 Alameda Diablo, in the fall of 1981. Thorough and scholarly, Blackmur's social history has textual punch and tasteful pictures. This volume is built on the framework Blackmur provided. His shoulders were its launching pad.

In 1975 there was a big push to save Diablo from being swallowed up by Danville or Blackhawk by incorporating as a city. Paul Cortese and Steve Jones chaired a committee to draw up a petition to present to LAFCO (Local Agency Formation Commission). (See page 184.) The committee asked Arnie to write a section on Diablo's history as a part of the petition. His book developed from that beginning.

He said, "For my book, I planned to write an opening section and have four or five others help me—one writing about houses, one the Club, another the DPOA and DCSD, etc. Then I realized that wouldn't work. If there was going to be a book, I'd have to do it."

Carol Sconyers, DPOA President, and others encouraged Arnie to do it. Ridley Rhind said his company, Ampex, would publish it, and Arnie said, "That provided the motivation." He selected Julie Rhind as his editor because he admired how well-read she was. Julie said, "I was so surprised when he asked me. I'd never been an editor. Ironically, since then I've taken courses in editing. My special contribution was to say, 'you can't stop with ancient history; you've got to bring it up to the present too.'"

Ampex had its own presses for in-house publications but had never done a book. "The workmen were excited about the project," Ridley said. He told Arnie, "You write it and I'll publish it." Arnie, a high school history teacher, spent the summers of 1978, '79 and '80 researching, photographing, collecting pictures and interviewing.

Arnold Blackmur in his Diablo Country Club sweater.

THE CONTEXT A former movie star dominates the political and economic scene. Ronald Reagan, "the Great Communicator" convinces Americans that trickle down economics and a military build-up are the keys to strength at home and respect abroad.

Yuppie families populate suburbia, supermarkets and shopping malls. Cable TV is in the marketplace, extending, expanding, and enriching entertainment and educational choice. Video cassettes make home movie viewing popular.

Computers are revolutionizing how we communicate, do business, fly airplanes, run rapid transit systems, and educate our children. Kids are hooked on video games.

Pro basketball and football dominate the sports world thanks to TV. The 1989 World Series is a transbay event, Giants-Oakland A's. The first game at Candlestick Park on October 17, 1989 is interrupted by the 7.2 Loma Prieta earthquake at 5:04 p.m.

Women and gays compete for political support in their fight for equality. AIDS becomes pandemic threatening homo- and heterosexuals alike; Japanese and German automobiles outsell American cars as world markets expand and business becomes international.

In Old Diablo, is published, the Chalet becomes a condominium and the clubhouse is restored.

Ampex charged the DPOA $6,000 for 2,000 copies. Arnie sent two copies to every public and private school in the area. For the next several years, at DPOA annual dinners and ice cream socials, *In Old Diablo* was featured with Arnie on hand to autograph copies. Residents new to Diablo were given copies by the Welcome Wagon Committee. The Club bought copies to give to new members.

When asked about finances, Arnie replied, "It was sold for $10 a copy and I assume the DPOA made some money but I don't know and I wouldn't know who to ask. I did it as a community contribution. It has served to remind me that Diablo has a colorful past and memorable present."

Suzanne Guinivere was the DPOA's Secretary and recalled a discussion about the amount of unexpended money in its bank account. It had been accumulating for a number of years in anticipation of doing something major with the entrance to Diablo. Now the Board was in a bind because the accumulated amount might place its tax exempt status in jeopardy.

"At that 'moment in time,'" recalled Suzanne, "the idea of publishing Arnie's book surfaced. It was the answer to the Board's dilemma and a way to recognize Arnie's contribution as a DPOA past President." She "thinks" the DPOA got its money back from the sale of the book but doesn't know. "This might have the makeup of a Diablo scandal. Call it 'Bookgate'," she said with a laugh.

The author called Arnie to talk about his book and his years in Diablo. He responded with a letter, dated February 8, 1994, shown on the next page.

THE GATHERING STORM The eye of a storm is at the center where all is calm while around it, fury and chaos rage. This may be likened to the situation in Diablo, 1984-1987.

The storm was about the clubhouse:

- Restore the present one, or
- Raze it and build a new one near the present site, or
- Abandon it and build on the knoll by the 10th tee.

This was a hurricane whose force split households, life-long friends and Club members living in Diablo from those not living here. Few, if any were in the calm of the eye.

The gathering storm began on November 25, 1984 as a light breeze billowing from the annual meeting. President Lynn McCoskey had discussed the problem of "our aging clubhouse" and proposed ways to rebuild it in another location. The majority of those present, however, favored restoring the clubhouse. In December, the board polled the members and Lynn reported: "From the members, it is

45 West Sheffield Road
Great Barrington, MA.

Dear Jim,

Here are some thoughts and recollections about Diablo as Jean and I remembered it.

When we moved there in the summer of 1973, it had a definite small-town atmosphere where many knew each other, and families had lived there for years. There were relatively few houses for sale—people just didn't move out. The houses were by and large a mix of former summer cottages and '50s ranch style—there were few truly elegant homes.

Living on Alameda Diablo gave us the opportunity to see and hear much: young children like ours, selling lemonade and vegetables on the street, and hearing the clippity-clop of horses' hooves on the streets as there wasn't much traffic then. We remember kids going to Diablo Lake to catch frogs and fish.

We joined the Club and have many happy memories watching the kids in swim meets and tennis tournaments and Jean and I going to neighbors' homes after Twilight Tennis. The Club was relatively inexpensive and quite informal—it was certainly not fancy and one might call it "faded."

Kids took the bus to school, and used to wait for it at the bus shelter. Parents and dogs would plan their daily activities around the comings and goings of the bus.

The small-town atmosphere was best illustrated by such events as the dedication of the new Post Office and the annual Ice Cream Social.

Diablons were fiercely proud of the uniqueness of the community and resisted attempts to merge with other communities. The DCSD and the DPOA combined efforts to preserve Diablo's independence.

In the 1980s there was a burst of new home construction as well as large-scale remodeling. The new homes were elegant and expensive. The remodeling was on a grand scale, converting former cottages to two-story mansions. All this, of course, resulted in a rapid escalation of property values.

The people buying the new homes or upgrading old ones were young and successful. Diablo was being populated by a new generation.

Now there were fewer horses on Alameda Diablo and in their place came Mercedes and BMWs—I saw this as I mowed my front lawn. The school bus was gone which meant more traffic as mothers drove their kids to and from school.

Finally, we could see a change in the atmosphere of the Club. The extensive remodeling made it a truly lovely and elegant Club.

Yes, Diablo has changed, but it still has an irresistible charm—it is even more of an enclave, surrounded by endless suburban squal! And the people continue to be dedicated to preserving and maintaining its uniqueness.

Jean sends her love to you and Dorothy.

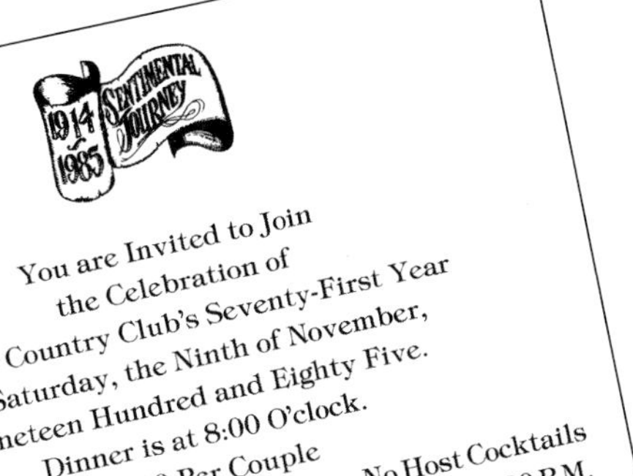

Harry Timmermans.

obvious that two-thirds of our members like the present clubhouse where it is and are willing to underwrite the cost of remodeling, assuming the financial arrangements are reasonable." (1)

DEVELOPING CONFLICT By January 1985, it was clear that the Board was going ahead with plans to rebuild rather than restore. With the exception of Vice President Larry Ives and Director Art Johnson, the rest of the Board was against restoration. In an effort to sensitize the Board to the historical interest of Diablo members and residents, Lynn was invited to a meeting at a Diablo member's home. The minutes of February 27, 1985 stated, "An informal meeting with President Lynn McCoskey (was held) at a member's home. Those present protested that the Board was not doing anything about restoring the present clubhouse, not following the vote in favor of restoration, and ignoring the historical significance of the clubhouse." Members living in Diablo were the backbone of what became known as the restoration drive.

During the next several months the storm became a gale with the press reporting, "tidal waves in the East Bay community of Diablo." Now the drive to build a new clubhouse was being challenged by a protest block led by Harry Timmermans. He was aided by Vice President Ives, and supported by Diablo members and residents. Harry and his wife Anne had been active members and residents since 1979 (1834 El Nido). Like his fellow Diablons, Harry was dedicated to restoring the clubhouse as an historical site. As a former President of the DPOA and WWII Air Force Colonel Wing Commander, he was an experienced leader with a large following.

The Board firmly believed it had been elected to make decisions on behalf of the members and it was encouraged to take this stance by its Legal Advisor Jeryco Peterson. At the June 26 meeting, the appointment of a *new* Clubhouse Construction Committee was approved. Also approved was $5,000 for initial surveys, soil samples and for soliciting building designs from interested architects. In the August, 1985, *Inferno,* President McCoskey reported the Board had "approved the construction of a *new* clubhouse and assessed each regular member $3,000 to keep this effort in motion."

Swirling through Diablo were two collision-bent gales: "raze and build" vs "restore/renovate." Cliff Gant, 1976 President, went to the September 25 Board meeting as a "friend of the Board" to strongly recommend that it "allow the members to vote at a special meeting on whether they favored building a new clubhouse or restoring the present one."

The September 29, 1985 special meeting revealed the storm had reached hurricane proportions.

NOVEMBER 26, 1985

COUNTRY CLUB DIVIDED OVER ITS CLUBHOUSE

Old facility may be razed

By Martha Ross
Staff writer

DIABLO — The split among members of Diablo Country Club over the future of their clubhouse is even apparent in the upcoming annual board of directors election.

Three candidates who have worked on the committee to save the century-old clubhouse are challenging three candidates nominated by the board of directors.

"I'm unhappy with the direction the board has taken, or I wouldn't be running," said candidate Mathew Chandler, who is running for one of three spots on the nine-member board.

Members will be mailed ballots that must be returned by the Nov. 24 general meeting, when the election winners will be announced. Board members serve three year terms

Members who want to save the clubhouse or at least want a new ballot to decide its fate have leveled accusations of misrepresentation and prejudice against the present board of directors for its vote in July to raze the building and replace it.

Chandler's cause is joined by Henry Timmermans and William Potts.

The directors' nominating committee asked Ken Fraser, Niles Lawson and Mike Stead to run.

"We would bring new blood and provide a different opinion," said Timmermans, a 9-year Diablo resident. "It's in the best interest of the membership to have a board consisting of representatives of a different viewpoint than those on the board at the present time.

"Unanimity is not necessarily the best form of government," he added.

Fraser served on the board from 1976 to 1979 and currently heads the Long Range Planning Committee, which has been looking toward constructing a new clubhouse.

"I was asked to run," Fraser said. "They felt I could aid the club. But under the conditions, I'm not so enthused about being a member (of the board)."

But Fraser said he hopes the election will be a step toward a reconciliation.

Board president Lynn McCoskey, who has said he has not decided whether to remain on the board, said the election has nothing to do with the clubhouse dispute.

Timmermans agreed the election is one way to "bring the club back together," but added that a new ballot on the clubhouse is a necessary part of any reconciliation.

"We feel the membership should have been fully informed of various cost options available," Timmermans said.

MEMBERS OF COUNTRY CLUB TO RECEIVE $3,000 REBATE

DIABLO — Diablo Country Club's board of directors voted Wednesday to return the fees members have been charged to cover the costs of building a new clubhouse, said president Lynn McCoskey.

But McCoskey would not comment on why the board reached this decision.

Clubmembers have protested the $3,000 fees and expressed their views loudly at a special club meeting on Sept. 29. They said they objected to the board collecting money when the decision to build a new clubhouse was in dispute.

"They asked for the money at the wrong time," said Henry Timmermans, who has been active in the save-the-clubhouse campaign. "They hadn't offered us any definite plan. We didn't know what it would be in design or size."

McCoskey said about 90 percent of the 462 voting members have paid the first two installments. But he said he had no idea when members would get their money back.

DIABLO COUNTRY CLUB

OFFICIAL BALLOT

Please read entire ballot before voting

PART I

Note: All proposals are subject to obtaining all necessary governmental agency approvals, permits and clearances required by law.

• If you vote to approve one or more proposals, please rank each proposal you approve in the order of your preference ("1" is the proposal you favor most).

• If you vote to disapprove, do not rank that proposal in the "Approved" column.

PROPOSAL	Approve	Disapprove
A Renovate/remodel the present clubhouse, improve tennis facility on same site.	☐	☐
B New clubhouse on or near tenth tee knoll. Improve tennis facility at existing site	☐	☐
C New clubhouse on or near present site. Improved tennis facility on same site.	☐	☐
D Maintain present clubhouse and tennis facility without remodeling.	☐	☐

PART II

ASSESSMENT AND DUES INCREASE FOR PROPOSALS: A B C

Vote your approval or disapproval of special funding needed in the event Proposal A or B or C obtains winning approval of the voting members. Special funding needed is based on preliminary estimates, and a final bid exceeding the preliminary estimate for the winning proposal will not be accepted without majority approval of the voting members. Vote your approval or disapproval of each by entering an "x" in the boxes below. You may approve or disapprove more than one. You may approve or disapprove **all** special funding required to fund the proposal obtaining winning approval of the voting members by entering "x" in all three boxes under the appropriate column.

PROPOSAL	Approve	Disapprove
A **Regular and Junior Exec.:** Assessment: $3600.; Capital Improvement Dues Increase: $40. **Non Resident Regular:** Assessment: $3600.; Capital Improvement Dues Increase: $20. **Tennis:** Assessment: $1800.; Capital Improvement Dues Increase: $20.	☐	☐
B **Regular and Junior Exec.:** Assessment: $4200.; Capital Improvement Dues Increase: $40. **Non Resident Regular:** Assessment: $4200.; Capital Improvement Dues Increase: $20. **Tennis:** Assessment: $2100.; Capital Improvement Dues Increase: $20.	☐	☐
C **Regular and Junior Exec.:** Assessment: $4600.; Capital Improvement Dues Increase: $40. **Non Resident Regular:** Assessment: $4600.; Capital Improvement Dues Increase: $20. **Tennis:** Assessment: $2300.; Capital Improvement Dues Increase: $20.	☐	☐

Members were deeply polarized. The depth of the chasm is shown by noting that the call for this special meeting did *not* come from the Board, but from a petition signed by 172 members. A poll was taken at the special meeting with these results:

– Raze it and build near the same site—187.

– Restore present clubhouse—199.

Now the raze and build block was unintentionally undercut by E.G. Craig. He offered to build a new clubhouse on the knoll by the 10th tee, thus making Diablo like other clubs with front and back nines beginning and ending at the clubhouse. The Craig proposal, leaving the present clubhouse to become a tennis, swimming, and recreational facility, added another dimension to the uncertainty.

BALLOT CONFUSION The Board's steadfast course to raze and build finally collided head-on with the restoration drive. The Club has no record of the results of a ballot taken on May 25, 1985. It was a confusing ballot. On the first half of the ballot, members were given the choice of voting for (1) "a new clubhouse as recommended by the Board of Directors, or (2) a remodeled clubhouse, or (3) neither of the above." A vote for 1 (new clubhouse) or 2 (restore) also was a vote for a "$3,000 assessment of regular members, $1,500 for associate members and a dues increase of $10-$40 for all." On the second half of the *same* ballot, members *again* were asked to vote:

"( ) A. A new clubhouse on or near the present site.

or

"( ) B. A new clubhouse at #10 knoll site."

The obfuscated ballot prompted legal action and a suit was filed.

The minutes of the October 17 Board meeting stated, "Jeryco Peterson (the Board's legal advisor) reviewed the results of the court hearing in the suit against the Club by Neufeld, Stone, Pianalto and Davies, (asking for a freeze on funds for planning and demanding a vote of the members on a clearly stated ballot). Judge Dolgin believed the Club should resolve its own differences. The Judge will not issue an opinion for 90 days." The court decision strongly suggested the Board reconsider its stand.

The Judge's message was understood. At the next meeting the Board approved a motion to rescind the $2,660,259 contract to build a new clubhouse. This was followed by another motion to return members' assessments.

EQUALITY AND FAIRNESS The following month the Board authorized $30,000 to pay for architectural drawings and site plans for a new clubhouse and another $30,000 for drawings and plans to restore the present clubhouse. E.G. Craig agreed to fund studies of his own proposal. President McCoskey appointed a committee to see that plans and designs of the three alternatives followed the same parameters. The Board named an independent cost estimator to review each proposal, and authorized the hiring of outside legal counsel to guide members in making a decision on the three options. A Los Angeles firm was retained to provide "a professional and unbiased discussion of the issues..." Their 50-page analysis of the three options was itself controversial. The Board provided for the chairmen of the three committees to approve the ballot design and voting procedure and it appointed an independent accounting firm to count the ballots. Each group mailed plans and brochures to members and developed models of its proposal. April 27-30 was set aside for members to examine sketches, plans, designs, models, and estimates.

For some unknown reason, Club minutes fail to mention the results of this momentous vote. Anne Timmermans, however, had a copy of the June 4, 1986 memorandum to the Board of Directors from the accounting firm of Blanding, Boyer and Ryan, the firm hired to conduct the voting and count the ballots. Their letter said, "Of 395 valid ballots 222.5 (58%) voted for restoration, 73 (19%) for a new clubhouse near the present site and 85.5 (22%) for a new clubhouse by the 10th."

Contracts were signed with architect George Swallow for design services and with Torre Construction for building. Activities in the clubhouse ceased January 1, 1987. Restoration work began in February with temporary buildings erected on the upper parking lot for office, Pro Shop, and food service.

The three-year storm finally subsided, and the path was cleared for a restored clubhouse that opened its doors with much fanfare for Christmas, 1988. It took time, effort, leadership, patience, persistence, the rebuilding of trust and goodwill, and $6.2 million. The result: Diablo—both Club and Community—has a beautifully restored historic clubhouse.

Results of the balloting from Blanding, Boyer and Ryan who verified the results.

BLANDING BOYER & RYAN

June 4, 1986

To the Board of Directors of Diablo Valley Country Club:

We have counted the ballots in accordance with the latter of instructions we received from Mr. Niles V. Lawson dated May 15, 1986.

The following represents the results of the Balloting which ended May 29, 1986:

	Number of Ballots	Percentage
Received Timely	402	
Incorrectly Filled Out Top Half — Disqualified	3	
Empty Envelopes Received After Due Date	2	
Results of "First Ballot"		
Proposal A	200.5	50.25
Proposal B	71	17.79
Proposal C	82.5	20.68
Proposal D	45	11.28
Results of "Second Ballot" (Using 381 Ballots since 18 voters did not give their second choice.)		
Proposal A	222.5	58.40
Proposal B	73	19.16
Proposal C	85.5	22.44
Results of Assessment and Dues Balloting:		
Funding A	273.5	61.74
Funding B	132	29.80
Funding C	152	34.31

(All 402 timely ballots were used for the assessment and dues balloting. The percentages are the positive ballots divided by the eligible voters, 443 which includes 38 half votes.)

The balloting went very smoothly which is a compliment to the membership of the Club. The ballot was fairly complicated yet only three of those received timely had to be disqualified. We are sure that having both sets of issues decided with this ballot will greatly help the board of directors.

We appreciate your having selected our firm to help you with the counting and coordinating of the ballots.

Please do not hesitate to call if you have any questions.

Very truly yours,
Blanding, Boyer & Ryan

Ronald Boyer

Ronald G. Boyer

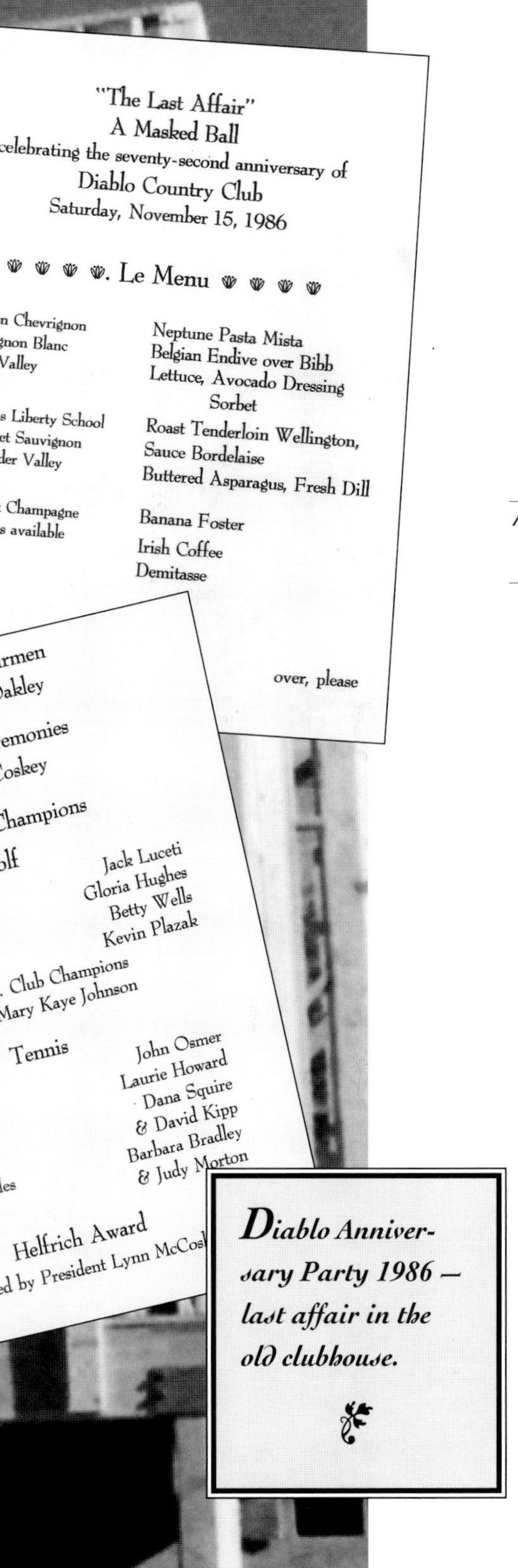

"The Last Affair"
A Masked Ball
celebrating the seventy-second anniversary of
Diablo Country Club
Saturday, November 15, 1986

Le Menu

Vichon Chevrignon
Sauvignon Blanc
Napa Valley

Neptune Pasta Mista
Belgian Endive over Bibb
Lettuce, Avocado Dressing
Sorbet

Caymus Liberty School
Cabernet Sauvignon
Alexander Valley

Roast Tenderloin Wellington,
Sauce Bordelaise
Buttered Asparagus, Fresh Dill

No-host Champagne
selections available

Banana Foster
Irish Coffee
Demitasse

over, please

Honorary Chairmen
Jack and Vi Oakley

Master of Ceremonies
Lynn McCoskey

Our 1986 Champions

Golf

Men's Champion	Jack Luceti
DWGG Champion	Gloria Hughes
Holyniner Champion	Betty Wells
Junior Champion	Kevin Plazak

Mr. & Mrs. Club Champions
"Dub" & Mary Kaye Johnson

Tennis

Men's Singles	John Osmer
Women's Singles	Laurie Howard
Men's Doubles	Dana Squire & David Kipp
Women's Doubles	Barbara Bradley & Judy Morton

Helfrich Award
Presented by President Lynn McCosk

The massive renovation project in the mid-1980s that resulted in the beautiful facility members enjoy today. COURTESY STEVE DOWLER.

Diablo Anniversary Party 1986 — last affair in the old clubhouse.

The temporary "clubhouse" in the upper parking lot served as golf Pro Shop, office and dining room while the clubhouse underwent construction.

1992 INTERVIEW WITH LYNN MCCOSKEY

Lynn McCoskey spent five years on the Board of Directors, 1982-86, three as President. "Many asked me why I was President for three years. I did it because I was there when we began to consider 'our aging clubhouse.' Once the issues heated up, there was no way to escape. Suddenly I had invested a lot of time and energy; then the seat became so hot, no one would touch it. By the time everything calmed down, I was into my third term and the second of a three-year term on the Board. I resigned in 1986 when the dust settled.

"By 1983, it was obvious members wanted something done about the clubhouse. The key word was SOMETHING but there was little agreement on what that something should be. It's normal for members to see their President as the responsible person. He gets the credit as well as the blame. I believed it was the President's job to represent the opinions of the members. That's what I thought I did. Some say I reflected my own opinions, not those of the members. What we might have done better than we did was communicate more often and in a better way. But that's 20/20 hindsight."

Lynn still thinks a new clubhouse would have satisfied most members and cost about half as much as was spent on the restoration. "Like the Chalet restoration, costs escalate," he said. "Until you take the boards off the wall you don't know what's behind them. Restoration always costs more than building new and you can seldom get a firm bid. As it turned out, Diablo has a beautiful clubhouse that the members like, despite the outlandish expense."

From the outset, Lynn wanted a new facility. But Diablo member-residents were more interested in restoration that would enhance their community as did the Chalet reconstruction.

CHALET RESTORATION The Chalet is a Diablo institution. Built in the midst of WWI—a 1917 gem—it has housed Club members and their guests, WWII construction workers, telephone girls, and Navy officers, Club employees as year-round residents, weekend party-goers, the Post Office and Golf Pro Shop. Today it houses eight three-story condominiums. It also generates income for the Club.

Founder RN Burgess envisioned castles on Mt. Diablo—one for himself, one for his partner William Randolf Hearst—and appropriately named his country club the Mt. Diablo Club. When it was time to erect a resort hotel, it had to be a Swiss chalet.

November 20, 1985

To The Members of Diablo Country Club:

In my letter to you of October 25, 1985, you were advised of the formation of a committee to meet with members opposed to the results of the May ballot and the actions of the Board to implement the construction of a new clubhouse on or near the existing site. The purpose of this meeting would be to find some common ground for moving forward.

I am pleased to inform you that the Board committee consisting of Marty Fowler, Dave Lamson and Bob Jones met with representatives for a Fair Ballot consisting of their Chairman, Cliff Gant and their three candidates for the Board — Matt Chandler, Bill Potts, and Harry Timmermans on November 7, 1985. Their discussions were friendly, open, frank and appreciative of the views and goals of each group. Members of each group also felt that progress was made towards finding some common ground for the formulation of a new ballot to replace the May ballot.

As a result of this meeting, the Board has established the Clubhouse Remodeling Committee as a Board committee with funding sufficient to hire outside firms to develop remodeling plans complete with drawings and cost estimates. The committee will consist of Chairman Harry Timmermans, Don Barrie, Carl Olson, Cliff Gant, Lee Hunt, Dan Neufeld, Abe Pianalto and Bill Potts. V.O. Smith will act as liaison with the Clubhouse Construction Committee.

A second meeting was held on November 16 and the attendees, consisting of Cliff Gant, Harry Timmermans, Abe Pianalto, Ken Fraser, E.G. Craig, Dave Lamson, Marty Fowler and Bob Jones, mutually agreed upon the following:

1. That whatever direction the clubhouse takes, considerations will include a long range view, construction be of quality and overall costs be within reasonable time limits.

2. That the presentation to the membership include a third option: a clubhouse at the 10th tee knoll site. Inasmuch as this proposal is an independent one, this option will be funded by E.G. Craig.

3. That all presentations be ready April 1, 1986.

After the presentation by the three committees, representatives of each group will be available at the clubhouse each evening for one or two weeks to answer specific questions that individual members deem necessary. You will have an opportunity to view site plans, plot plans, elevations, renderings, description of quality and type of materials, cost estimates, dues and assessments necessary to execute each alternative. Additionally, estimates of rates and terms of any loan will be disclosed. The Board will closely monitor the progress made by each of the committees and will keep you regularly advised of the information as gathered.

It is the desire of the Board of Directors that all members have sufficient time to seek out information in order that they may make an informed decision relative to the clubhouse. At the conclusion of the informational period a ballot on which all groups have had input, and which will replace the May 1985 ballot will be sent to the membership to determine the final directions of Diablo Country Club.

It is our hope that once the final decision is made, all members will rally behind that choice and work together in a spirit of co-operation to expedite Diablo's new direction.

Sincerely,

Lynn E. McCoskey

Lynn E. McCoskey,
President

Red Horse Apartments.

Beth Hearn and Dorothy Petersen, who have, respectively, summered and lived in Diablo longer than any other Diablons.

Designed by Arthur Benton, a distinguished Los Angeles architect, it contained 14 one-, two- and three-bedroom suites, each with a dressing room, bath and separate entrance. At the dedication on July 22, 1917, the suites were sold at auction from $2,830 to $5,224. Bill Thomas (William P. Thomas, M.D. of Los Altos), who with his sister Beth (Mrs. Norman J. Hearn) began staying at the Chalet in the summer of 1925, remembers it clearly, "There was a balcony running along the back connecting it to an open passageway over the creek to the second floor of the clubhouse (now a private residence at 1925 Alameda Diablo). We'd go there for our meals because there were no kitchens in the Chalet. Besides, mom didn't want to cook. She was on vacation too. When our parents, Fred and Alice Thomas, built our summer home in 1929 (at 2043 Los Callados) we stayed there, but I still had friends in the Chalet. It was such a handy spot and a center of activity."

Simultaneously in 1917, Burgess built the Red Horse Tavern (now The Red Horse Apartments on Avenida Nueva) also to house Club guests as well as travelers and the many visitors coming to see his exciting new vacation spa.

Beginning with the Great Depression of the '30s, the Chalet became an ever-increasing problem. Except for awhile during WWII when it served as temporary housing for construction crews and later the telephone girls from Camps Parks and Shoemaker followed by Navy officers and their families, parts were used only occasionally. At times members and their guests would stay for short periods of time. Carol Jones recalls a friend's experience, "...We stayed in the Chalet for several days while moving to Diablo. I remember it was nicely furnished, but smelled a bit musty from lack of use."

Later several members who rented a suite added a kitchen and made the Chalet their home. Among those were Maude Pratt, the driving force behind the Lou Armstrong Memorial, the Bailey Justices and Benji Hendricks. For a brief time in 1948, the Chalet housed the Post Office while the old milk barn was being readied for it. For a long time the lower corner near the present clubhouse was the Golf Pro Shop. This site was abandoned in 1965, when the new shop near the first tee was completed. Today, that building is the home of the Post Office.

During all these years, the Club considered alternatives. John Price, a member since 1955, recalled, "We often talked about making the Chalet into apartments but all we could do was dream about it because the Club was barely able to pay its monthly bills. It was real tough just getting and keeping members."

Paul Cortese moved to Diablo in 1967 and joined the Club. By 1976, with children going to college, he began looking for smaller quarters. Adequate smaller homes, however, were not then available in Diablo and he considered moving into the Chalet. Instead he decided to buy and demolish it and build condominiums. To that end he began to negotiate with the Club.

Fred Bennett and later Jack Hughes, the 1977 President, and the Board of Directors preferred; 1) The land be leased, not sold, and 2) For historical reasons the exterior remain as is. What resulted was a land lease for 50 years with three, ten-year options. Paul resigned from the Club Board of Directors to avoid even the appearance of conflict of interest.

He hired architects and engineers to reconstruct "from the ground up" eight condominiums of 2,400-4,000 square-feet each. In general, the plans specified a ground floor for storage, a game room or bedroom, and a bath; a first floor with an entry foyer, living and dining rooms, den, kitchen and breakfast areas; and a second floor of two bedrooms and two baths.

The Club held a sale when the Chalet was gutted. Dave and Tim Rei remembered carrying a sink and kitchen cabinet purchased by their parents, Bill and Ginny, to the family's guest house where they are still in use. The Reis also bought a dinner plate bearing the insignia of the Red Horse Tavern.

"From the ground up" meant redoing the foundation. Paul hired Vern Ryan, a well-known Danville builder. Vern was familiar with Diablo, having built homes for the Ives, Neufelds, Olivers, Shanks and Stones. He was not prepared, however, for the challenge of the crumbling foundation. He commented, "Every time we dug with a shovel or pounded with a hammer, something unknown and unexpected happened." When the foundation was finished, so was he.

Paul hired the M.G.C. Construction Company of San Leandro and the rebuilding took off. "'Took off' is right," said Paul. "That's exactly what the costs did too, despite a contract with a firm price." When the job was completed, two years later, the costs were 50% over bid. There were $500,000 of unexpected, unforeseen and disputed overruns that were settled later through arbitration for about half the amount. "What headaches, hearings, legal fees. What a disappointment," said Paul, "We had eight lovely condos worth around $400,000 each, instead of our projected $300,000 and it took from 1978 to 1982 to get it done."

SALE TO MEMBERS Another part of the Cortese/Club agreement was that members had first refusal rights and that the buyers be limited partners. Club members were notified of the sale. The

Paul Cortese, board member in the '80s, was the prime mover in the restoration of the Chalet.

The insignia from the dinner and steak plates of the Red Horse Tavern.

COURTESY OF BILL AND GINNY REI

President Jim Hague.

July 1977 *Inferno* stated that the drawing established the following priority list: Cortese, Mainhardt, Smiley, Jackson, Busch, Magrath and McFarland. An agreement was negotiated among the limited partners to take care of maintenance, repairs and gardening. Paul commented, "Wisely, we chose Nancy Magrath as the chair, thus assuring that all our future problems would be readily taken care of."

Jim Hague, 1978 President, who was deeply involved in the Chalet's rebirth along with Phil Hammond and Frank Schmitt, said, "It was an ordeal for all of us but well worth the effort—getting us out of a 1970s fire trap and into a modern gem that preserved its architectural integrity. Paul Cortese had the vision and the know-how to get the job done. He stands tall for business acumen and social conscience."

The Club gets $33,295 per year income from the land lease, a reliable and stable profit center. All members benefit and all of Diablo benefits by having a rebuilt Chalet beautifying the community.

THE FULL CIRCLE

Cecil Ryder said he was glad the new clubhouse had a dumbwaiter for the men's locker room. He commented, "It was a long time coming. Early in the '60s, I figured out where a dumbwaiter could be put and told Larry Curtola about it even though he didn't own the Club anymore. He said, 'Makes sense,' and went with me to see how it could be done. He got a bid for $2,000 to have the dumbwaiter installed but the Club's directors turned it down." Because of that decision the dumbwaiter had to wait 30 years but was finally installed during the restoration.

Cecil and Helen still occupy their home on Diablo Road. He is now 88 and not only maintains his house but is also an avid gardener. All who pass the house across the road from Diablo Nursery enjoy his spring garden bordered by giant sunflowers.

Cecil Ryder in his Diablo Road garden.

ADDENDUM TO THE RESTORATION DECISION
FROM CLUB RECORDS

"A" July 8, 1987 *To*: The Membership
From: Mike Stead

"Enclosed are the results of the Ballot for the Assessment of June 19th. The proposition did *not* receive the necessary 218 votes to approve the assessment. (As a consequence) At the special meeting on July 6, 1987, your Board . . . voted to:

1. Discontinue all further action with regard to the clubhouse renovation.
2. Advise the General Contractor his firm offer cannot be accepted.
3. Initiate steps to terminate contracts currently in effect. President Neils Lawson has resigned. This is a tremendous loss to the Club."

"B" July 9, 1987 *To*: The Board of Directors
From: Lloyd Ives, Member #88

"Pursuant to . . . Article VIII, Sec. 2, of the By-Laws . . . the undersigned members hereby request the Board of Directors to call a Special Meeting of the membership (to):

1. Review the results of the Ballot for Assessment June 19, 1987.
2. Review the Board's decision to discontinue all further action with regard to the club house renovation.
3. . . . present a new ballot to the membership as expediently as possible."

(Signed by 10% of the members.)

"C" July 21, 1987 *To*: The Membership
From: Lloyd Ives, Member #88

The undersigned are writing you in support of the $900 assessment mailed . . . July 23, 1987, for your approval. "While we may not agree with some of the cost incurred, we do *not* feel that the membership has a reasonable alternative . . . If the remodeling project is not pursued, the $725,000 already committed will be lost . . . We do not consider this to be a fiscally responsible alternative."
(Signed by 41 members.)

"D" July 23, 1987 *To*: The Membership
From: Michael T. Ogles, Secretary, Board of Directors

"...notice is hereby given . . . to assess each regular member as follows:-A Capital Assessment for the clubhouse renovation in the amount of $900...Attached is the official ballot . . . In order to become effective, a majority of members . . . must be obtained . . .. Disapproval will end the clubhouse renovation..."
(Assessment was approved by a majority of the membership.)

DURABLE DIABLON: LARRY IVES

Name a Club committee—Entertainment, House, Long-Range Planning, Membership, Security—and Larry Ives, "Mr. Diablo"—has served on it. He also served on the Board of Directors, 1983-86, was Vice President, 1983-86, and for nine years represented Diablo in the North and East Bay Association of Country Clubs.

A member since 1965, Larry has been an avid petitioner for causes at the Club and in the community. In Diablo he has been President of both the DPOA and the DCSD. He was on the original San Ramon Valley planning committee, a precursor of the San Ramon Valley Area Planning Commission which advised the Board of Supervisors. He was a member of the group that recommended those appointed to the first SRVAPC. He was also on the committee that developed the County General Plan.

When his term expired on the Club Board in 1985, he petitioned for the restoration of the clubhouse. In the days before the golf course was fenced, Larry organized a marshaling group to keep unauthorized golfers from playing. He remembered, "Al McCarron, Larry Curtola, and Neil (Tommy) Thompson and I took turns patrolling the course everyday in our golf carts."

The first challenge Neils Lawson faced upon assuming the Presidency in 1987 was a proposal to assess members $900 to keep the clubhouse restoration on schedule. Neils was shocked when the assessment was defeated. He took this as a vote of no-confidence and summarily resigned. Larry immediately drew up a petition asking for a special meeting of the Board to vote again on the asssessment. Then he sent a letter outlining why members should approve it and this time the vote was positive. The rebuilding continued as planned (see page 188), even though in Neils Lawson the Club had lost a valued member and respected leader.

During WWII, Larry was a pilot for the Air Transport Command and later a TWA captain. He was once assigned to fly a DC3 on a whistle-stop trip for Vice President Richard Nixon during the 1960 Nixon-Kennedy campaign. Larry was to fly the Vice President to a series of destinations from Kansas City including Richards, Missouri. The Richards "airport" consisted of a grass strip and had no lights or radio communication. Larry explained to Nixon a night landing there was unsafe and suggested they fly to Des Moines, Iowa. Nixon first offered an unacceptable alternative then angrily called TWA headquarters in an effort to reverse Larry's decision. After more discussion Larry informed Nixon, "We

INCOMING PRESIDENT of the Diablo Homeowners, Lloyd Ives (R) accepts the amended by-laws from outgoing prexy Robert Tiernan at the group's first meeting of the year. The new slate of officers includes Hal Sconyers, vice president; Joe Kris,treasurer and Phylis Alexanderson, secretary. The board of directors consists of Bill Cronin, Elizabeth McSherry, John Roberts, Beverly Unger and Al Rubey.

Bob Tiernan passing the presidential mantle to Larry. (DPOA, 1968)

Neil (Tommy) Thompson. COURTESY LARRY IVES.

Lyle Wehrman, Golf Pro at the time, presents Larry with a trophy for one of Larry's three holes-in-one, below.

Larry's last flight, in the left seat of a TWA 707 enroute to Lisbon, Athens and New York. Connie temporarily occupied the co-pilot seat. March, 17, 1976. COURTESY LARRY IVES.

Connie, Chris, and Larry. May, 1976 when Chris was commissioned a Naval Officer. He later was a Blue Angel who performed during Fleet Week October, 1985. Chris was sworn into the Navy as an Ensign by Diablon Admiral Robert E. Tiernan.

will not land in Richards. I do not want to mislead you." Larry and Nixon took their leave in Des Moines on less than friendly terms. Nixon later lambasted Larry and TWA in radio and TV broadcasts.

Larry appeared on "60 Minutes" with Mike Wallace in 1973. He met Mike in Tel Aviv when the 707 Larry was flying was delayed. Mike's 747 flight also was on hold and Larry offered him a seat on his plane bound for Paris which Mike accepted.

Their conversation turned to jet lag, which Mike noted, "... impacts on my life and work." They continued exchanging experiences and Larry offered solutions. Mike said, "This might make a story" and later got CBS to arrange with TWA for Mike to shadow Larry on one of his round-the-world flights. Later Mike and the 5-member CBS crew came to Diablo to interview and photograph Larry on the golf course.

Cheri Ives with the gourmet dinner she prepared for her parents' 40th wedding anniversary.

In 1961, after defeat in his run for mayor of Ann Arbor, Michigan by only a few votes, Larry, Connie, and their children, Cheri and Chris, decided to move to the Bay Area. Larry first heard of Diablo from a fellow pilot who was building a house on Caballo Ranchero Drive. He visited the area on a cold, rainy February day and was not favorably impressed. Some months later, however, while checking out Round Hill, he took another look at Diablo and decided this was the place for the Ives family.

As President of the Diablo Property Owners Association in 1968, he became involved in the move to form the Diablo Community Service District to take care of security and road maintenance. He appeared before LAFCO (Local Agency Formation Commission), whose approval was necessary. But the Commission recommended against it. Larry responded by obtaining residents' signatures on a petition in favor of the new district. He presented it to the Board of Supervisors as convincing evidence of property owners' wishes. The Board agreed and the district was voted in at the November 1968 election, again over the objection of LAFCO.

Larry was named General Manager of the District and later served on the Board and as President. He was active in the debate over gating the community, a controversial issue for club members, particularly those not living in Diablo, as well as for the community.

His latest contribution has been as co-editor of the *Inferno* with Audrey Barrie and Ann Timmermans and more recently with Roseanne Ogles and Jan McGlynn. The pictures during those years are the result of Larry Ives' photographic skills.

Of his many honors, he said, "You'd think my most memorable moment would be when Marsh Freeman, DPOA President in 1971, came to me asking who I thought should receive the first Outstanding Citizen Award. I said Bob Tiernan. So naturally I was amazed when they chose me. As proud as that made me feel, my fondest memory is when the DCSD presented me with a plaque on my retirement from the Board, December 9, 1985."

That says it all for Mr. Diablo.

DURABLE DIABLONS: JOHN AND SHIRLEY OSMER

The opinion is unanimous—the Osmers are Mr. and Mrs. Diablo Tennis. Since moving to Diablo in 1968, they have been the Club's most persistent players, most consistent winners and one of the Community's most friendly, helpful couples.

Asked to tell her most memorable experience Shirley said, "It was the family tournaments: mother/son, father/daughter, husband/wife, and best of all the junior/senior mystery mixed doubles." This is when partners are drawn out of a hat. "Players—the young and the old—devote the entire weekend to play, because no one knows how far he'll go or how long she'll last. Watching play was a big attraction too—a weekend of family fun."

John's first thoughts were the husband/wife tournaments. He remembered one in 1974 with Don and Marjorie Kinkel. The Osmers won a very close match. When Shirley didn't respond as enthusiastically to this remembrance, John said, "Well, mixed doubles was fun up to a point. Undoubtedly it put a strain on some marriages."

John's second remembrance was the Tennis Balls—those rollicking Friday night dances which included low-skill sporting events during the dances.

He fondly recalled the first time he played in the A's for the Club Championship. This was in 1972 and his opponents were players of the stature of Marshall Freeman, Don Kinkel, Bob Tiernan, Semmes Gordon, Lee Schneider and Jim Mandley. His first father/daughter final was when Susan was 12 (1973) and they played against Jack and Jill Toney.

"One tournament we can't do anymore," said John, "is the Calcutta." Friday evenings were spent in the Club's main dining room with everyone betting on a team, then groups would combine their money on particular teams and turn out on Saturday and Sunday to see the results.

Another type of play the Osmers liked that isn't done now is exchange tennis. During the sum-

Whereas, as President of the Diablo Property Owners Association in 1968 Larry Ives worked zealously to obtain the approval of the County Board of Supervisors for the formation of the Diablo Community Service District and a subsequent election to authorize it,

and

Whereas, he served as the unpaid General Manager of the District during its formative years,

and

Whereas, he was appointed as Director of the Diablo Community Service District in 1976 and reelected in 1977 and again in 1981,

and

Whereas, during those nine years, he provided outstanding service to the community of Diablo as District Road Commissioner, Treasurer, Vice President, and President,

and

Whereas, during those years, his leadership won for him the affectionate appellation, "Mr. Diablo,"

Therefore be it resolved that the Board of Directors salute Larry Ives in recognition of his outstanding service to the Diablo community by the adoption of this resolution.

Shirley and John as tennis spectators.

Shirley and John, happy competitors.

mer, teams from Diablo played at Round Hill one evening, for example, and vice versa the next week. "We just don't do that any more," said Shirley.

LEARNING THE GAME Shirley talked about their learning how to play tennis and how helpful Jean and Sam Ditto were. "They were on the courts every Sunday—to play with any and all comers. It was a boost for us beginners because neither John nor I had played until we joined in 1968."

She remembered their first Thursday evening tennis in 1969. "It was Hal Sconyers' 40th birthday and the dinner was at their house. I'd just started playing and John was dividing his time between learning golf and tennis. He had so much fun that night—the players were so companionable—he gave up golf to concentrate on tennis.

John was elected to a three-year term on the Club Board in 1974. "It was a bit discouraging," he remembered, "because some Directors resented the great interest and popularity of tennis. They had no concept of members spending money at the Club and yet not crowding the fairways. However, the three Presidents (Hank Steinback, Frank Schmitt, and George Padis) were understanding and supportive."

During those years, flood lights and courts six and seven were added. In those days, playing time was in such demand that a reservation system was established using three pegs on the metal fence for tennis racquets. Each was numbered and when players arrived with the courts full, they hung their racquets on the empty peg and waited their turn.

Shirley said, "Maybe John and I have been the most involved tennis couple over the years, but Mel Toney surely was the strongest influence." There were six Toney children—Jack II, Marcia, Melissa, Mark, Jon, and Jill. They all were good players and Mel and Jack were always there (meaning in and around the courts) to see that their children received their fair share of instruction and quality playing time.

A big plus today is the new tennis facility. It's a far cry from the old pro shop where an outhouse type bathroom was up the hill behind the swimming pool. Nancy Rubey wallpapered it every year so at least the interior was presentable!

The Osmers' investment in tennis has paid off handsomely. It has become their consuming interest and chief leisure activity. They are recognized as the Club's premier players. They have taken their talents around the world—Sweden, Italy, Yugoslavia, Australia, Bora-Bora—clearly Diablo's *Mr. and Mrs. Tennis!* And they have given unstintingly of their time and interest to make Diablo a better community and an ideal place to live.

It was a beautiful spring afternoon in the late '20s. We strolled along Alameda Diablo and passed William H. Oliver's Italian villa (1699) and the Jensens' English cottage across the street (1700). As we admired the huge oaks that were in full leaf, we thought how good the new paint job looked on the Bulls' Dutch colonial (1717). Further up on the other side of the street we passed the Hales (1830), then gazed admiringly at the twins—the look-alike homes of Jenkin John and Henry Melvin (1842 and 1850).

We arrived at our destination, the Hunts' arts and crafts style beauty at 1833. We're stopping there to look in on a meeting of Diablo's "power brokers"—the Hales, Hunts, Olivers and Herb Hall whose summer cottage was a long walk away—1778 West Salida (Club House Road).

That was a leisurely stroll in '29, but now it's '94. The owners have changed. But the homes are still there, as these pages prove, a selection of 20 from among the 40+ built in the 1920s.(1)

Chapter X: TWENTY FROM THE TWENTIES

THE MEHRANS
1699 ALAMEDA DIABLO

In 1916, William H. Oliver built this beautiful example of Italian Moorish architecture and occupied it as a vacation home until 1941. Then it was purchased by Emil and Esther Hagstrom. Emil owned a chain of East Bay grocery stores and was an avid horseman.

The Mehrans purchased it in 1965, raising their two sons, Casey and Alex there. Masud and Maryam added a pool and cabana and restored the house with Persian touches. There are two columns supporting a frieze near the barn that once graced the reviewing stand of the old race track.

Jane Friden, who lived across the street (1720) wrote, "The Hagstroms were a wonderful couple and so was their daughter, Tootie, whom we loved. Stanley and I spent many happy hours in Emil's study and their elegant, old-world dining room. When Emil died, brokenhearted Esther sold the property."

Emil, who purchased an additional six acres from the Club in 1941 for pasture and open space, kept trotting horses and carriages. He was very generous about giving rides to children to and from the Club, especially on special occasions such as holiday weekends.

Ashley Stone and her younger sister, Ann, recall how Emil Hagstrom used to hitch his white horse to a buggy and ride through Diablo each Sunday afternoon. They also fondly remember Christmas caroling on horseback through Diablo. The carolers always saved the Hagstroms' as the last stop of the evening because he came out to pat their horses while his butler Otto passed platefuls of goodies.

THE MARKSTEINS
1734 ALAMEDA DIABLO

This arts and crafts design country cottage on a two-acre plot was built in 1923 by the Stuart Hawleys of the Carter-Hawleys-Hales stores chain. They were succeeded by Chester and Mary Eschen who lived there for 25 years, followed by Ron and Jenifer Beardslee for five years. Ron was responsible for the hand-laid circular brick driveway that is a prominent feature of the front yard. The Johnsons who owned it next did an extensive remodeling before selling to Bob and Brenda Markstein in 1987. The Marksteins did more extensive remodeling, adding a two-story guest house with clear grain fir ceiling and walls to match the original walls of the living room. A new family room is of the same wood. The interior walls of the living and family rooms are hand painted.

In the '20s, this home was the ladies' 19th hole. The original living room floor was pock-marked by golf cleats as evidence that "this cottage was a place to come to and relax, have a drink and a card game, before going to the Lake," said Brenda.

The residence has four fireplaces. The one in the living room was built with stones brought from Yosemite by the Hawleys. In addition to a number of beautiful old oaks, the exterior features a vegetable garden, green house, and orchard accessed by a trellised bridge over Green Valley Creek.

Brenda said, "We love this property and realize how fortunate we are to bring-up our children and grandchildren here."

THE CRONINS
1700 ALAMEDA DIABLO

This English cottage was built in 1921 and owned by the Jensens, who were related to the Olivers. Letts Oliver originally had purchased the three-acre lot from RN Burgess before WWI. Bill and Janet Cronin bought "Friendly Oaks" in 1957. The house has had only two owners in its 73-year history. The living room is designed to resemble a ship's cabin. Several porches have been enclosed for year-round use. One had been Jensen's experimental lab where he invented the Jensen speaker used in radios. There are five bedrooms, a den, dining room and large 1920s kitchen. In the interior is a hidden room, originally built to store liquor during Prohibition. There is also a detached three-bedroom guest cottage.

"Friendly Oaks" originally had five large oaks purported to be 300-years old. One crashed into the pool, one on the guest house, one in front of the house, and another one barely missed the house next door. "Friendly Oaks," said Janet, "did not have friendly oaks."

The Cronins added a master bedroom in 1957. Other than that the house remains true to the period in which it was built. Janet concluded, "We have purposely left it old fashioned. Our children and grandchildren love it just the way it is."

THE PELANDINIS
1830 ALAMEDA DIABLO

The William Hale family who lived here on this two-acre site from the '20s to the '60s, made their mark on Club and Community. They are referred to numerous times in this volume. Known as Thimble Farm, the Hale property was bought by Tom and Sandi Pelandini in 1978. They followed in the Hale tradition as community leaders.

The house, built of redwood, and designed by Bernard Maybeck is in the art and crafts style. Originally it was a summer cottage with two sleeping porches and another that was used as a dining area. The Hales added a dining room in 1951 when the home was featured in the December issue of *Sunset Magazine*. In keeping with its name, Thimble Farm, the Hales kept horses and were ardent and enthusiastic riders.

In 1993 the Pelandinis renovated the kitchen and dining room and moved the original two-story barn down from the pasture next to the house and converted it to a carriage house.

In the late '30s when Bill Hale, Jr. was a Cal student, the old homestead was the center of many frat parties that as often as not ended up at Diablo Lake.

THE MILKS
1833 ALAMEDA DIABLO

This unusual home was built in 1921 for Hubert and Elizabeth Hunt of Piedmont on what was originally three lots. On the west half-acre was a brown-shingled guest house for the Hunt children, now a separate residence. The Hunts named their summer villa Miraflores because of Elizabeth's love of flowers. The architecture is an example of the arts and crafts style so popular then, and was the work of architect Bernard Maybeck. In 1931, it was purchased by Herb (Gray) Hills of Hills Brothers Coffee who was prominent in the affairs of the Club for two decades. Frank and Margaret Helfrich purchased it in 1954 and lived there for 32 years. Their three children, Frances, "Gus", and Erick (see page 101) were prominent in Club and Community during the '60s and '70s. In 1986 George and Shirley Hare purchased it and began an extensive restoration and remodeling program.

They moved out of the house for a year while the work was done under the direction of architect George Swallow who restored the clubhouse (see page 138). A second story bedroom suite was added, and a new kitchen, pantry, and laundry. The former kitchen became the family room, the former family room, a dining room. The unusual brocaded board and batten paneling, plate rails, and cathedral ceilings in the dining room and entrance hall were designed to match the original treatment in the living room and library.

To everyone's regret, the Hares decided to find a smaller home in 1992. The present owners, Sam and Mary Milks, and their children Ben and Katie, are a welcome addition to Diablo.

THE HEARNS
2043 CALLE LOS CALLADOS

This French Provincial home dates from 1929 when it was built by Beth Hearn's parents, Fred and Alice Thomas. It's the only Diablo home owned by the same family since it was built and the only one continuously used as a summer home. Designed to be cool (no air conditioning then), hollow tile masonry was used, cross ventilation provided in every room, and a central breezeway between the kitchen, dining room, living room area and the bedroom wing. A guest house was added in 1937, a swimming pool and cabana in 1973.

Beth and her brother Bill Thomas are featured repeatedly throughout this book.

THE BIRKA-WHITES
2166 ALAMEDA DIABLO

This 70-year old classic Dutch colonial is called Gablewood because of the numerous gables, including one pillared over the front door. The house was built in 1924 for the Dolges. In 1987, David and Elizabeth Birka-White purchased it and quickly became active in community affairs, a tradition inherited from the 24 years of residency by the previous owners, Semmes and Peggy Gordon. The Gordons owned and edited the Valley's weekly newspaper, *The Valley Pioneer*, and acquired their activist tradition from Munce and Suzy Baldwin who enjoyed a busy two-year stay, 1960-62.

Located on an acre and a half of redwoods, oaks, and gardens, Gablewood also has seen lots of remodeling. The latest was done by Dave and Liz when they enlarged the family room and entry, converted the garage to a billiard room, and added a separate garage. If walls could talk, this place would have a lot to say—all of its owners have been popular party givers.

Herbert Hoover's well-known visit to this beautiful house in 1928 is told elsewhere in this book. (see page 26)

THE FIELDS
1817 CALLE ARROYO

Bob and Marcia Field, with Camie, 14 and Blake, 9, have lived in this, the original Burgess home, since 1992. The traditional English country design is the creation of the famed architect George A. Applegarth who also designed the Palace of Legion of Honor in San Francisco. The well-known Thomas Church was the landscape architect.

The Fields have done extensive remodeling and restoration. The interior is a veritable treasure to behold and the exterior has been restored to its original charm. Marcia said, "After we purchased the home, I opened a closet and there was another bathroom." During the restoration, behind a wall, they discovered a 1906 gun, rusted and unworkable. Unusual for Diablo homes, it has a partial basement in which there is a 1915 coal burning furnace. Bob said, "Some day, I'll make this area into a wine cellar."

A legend about "Fairway Oaks" is that Shirley Temple Black stayed overnight after attending a Club party. In another version of the legend, Shirley spent her honeymoon here.

THE REIS
1740 CLUB HOUSE ROAD

This interesting two-story home was built in 1925 on a two-and-a-half acre plot for Charles and Mary Mills Elliot of Piedmont. Mary also originally owned the property where the La Cava, Marcotte and Miller houses now stand on Club House Road. Of Mediterranean design with red tile roof and a six-arched loggia beneath the front porch, it has 11 rooms, 4 ½ baths, a basement with a steam heat furnace and a detached cottage. Originally the cottage was servants' quarters but now is a guest house. The Elliots had no children but Charles often invited neighborhood children to view the heavens through his telescope that was mounted on the concrete roof of the servants' house. Bill and Ginny Rei purchased the property in 1959 and moved in with their four children. After a fifth and sixth child arrived they added 1,200 square feet.

Charles Elliot was known for racing his sporty Cord from Elliott's (no relation) Bar in Danville to the Dublin Corral. Mary entertained often at the Club and insisted on a round table because of her belief in occultism.

THE LA CAVAS
1752 CLUB HOUSE ROAD

This Spanish Mediterranean villa dates from 1924 when it was built as a summer retreat. In 1939 the Samuel Abbotts purchased it. Their neighbors to the west were the Halls (see page 28). In 1945 a well-known sportsman, Eric de Reynier was the owner. "Casa del Sol" was purchased by Edward and Consuelo La Cava in 1957. They doubled the size of the house to take care of their growing family of four children. The remodeling was designed by Jack Lee and Paul Ryan who were the architects of St. Mary's Cathedral in San Francisco. "House in the sun" features Mexican tiles throughout, arched windows, white-washed brick walls, and an indoor atrium. A horse barn on the premises overlooks the 2nd fairway. It was the center of interest for the La Cava daughters, Stefania and Nicole, while the pool with its cabana/guest house kept sons Vince and Ward occupied.

Connie said, "Many colorful stories have been told about the early days of our home. One we have verified is that a Navy Admiral lived here during WWII. All the other tales we haven't been able to verify, such as a suicide, illicit romances, and other goings on."

THE ALIOTOS

1778 CLUB HOUSE ROAD

Herb and Susan Hall made the two-hour trip from Piedmont in their LaSalle touring car in the spring of 1925 in search of a summer and weekend retreat. They fell in love with four acres on the second fairway of Diablo. It had only a one room cottage on it at the time, and while the Halls added on and built two other guest houses, eight-year old Myra Mae enjoyed the balmy Diablo nights from her "tent room" in the garden.

The Halls sold the property to Leigh and Ginny Freeman in 1968. Ginny was ecstatic about living in the charming, secluded cottages. Sadly, in April Ginny died after a sudden illness. Leigh moved in with his three children and was joined by his second wife, Susan, in Nov. 1969. In Jan. of 1976, Leigh and Susan bought the Sconyers' house also near the tennis courts. The cottages stood vacant until they were sold to a European buyer in absentia. Unbeknownst to the Freemans, the buyer was a developer who had planned to tear down the structures and build four homes on the estate.

A month later, Joseph M. and Michele Alioto saw the property. They fell in love with its charm and character, and purchased the property from the developer. In keeping with the original motif, they imported palms, succulents and other plants that are indigenous to both Diablo and Mexico. They also imported tiles, artifacts and other original art work from Mexico, and have created a beautiful summer retreat from their home in San Francisco. The Alioto children, Michela, Angelina, Joseph Jr. and Alexander, have 33 first cousins. Their home has become a site for festive family barbecues for the Alioto-Driscoll family.

THE MILLERS
1812 CLUB HOUSE ROAD

The Kahls built this French country summer cottage overlooking the 3rd tee shortly before WWI. It has been a house that grew like Topsy, with each owner adding and remodeling. The Hendricks—Joe was Club President in 1953—and Benjie Giradelli Hendricks owned it as a summer house for 47 years. Bob and Jinny Cuenin lived there from 1970-81, followed by short stays by the O'Briens, (80-83) and Tinneys, (83-91). Then Jeff and Karen Miller purchased it. Jeff is the oldest of Bob and Patty Miller's five children. (1857 El Nido)

Jeff and Karen added a study, master suite, two bathrooms, breakfast nook/ kitchen annex and laundry room while expanding the family room, dining room, two bedrooms, and garage. This extensive remodeling was all done to match the original style because, "We didn't want our new home to look new," said Karen.

When the Cuenins lived there, Bob and his tennis buddies usually played on courts six and seven because it was cooler on warm mornings. When the matches were over, they headed for a cold beer at 1812 Club House Road and the Cuenins' refrigerator out by the pool, "because it was closer than going all the way up to the Club," said Bob. He adds quickly, "And also because it was cheaper—for them."

THE KNOEDLERS
1717 ALAMEDA DIABLO

The Knoedler family, Peter, Mary and their three children, Pete, Amy, and Stephen, have lived in this home since 1970. They purchased it from the Stotts who bought it in 1940 from the original owner and builder Edwin Bull. The building date is 1915 making it one of Diablo's first summer villas. In its 79 years, there have been only three owners.

The house is a traditional Dutch colonial with white shingles and green shutters. There also is a matching guest cottage. Edwin Bull was RN Burgess' manager of the Villa Properties Inc., so he was on the ground floor in site selection and picked a lot that overlooked the 17th fairway.

The Knoedlers remodeled in 1984, enlarging the kitchen and installing a master bedroom overlooking the golf course. They also had keys made—the Stotts had never locked their house in the 30 years they lived there. On the second floor at the back adjacent to a sleeping porch, there was a huge 'gang' shower with sheet metal walls. Mary said, "We were told our house was used as an R and R spot—a club for officers in WWII."

Twelve years ago an elderly gentleman stopped by and introduced himself to Mary and Pete. It was William Oliver who had come by to see the house his father, William Letts Oliver, had built next door (Mehrans). "What a treat to meet him," said Mary. He told her his father also built the house across the street (Cronin residence). He said he remembered the redwood tree in the Knoedler's back yard as being as tall as he was then. He couldn't believe the size it had become.

THE PEDERSENS
1671 EL NIDO

Chris and Kim Pedersen purchased this home in 1990. The original structure, which now encompasses the lower wing of the house, was built by Carrie and Dan Cook in 1879 as the dairy for the Oakwood Stock Farm. Reminders of this early period as a milk barn are the insulating 14" walls and the stone pit under the living room that was used to keep the metal cream cans cool.

During World War I the dairy closed and the building was annexed to the Club. Beginning in 1953, it housed the Post Office for 23 years. Then George Fortado purchased it from his brother-in-law, Larry Curtola, in 1974. Fortado created a home using the original milk barn as its centerpiece. With the addition of the Pedersens' third girl in January, 1994, Chris and Kim plan a second phase of construction.

THE RIDLEY RHINDS
1750 ALAMEDA DIABLO

This early California style home designed by architect Henry Reimer of Piedmont was built in 1928 for Henry Nichols. Only three other families have owned the house. The Nichols owned it for 19 years before selling it in 1947 to his niece, Myra Mae (Hall) Abbott and her husband Sam (see page 28). They owned it for another 19 years before selling it to Don and Marge Kinkel in 1966. Ten years later Ridley and Julie Rhinds moved in.

The outstanding feature is the central courtyard. It was designed this way because the Nichols had gone to Mexico and found the idea of an inner courtyard both practical and attractive. It makes a wonderful outside room for living and entertaining much of the year. The Abbotts added a master bedroom suite and a dining room. The Rhinds modernized the kitchen and put in a swimming pool.

The Abbotts added a stable and kept their Arabians there. On Christmas eve, they brought their horses into the living room—reminiscent of an Arabian tradition of bringing their horses into their tents. Since then the stable has been rented as neither the Kinkels nor Rhinds kept horses. Julie wrote, "We have been told it's one of the 'the best horse facilities in Diablo.' We have enjoyed the friends we've made through the stable—children, horses, and adults.

"Casa Sal Si Puedes, our name for the property, means 'Leave if you can.' I like to think all the previous owners would approve of the name, as it's not an easy house to leave."

THE DONLEYS
2139 ALAMEDA DIABLO

This attractive summer cottage was built in 1920 for Dr. and Mrs. Charles Morey. Charles was one of the early leaders in developing the Club. Mrs. Morey was the oldest living resident in Diablo in 1967 when the Donleys purchased the home. Henrietta—"Henrie" to her friends—Morey then lived next door at 2145, the Ragusa property. Prior owners to the Donleys were the O'Connors, Cairnes, and Starr Hornby families.

Gabby Hayes, a well-known cowboy actor in the '30s and '40s was a frequent guest between 1928 and 1935.

THE GUINIVERES
1607 CALLE ARROYO

This home was an English gardner's cottage. The garden was in the center of the racetrack. From Mt. Diablo, the center looked green because of the fresh fruits and vegetables grown there which were served regularly in the Club's dining room.

The cottage was moved to its present location by the Carlyles in 1917. Twenty years later, the Mills bought it. In 1956, the Farrells purchased it, selling it to the Guiniveres 19 years later. In total, there were only four owners in 77 years. Coincidentally, three owners have been mining engineers including the present one, Rex Guinivere.

Several years ago a man stopped by and introduced himself to Rex. It was one of the Carlyles' sons. He wanted to see how the 'ol homestead' looked. He said he loved the place so much that when his parents put it on the market, he did everything he could to prevent the sale. He even took prospective buyers down into the partial basement to show them a wide crack in the wall saying, "You don't want a house that looks like this!"

THE SCHARNELLS
2154 ALAMEDA DIABLO

Rob and Deborah Scharnell purchased this 1928 gem from John and Earlene Roberts in 1988. They are only the third owners of this one acre property which spans from Alameda Diablo to Mt. Diablo Scenic Boulevard. It was designed and built by Berkeley architect Thomas Corlett. The house, which includes a separate guest cottage and a garage with adjoining workshop, was used as a summer home by the Corlett family. The Roberts added a two-stall barn and paddock. The house is only one of three original Diablo homes which remain unchanged to this day.

Corlett was meticulous in his design and hired the finest craftsmen. From Alameda Diablo the house looks quite simple, but very intricate details were used in the construction. An example is the shutters which cover each of the double-hung windows. Each has a unique scene carved on it, such as the cow jumping over the moon, a man and women gardening, squirrels, and acorns.

The house is constructed of clear redwood, and Corlett used random-length teak imported from the Phillippines for the floors. He installed a gas-fired boiler, a state of the art heating system at the time. In addition, there is a large fireplace in the living room that has an adjoining fireplace servicing the outside porch. This is a special treat on cool evenings and is the center for outdoor entertaining.

As a child, Rob lived in the Diablo Hacienda subdivision, which was built on the Oakwood Farm's racetrack. He said, "Diablo had a mystical quality about it and I decided then, I'd like to live there someday. Now I'm lucky to be able to—a dream come true."

THE MINORS
1925 ALAMEDA DIABLO

Jim and Shelley Minor purchased this treasure—a classic Italian Renaissance Victorian—from the Deckers in 1984. The Deckers lived there 12 years (1972-83) having bought it from the Curtolas in 1971.

This three-story 6,000 square foot brick beauty was built in 1879 as the home of the owners of the Oakwood Stock Farm: Dan Cook, 1879; Seth Cook 1881; Louis Boyd, 1889. It was their home and social center where much entertaining was done in the early days of Diablo.

The house served as an Inn for several years but beginning with the '20s, it became the much revered and fondly remembered Diablo clubhouse of the '20s, '30s, and '40s.

In 1948, when Larry Curtola purchased the Club, he converted the clubhouse into a private residence for his family, using paneling and marble from the Cowell estate in San Francisco. He, Betty, Corrie, Connie and Chrissie lived there for 23 years. The Minors have added a three-car carriage house and an outdoor cabana and entertainment area near the pool. They have also re-established the original stock farm name of Oakwood.

Today this elegant home, filled with artifacts appropriate to its day, sits proudly in its traditional gardens in a manner befitting its historical importance.

THE CORTESES
1843 CALLE ARROYO

Michael and Camille purchased this 1926 New England cottage in 1990 from the Shearers who had lived there since 1977. The original owners, Dr. Edward and Edith Love bought the house for $4,000 in gold. In its 68 years, there have been seven owners.

The Shearers spent two years remodeling and refurbishing, making the house what it is today. They took great care to preserve its woodsy charm, while adding nearly 1,500 square feet.

The Corteses are at the end of a two-year landscape project. Up to this time, the property was basically an olive orchard leftover from one that had covered all the acreage around including the tennis courts. Mike and Camille's goal was to open up and level areas of the yard, making it more accessible from what was previously a dark and unutilized hillside.

Mike said, "The property was once the location of a large group of eucalyptus trees. The creek was filled with about 75 cords of wood when the trees were cut down in 1991. The trees were home to great numbers of roosting turkey vultures. As a child growing up in Diablo, I remember one early evening walking along the golf course and looking up to see the sky blackened with what seemed like a hundred vultures as they simultaneously took flight to escape a cracking eucalyptus branch. Now the number of roosting vultures has dwindled to 10 or 20."

THE TWINS These charming English cottage twins were built in 1917 by a wealthy San Franciscan for his married daughters. They were connected by brick terraces with a tea house in the center. A portion of the terrace still exists. Both houses span Green Valley creek and have managed to remain undisturbed by either flood or drought.

THE HOLTS
1850 ALAMEDA DIABLO

Henry Melvin and Jenkin John were the original owners of the twin cottages in 1917. The Holts purchased this one in 1982 from the Baenders who had lived there since 1959.

There was a guest house that is now a family room and master bedroom. At one time, it was a toolshop. Extensive remodeling and landscaping has been done by the Baenders and Holts. But from the front, the place still has its original 'old world' charm.

THE GARONS
1842 ALAMEDA DIABLO

This twin has been owned by Edward and Rowena Garon since 1989. Bob and Lucille Armstrong made the house famous as an entertainment center in the '50s and '60s. Dr. Dar and Ellie Datwyler purchased it from the Estate of Lucille A. Armstrong in November, 1969. They lived there for 20 years with their four children.

The major renovations to the home were done by the Datwylers approximately 25 years ago when they more than doubled its size while carefully preserving the original ambiance including such features as hardwood floors, oak wainscoting, wood sashed windows and French doors. A portion of the house was engineered and built over the creek to allow the creek to maintain its flow through the property; multilevel decks were built to maximize the utility of the site and foot bridges were built outside that crisscross a meandering stream, a waterfall, separate pool area and gardens.

THE ROAD TO RESPONSIBILITY

For 82 years Diablo struggled for water, sewers, security, roads, postal service, incorporation as a city, and for a voice in public affairs. In this sense its story is the story of every community.

In the beginning, everything belonged to RN Burgess—the Club, the land, the lake, the swimming pool, golf course, Post Office, racing road to the summit of Mt. Diablo, country lanes meandering to the Club from summer villas. He provided the water through an ingenious system of pipes from Mt. Diablo springs. Whenever things needed fixing—water lines, roads, buildings, whatever—he saw to that too. In time, however, the residents began to exert themselves. Some residents began collecting money from neighbors to fill holes in the roads. Those who didn't pay rode free. It was disheartening to drive on a smooth section of a Diablo road and then have to maneuver between pot holes and ruts.

By 1929 the road freeloaders had become a problem. Roads to some homes were repaired while those to others were a disaster. The DPOA (Diablo Property Owners Association) was formed, and with its power of persuasion and pressure, maintained the roads through the '30s. With the bombing of Pearl Harbor, December 7, 1941, the scene changed. Clubmen went to war and most of those on the home front had only "A" gas coupons and couldn't drive to Diablo. Vacant summer homes were rented to Navy officers and they used the Club as guests. This influx marked the beginning of year-round residency. For the first time, Diablo's roads were being used 365 days a year. There was no maintenance because men and materials had gone to war. By 1945 Navy personnel began leaving, and little by little the summer villas were reclaimed by their owners or sold, despite the fact that the roads were in deplorable condition and worsening daily.

BRAY BREITWIESER COSTANZA BRAY

A Professional Corporation
ATTORNEYS AT LAW

Mr. James Stone
P.O. Box 374
Diablo, CA 94528

November 12, 1991

Dear Jim:

The antecedents of the Diablo Community Service District lie in the road system in Diablo. Back in the 1920's and 1930's, one or more of the homeowners would start knocking on doors to try and collect enough money to repair the roads within Diablo. As you might imagine, some residents contributed and some did not. Also, at that time, many of the homes were summer homes for Oakland and San Francisco residents and consequently, they were not very motivated to spend more money for the roads at a country home. A more formalized arrangement was necessary and this lead to the formation of the Diablo Property Association in 1929. Apparently, the Property Owners Association did tolerably well until after World World II when it was recognized that the roads needed major repair. In addition it was decided (I don't know whether voluntarily or required by the County) that Diablo should annex to Central Contra Costa Sanitary District. At this time, the roads were in a deplorable state and there were no sewers. As a result, the Diablo Public Utility District was created and immediately put out two bond issues. One was for the purpose of raising money to put the roads in shape, and the second funded the construction of the sewer system so that Central San would annex the Diablo area. Frank Bray [legal counselor for the DPUD] tells me that about this time, the County was willing to take over the maintenance of the roads after the rehabilitation resulting from the bond issue. Although I do not know what the criteria for county roads was at that time, clearly the Diablo Roads would not have met county standards. Nevertheless, the County was still willing to take over the maintenance of the roads. However, some of the residents, including Bill Hale, Sr. objected and ultimately the assumption of maintenance responsibility was abandoned by the County.

Very truly yours,

Richard J. Breitwieser

COMMON CAUSE

In 1949, the DPUD (Diablo Public Utility District) was formed. Its first order of business was to sell bonds to repair the roads and install sewer lines. The DPUD's legal advisor was first Wakefield Taylor, later a Justice of the District Court of Appeal, then John Baldwin, later a Congressman, followed by Frank Bray during the '50s. Dick Breitwieser was appointed in 1965. Dick remarked, "The Board always met monthly in Art Mohr's home at 2061 Casa Nuestra. Art was the perennial president; he covered the agenda in about 20 minutes and the rest of the meeting was Diablo talk between Directors Jack Imrie, Al Layton, Bob Cuenin and Joe Ragusa." At Dick's first meeting, Bob Cuenin was named Secretary. He said, "Okay, but remember I fill teeth, I don't take minutes." So Dick became the "minute man" and has been to this day.

When the University of California's Free Speech Movement hit the Berkeley scene in 1964, the social mores of America began to split at the seams. Diablo, and the Club in particular, became the target for tomfoolery, bashing, arson, vandalism and burglaries, especially on three-day weekends and holidays such as Halloween. The DPUD's charter was roads and sewers, so Art Mohr asked Dick Breitwieser to make inquiries about an organizational arrangement to deal with security. Dick proposed a service district. At the same time, Bob Tiernan, DPOA's President, was looking into the matter and he came up with the idea of replacing the DPUD with a service district empowered to provide security. He met with the DPUD Board, everyone agreed, and Dick prepared the necessary papers. It then fell to Larry Ives, who succeeded Tiernan as DPOA President to follow through. He met with county officials and successfully presented the plan before the Board of Supervisors in Martinez, along with a petition signed by most residents of Diablo and the Club's Board of Directors (see next page).

Diablo District Directors

Completing their first year of service is the Board of the Diablo Community Services District, which meets the first Monday of each month. Pictured, from left, are Joseph Ragusa, Dr. James C. Stone, president William F. Cronin, Robert Tiernan and Richard Breitwieser. Not pictured are board member John Imrie and Larry Ives, general manager.

DISTRICT CUTS DIABLO TAXES

The Diablo Community Services District, the successor to the Diablo Public Utility District, has since it went into operation on Oct. 1, 1969, done something unheard of in this day of skyrocketing taxes. They reduced the tax rate!

In presenting their proposed tax rate for 1970 to the Contra Costa Auditor's Office, the budget showed a reduction from .68 cents to .58 per $100 assessed valuation.

A tax reduction didn't curtail services, since a private patrol service was engaged for the Diablo community that has proven extremely successful in the reduction of vandalism and burglaries. The patrol works in close cooperation with the Contra Costa County Sheriff's Dept.

Deputy Sheriff Wes Coy and the Diablo patrol car.

EXHIBIT "A"

CONTRA COSTA COUNTY
RECEIVED
JUNE 19, 1968

LOCAL AGENCY
FORMATION COMMISSION
PETITION FOR REORGANIZATION

In the Matter of the Reorganization of Diablo Community Service District and Diablo Public Utility District

a) This proposal is made pursuant to the District Reorganization Act of 1965.
b) Proposed changes of organization:
1) Creation of a new community service district to be known as Diablo Community Service District.
2) Dissolution of Diablo Public Utility District.
c) In addition to the existing boundaries of the Diablo Public Utility District, the proposed district will include the Mt. Diablo Estate Park Subdivision Unit No. 3.
d) The principal act under which the proposed community service district is proposed to be formed is the Community Services District Law (Calif. Govt. Code section 61000 et fol.) The description of the boundaries of the proposed district is attached hereto as Exhibit "A." A map showing said boundaries is attached at Exhibit "B." Both said exhibits are incorporated herein as if set forth in detail.
e) Petitioners submit conditions as follows: That the successor community service district shall succeed to all of the rights, duties and obligations of the extinguished Diablo Public Utility District with respect to the enforcement, performance and payment of the outstanding bond and contracts, and that furthermore the successor district shall succeed to all of the present, existing, contingent or future assets of said Diablo Public Utility District.
f) Reasons for proposal:
1) The area included within the boundaries of the proposed district is located in the unincorporated portion of the county and is some distance from any other center of population. The affected area includes the Diablo Country Club and quality single family dwellings. The area is subject to extensive acts of vandalism, and frequent burglaries. Experience has shown that the limited protection offered by the Sheriff's Department is insufficient to control the vandalism and burglaries.
2) With few exceptions, the roads within the proposed district are private in nature, but subject to a right of way reserved to the public. The roads are narrow and visibility is limited. The posted speed limit is 25 milers per hour, but experience has indicated that the posted speed limit (25mph) is rarely observed. Again, because of the limited patrols by Sheriff's personnel, there is no way to control the situation.

Since the area is primarily residential and recreational, the risk of personal injury and property damage due to vehicular traffic is inordinately high. The petitioners herein are convinced that both of the above situations can be significantly decreased if adequate control measures were adopted. The proposed district would employ a private patrol, equipped with a suitable vehicle, to make random patrols of the area. The only method to procure sufficient consistent income to support this proposal is through and by means of a tax assessment.

3) The Diablo Public Utility District was formed to provide and maintain suitable sanitation service to the area and to maintain said private roads. The said district incurred a bonded indebtedness to put the said sanitation facilities in a condition in which Central Sanitation District would annex the area, and this is now an accomplished fact.

Consequently, the main function of said Diablo Public Utility District is to maintain said roads within their boundaries.

The maintenance of said roads would be assumed by the proposed district as well as providing the required security as described herein.

Section 61600 of the Government Code lists the powers which can be granted to a community service district. If this proposed district is formed, the following powers would be requested:

1) Street lighting;.

2) Equipment, maintenance and administration of police protection or security systems-guard force to protect and safeguard life and property.

3) The opening, closing, widening, extending, straightening, surfacing and resurfacing, in whole or in part, of any street or road which is subject to a right-of-way by the public, but which has not been accepted into the county road system in such district, and the implementation of these safety measures deemed necessary to safeguard life and property.

4) The construction and improvement of bridges, culverts, curbs, gutters and works incidental to the purposes specified in the preceding paragraphs.

g) The Board of Directors shall be composed of five (5) members.
h) The chief petitioners are Lloyd Ives and Robert P. Tiernan.

WHEREFORE petitioners pray that proceedings be taken for reorganization as proposed herein.

Lloyd M Ives — Robert P Tiernan

LLOYD IVES — ROBERT P. TIERNAN

Petition for Reorganization of DPUD to Diablo Community Service District,

In 1968, Diablo voted to dissolve the DPUD and replace it with the DCSD (Diablo Community Service District) for the purpose of providing security, maintaining roads, and offering street lighting. Elected as Directors were Bill Cronin, Jack Imrie, Joe Ragusa, Jim Stone, and Bob Tiernan—all prominent in the drive to establish a publicly elected body to deal with Diablo's major problems.

The Directors selected Larry Ives as general manager and Dick Breitwieser the legal advisor and "minute man." Larry recalled, "It was difficult to get 100% community support because of the homeowners on Caballo Ranchero. That was a county, i.e., public road, and Caballo Ranchero residents had been traveling free over Diablo's 'private' roads." Some felt they liked the idea of having security, but objected to paying for roads that had been free. One week prior to the election, a meeting was organized at the Stones' Caballo Ranchero home. Of 19 homeowners, 15 *men* came to the meeting. At the height of Larry's pitch, a woman resident arrived daringly clad in the latest motorcycle fashion. While the men ogled and goggled, Larry called for the question. Later he said, "To this day, I'm not sure the guys knew what they voted for!"

The open space between the end of Alameda Diablo and the State Park was known as the 160. This area, popular with horse riders, was owned by Larry Curtola as part of his purchase of the Club in 1948. Very wisely, it was divided into 25 parcels of five to twenty acres each. These 25 sites were served by extending Alameda Diablo. After the extension was constructed by the developers it was taken over by the DCSD for maintenance. Looking ahead the District could foresee the time when many homes might be built in the 160, and made a contract specifying that no more than 25 residents could egress and ingress via Alameda Diablo. Bob Tiernan said, "In terms of controlling development, this was a momentous decision, benefiting the community."

The Club was a key player in this road to responsibility. As owner of the largest facility in the community, its members and guests use the roads more than the homeowners do. The Club occupies the largest piece of land, which happens to be covered with tennis courts, a golf course, pool, lake, open space—all "attractive nuisances." Thus the Club benefits most from a publicly recognized, reliable, professional security system. The Club's common cause contribution is 10% of the DCSD's income.

San Ramon Valley Times
Saturday, April 16, 1994

HOMETOWN

LOOKING BACK
25 YEARS AGO

Valley Pioneer
Wednesday, April 16, 1969

OK DIABLO SERVICE AREA.
DIABLO RESIDENTS WENT TO THE POLLS TUESDAY.

Ten candidates were vying for five seats on the board of directors for the newly formed Diablo Community Services District. Running were: William F. Cronin, John Imrie, Joseph A. Kriz, Edward W.E. LaCava, Arthur Mohr, Joseph Ragusa, Albert R. Rubey, James Stone, Robert Tiernan and Robert J. Wall.

Elected to serve on the first boards were Cronin, Imrie, Ragusa, Tiernan and Stone.

DIABLO, hard hit in recent Halloweens, has taken elaborate steps to curb vandalism this year. The property owners of the area have hired some 20 special deputies; have issued identification markers for the autos of Diablo residents only; and will post a guard at the gate from 3 p.m. to midnight who will allow no one other than Diablo residents entry into the residential community.

The Diablo "trick and treat" set has been advised to complete their rounds by 6 p.m. on Halloween.

Motorists are reminded to drive with extra care, since literally hundreds of small fry will be out trick or treating, some dressed in costumes that are difficult to see at night.

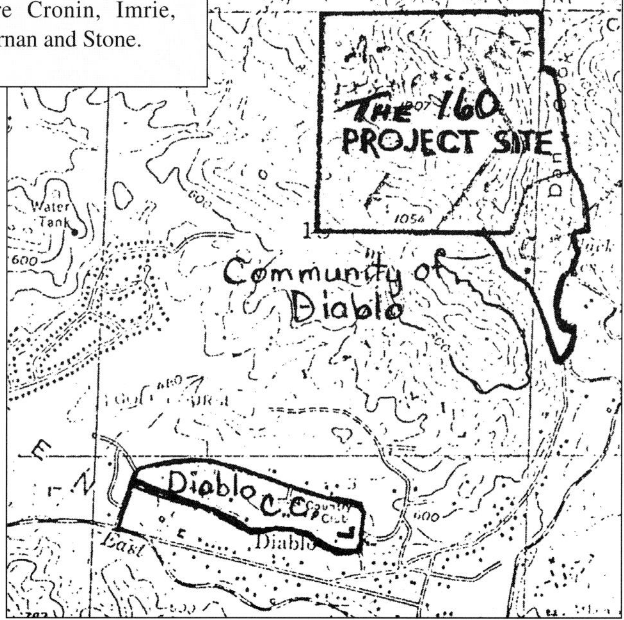

Map of the 160.

The Club and Chalet today.

THE NOBLEST OF THE ELEMENTS

"We never know the worth of water until the well is dry"—Thomas Fuller (1645)

It was a hot morning in July, 1958. Dorothy woke up at 6:30 a.m. just before the alarm clock went off, slipped out of bed, donned her bathrobe, and headed for the kitchen. She turned on the faucet to fill the coffee pot. There was an ominous yet familiar gurgling in the pipe. She turned the faucet off and rushed down the hall, calling, "Up, up everyone, fill the bath tubs, the buckets and the pots and pans while the water lasts. It's going to be another dry day on Caballo Ranchero. When you children come home from the Club this afternoon, be sure you each bring home a thermos of water."

This was any summer day, 1955-60, a real five-year drought! It occurred in Diablo each of those summers, despite heavy winter rains and deep snows in the Sierra.

In 1948, when Larry Curtola snatched the Club from the jaws of developers, he bought a country club, the Chalet, a golf course, swimming pool, two tennis courts, Diablo Lake, a huge horse barn that also housed a U.S. Post Office, and the Red Horse Tavern (where Club workmen and their families lived during the reconstruction of the Club). "I bought it for the land that came with the Club," Larry said, "in order to build houses. I really didn't care about running a country club, had no idea how to maintain a water system, repair a meandering network of driveways called roads or keep-up a rinky-dink sewer line."

Fixing up the clubhouse and the golf course were Curtola's number one priority—the other things could wait. Then he realized he couldn't redo the additional nine holes without more water. He then formed the Curtola Water Company and hired Betty Curtola's nephew, Charlie Howard, a young engineer, to oversee it.

Cecil Ryder, who was the Club's maintenance supervisor from 1935-1975, recalled, "We had 27 active springs in the mountains and four storage tanks with Diablo Lake as the main reservoir. Trouble was, those old iron pipes that brought the water down from the springs dated from before WWI. Much of my time was spent walking the lines to repair the leaks." Iron clamps were used, since this was long before the advent of plastic pipe.

Cecil recalled, "In summers, I always carried a shovel because of the rattle snakes. I tried not to surprise them 'cause that's when they'll most likely strike. Otherwise they'd just as soon leave you alone as you would them." One beastly hot summer day on one of his repair runs, Cecil bent down to drink some cool fresh mountain spring water. His partner in the truck hollered, "Look out Ryder, there's a rattler." Sure enough, there was one just six inches from Cecil's neck. His shovel quickly dispatched it.

When Larry asked Cecil his opinion about the adequacy of the water system, Cecil said, "It's O.K. for now," by which he meant it was adequate to water the first nine holes and the lawns and gardens of Diablo but definitely not for nine more holes, and perhaps somewhat questionable for drinking. So the Curtola Water Company built a 2-3 acre holding pond in the mountains to collect and store drinking water. But that still left the extension of the golf course in limbo.

Naturally, there was water under the golf course or under something, somewhere in Diablo. But several dozen drillings came up dry or with so little water it wasn't worth writing home about. The redoing of the golf course was still in limbo.

Horsemen familiar with the Mt. Diablo trails knew about Pine Canyon near the Castle Rock entry to the Park in Walnut Creek. It was renowned for its never-ending springs of fresh water, even in the hottest and driest summers. Larry learned that a group was interested in forming a Pine Canyon water district. He joined forces with them with the understanding he could have their overflow. "Golf course extension, here we come," he thought. Well, not quite, water doesn't flow over mountains.

It doesn't flow, but it could be pumped! Larry went to see Charles Fryer who owned the ranch between Pine Canyon and Diablo. Fryer refused to grant an easement for the pipeline. Curtola was defeated. In desperation he said, "So you won't give me an easement even though I'll pay whatever it takes, so what's next? Will you sell the ranch?" "Why not," said Fryer.

The deal for the Fryer ranch was sealed with a handshake. Larry purchased 2,500 plus acres and a spacious ranch house for $275,000. The extension of the golf course was assured. Engineers went to work and on August 19, 1951 at the 16th tee, where the new pipeline entered the golf course (and is still there) a grand celebration was held. Club president William Van Bokkelen extolled Larry's determination and foresight, predicting the Club's water problems had been solved. Or so he thought.

Builders, carpenters, electricians and plumbers were busy in Diablo during the early '50s, using the limited supply of water to build new houses, which had to depend on the Club's water supply. By 1956, the County refused to issue building permits without a hook-up agreement signed by the Curtola Water Company, but no more such agreements were forthcoming. The water system was overextended and a moratorium on development ensued. Builders were outraged and some residents too,

Larry Curtola and friends.

***F**ryer Ranch and water pipeline from Pine Canyon superimposed over modern map, opposite page.*

***M**t. Diablo State Park.*

not just because the water supply was unreliable, but also because of its quality. Several complained to County Health officials and the Curtola Water Company was required to truck in fresh supplies of water in the summer months. Beth Hearn recalled, "We had two water systems. One was inside, for our drinking water; one was outside, for irrigation, which came with polywogs and other 'wogs.' With one turn of the faucet, we had irrigation plus plant food."

LARRY CURTOLA Larry said this about himself, "I was so new at this business—being 'czar' of roads and water. One day a well-known company came by and offered to put in a new and better pumping system, I said, 'Sure, anything to improve the delivery of water.' Just before hook-up time, Cecil came to me and said, 'I wouldn't do it. Looks to me like the pressure will blow out all our pipe connections.'" Curtola approached the company's chief engineer, saying, "I'm not convinced your new system will work. Will you guarantee it and take full responsibility for what happens if it doesn't?" The hook-up ended before it began, and the new pump was dismantled and hauled away.

"Right in the midst of my water development efforts," said Larry, "I had this problem with the State Park people. They said I couldn't put in a particular trench for new pipelines needed to feed the golf course. I said, 'You guys have no right to stop me, I have a county permit.' They replied, 'This is a state matter.' And so it was . . . and Larry was stopped in his tracks for the time being, but only for the time being.

Bill Knowland, owner of the *Oakland Tribune,* was a Club member. He also was a member of the State Park Board. Bill told Larry to attend the next meeting of the Board. "I did," said Larry. "I got to the room around 9:30 for a meeting that had begun at 9:00. I was told my item had already been approved. Now I had a State permit."

In 1960 East Bay Municipal Utilities District took over and the Curtola Water Company was history. EBMUD installed its own lines and meters. The old system had seen too many miles. It had been established in the late 1800s and stretched from Green Valley School and Stone Valley Road to the top of Mt. Diablo. One of the features of the old Oakwood Farm had been a huge reservoir below the race track above where Stone Valley and Diablo roads intersect. In 1925, the Club (meaning Burgess) established a pumping station there that cost $50,000. It pumped irrigation water for the first nine holes of the golf course.

And that's how it all started—this saga about "the noblest of the elements is water." (Pindaros Pindar, 518-432 B.C. [Olympian Odes, Ode I, I, I])

INCORPORATION STUDY
FOR THE PROPOSED
CITY OF DIABLO

October 20, 1975

VIII. SUBMISSION OF THE STUDY

This incorporation study was prepared by a group of interested Diablo residents. Work was begun in 1973, and has continued steadily to the present, with countless hours spent on gathering, analyzing, discussing, and drafting the information contained in this study. Valuable information has been provided by Joseph S. Connery, Executive Officer of LAFCO, and other Contra Costa county officials. We wish to also acknowledge the help of the League of California cities and the Cities of Clayton, Monte Serno, and Moraga, which provided additional background information and support. The residents who participated in the study committee now respectfully submit this study to the residents of Diablo and, as proponents of incorporation, to LAFCO in support of the application for incorporation of Diablo.

ARNOLD A. BLACKMUR 1941 Alameda Diablo	JAMES C. STONE Caballo Ranchero
PAUL J. CORTESE 1720 Alameda Diablo	ROBERT P. TIERNAN Calle Arroyo
MARSHALL W. FREEMAN 36 Campo Pelota	WILLIAM H. HALE Diablo Road
DONALD H. HOFFMAN 1953 La Cadena	STEPHEN K. JONES 2688 Caballo Ranchero
PETER KNOEDLER 1717 Alameda Diablo	JOHN W. OLANDER Verda del Cienvo
JOSEPH RAGUSA Alameda Diablo	DOLPH C. SENASAC 8 Calle del Casarillos
NONA R. SENASAC	

Admiral Robert A. Tiernan.

Application for Incorporation of Diablo as a City, opposite page.

THE CITY OF DIABLO

By the '70s, the community was feeling pressured by competing outside forces. Alamo, Danville and San Ramon were talking incorporation and referring to certain areas as their "spheres of influence." Danville in particular eyed Diablo for takeover. The DCSD and DPOA came to life, and a committee to incorporate Diablo as a city was organized with Paul Cortese, DCSD past president and Steve Jones, DCSD president, as co-chairmen. Others were Arnie Blackmur, DPOA spokesman, Bill Hale, Don Hoffman, Pete Knoedler, Marshall Freeman, John Olander, Joe Ragusa, Dolf Senasac, Jim Stone, and Bob Tiernan. Dick Breitwieser served as legal advisor. The Club lent its considerable political support to the incorporation effort.

A 47-page document was prepared. It began by tracing Diablo's progress from Club ownership to the founding of the DPOA in 1929, DPUD in 1949, and DCSD in 1968. It outlined the town's physical features, the importance of the Club, income projections, budgetary provisions, and the rationale for cityhood—local control. The proposed city was to be governed by a five-member elected city council, one of whom would serve as mayor. The application was presented to LAFCO (Local Agency Formation Commission) and the case argued by Cortese with the assistance of attorneys Breitwieser and Tiernan.

LAFCO denied the request because the community of Diablo, "While a well-defined place of residency is too small to be a city." The unsuccessful drive, however, assured the continuation of Diablo as an unincorporated community, independent from the emerging cities.

Steve Jones, Co-chairman of Incorporation Committee. The other Co-chairman was Paul Cortese.

Rich Swanson, President, Diablo Community Service District, 1993–.

DIABLO POST OFFICE

Everyone has to go to the Post Office, since there are no letter carriers. This is one of the unique features of Diablo. The Post Office is the town meeting place—a spot to socialize, exchange ideas, and update neighborhood news. The history of this institution, like everything else about Diablo, is intertwined with the Club.

In 1912, shortly after RN purchased the Oakwood Stock Farm, he applied for a USPO. The application stated the Post Office would serve a community "near San Francisco" about 15 miles southwest of the San Joaquin River . . . and "adjacent to the terminal of the Oakland and Antioch Railroad and at a distance of 100 feet from the track." No mention was made of the size of the community, about a dozen residents.

The Post Office began operation prior to WWI and was housed in the old horse barn across from the Red Horse Tavern. The first Postmaster was John Curtis, who was also Burgess' superintendent in charge of paving the road to the summit. Postcards could be sent for a penny, letters for three cents. At the 1916 opening, it was anticipated there would be a rush to be the person buying Diablo's first stamp. Burgess ruled that lots should be drawn as the only fair way to decide. Unfortunately, he drew the lucky number himself!

When John Curtis finished the paving job, he was succeeded as Postmaster by Edwin Cooper (1918-1940) followed by his wife, Helen (1940-1955). Together their posting responsibilities spanned 37 years.

When Larry Curtola dismantled the horse barn in 1948 "before it fell down," he moved the Post Office temporarily to the Chalet, then gave it a permanent home in the milk barn (1953-1974). Many Diablons picked up their mail while riding their horses and tied up at the hitching post near the entrance. The Postmaster was Ethyl Stott (1955-1969). During her 14-year tenure, the price of a stamp for a first-class letter rose dramatically from $.06 to $.08!

Over the years, the Club had been ambivalent about where to locate the golf Pro Shop. It has been in the Chalet and the clubhouse. Finally, in September, 1964, the Club broke ground for a new facility on the site of the old tennis courts. It opened May 1, 1965, when Lyle Wehrman took over as the Golf Pro. As time went by, however, a consensus developed that it was too separate, "too far away

This sign was on the side of the old milk barn/Post Office, above. Note the building's wide siding.

Originally constructed as the Golf Pro Shop this building has housed the Post Office since 1974.

The Post Office was housed in the lower right corner of the old horse barn beginning in 1916, upper left.

The old milk barn later housed the Post Office, left.

LOOKING BACK 25 YEARS

In 1947, the Diablo post office was the subject of a feature story in the *Oakland Tribune.* Although Postal Service records refute some of the dates, the story is interesting for its local color.

It was headlined "Huge Stock Barn Houses Post Office for Tiny Diablo," and read: "Diablo, June 3— One of the last places anyone would expect to find a post office would be in a barn, and perhaps that's why few people other than the inhabitants of this small town know that what was once an imposing stock barn has, for 40 years, housed the Diablo post office."

The article went on to describe the tenure of Cooper and that of his wife, Helen, who took over after her husband's death. It said: "Mrs. Cooper specializes in service to her 'customers,' as she calls them, because 'we're just like one big family.' Mrs. Cooper's post office serves approximately 300 people, including the ranger station atop Mt. Diablo. During the war, her work was doubled handling the mail for Navy installations on Mt. Diablo.

"The huge barn was used 75 years ago by Seth Cook, who kept around 300 head of blue-blooded, standard-bred horses there.

According to Mrs. Charles Morey, a Diablo resident since 1916, postal facilities moved the first time into what was then the clubhouse for Diablo Country Club and is now the Curtola residence.

"The present post office building was once something quite different, according to Mrs. Morey. She recalled: 'At one time, it was intended that the club be self-supporting. We were to have our own vegetable gardens and farms and the present building was the milkhouse of the dairy. A Swiss, Mr. Hueber, ran the dairy for us. The little building has very thick walls and stored our milk products for us. It was in a different place then and didn't get moved until they wanted to change it into the post office.'"

When Mrs. Cooper submitted her typed description of the new site, some long-forgotten postal official wrote across the top "Not on map".

for ready access," and plans were made to move it back to the clubhouse. But the question remained, what to do about the building?

About this time, there were rumblings that the Postmaster General was going to close Diablo's Post Office because of inadequate facilities. Larry Curtola, who owned the milk barn, then sold it as a residence site rather than renovate it as a Post Office. (The barn is now the Pedersens' home at 1671 El Nido.) The April 1956 *Inferno* said of this event., "This will cut down considerably on the amount of traffic through the Club grounds." (There was a road in front of the Chalet connecting El Nido and Club House Road).

The DPOA (Diablo Property Owners Association), zealous to preserve Diablo's identity, joined forces with the Club and together they convinced Postal authorities that they should lease the Pro Shop as a Post Office. Steve Jones recalled, "Hal Smith had the right contacts with the government and Bob Wall of the Club Board supplied the leadership to make it a '. . . done deal.'" At high noon on August 21, 1974, the new Post Office was dedicated at a ceremony that featured an ice cream social, now an annual Diablo event. On hand for the dedication was Club President Frank Schmitt and DPOA past president Steve Jones—both active in the negotiations. The Master of Ceremonies was Carol Sconyers, the first woman president of the DPOA in its then 62-year history. Bettye Johanson, Postmaster, 1968-1981, accepted the building on behalf of the USPO, thus ending the Post Office's first 58 years living in a barn. Also ending after 58 years was the Post Office's free ride with the Club and later, Curtola supplying the building and utilities gratis. Larry recalled, "Each week, when the crew finished cleaning our home, I sent them up to the Post Office to give it a cleaning too."

Today a $.29 first-class letter is handled by Postmaster Cathy Cantu-Ott (1993-present), who succeeded Mary Lou Hodgson (1985-1993) and Ron Elisondo (1983-1985), all with the assistance of Diana Chavez and Sandy Patterson. In the past ten years, the number of boxes has increased from 480 to 562, the cost of a stamp from $.18 to $.29, the annual revenue from $90,000 to $130,000 and the personnel from one to three. All have that abiding interest in serving a community that is shrouded in history, prizes its privacy, and treasures its tranquility.

Celebrating its 75th anniversary in 1991, a commemorative postmark was introduced to honor the Diablo Post Office, thus ensuring its place in the 200-year chronicle of the U.S. Postal Service.

Bob Wall, Club Board member who was active in the successful negotiations for the new home of the Post Office in the Club's former Pro Shop, above.

Diablo's newest Postmaster, Cathy Cantu-Ott.

DIABLO PROPERTY OWNERS ASSOCIATION
DIABLO, CALIFORNIA

Dear Property Owner,

Individual letters to you all do not seem quite as necessary now that we have our new kiosk on which to post items of community interest. A special word of thanks to talented Ted Petersen & Associates for its attractive design and construction —a job well done for now and many years to come. The other construction projects are also under way: the remodeling of the bus shelter on Alameda Diablo and the possible installation of wooden street signs. There have been some delays, as is often the case with construction work, but we hope to have the bus shelter ready to use by the first rains and some trial signs up for a vandalism check very soon.

Some years ago the Diablo Patrol was hired as a method of controlling vandalism in Diablo, especially on Halloween. Recently there have been fewer problems from outsiders but we still have youngsters of Diablo families who are abusing private property, throwing water balloons into passing cars at the intersections of Alameda Diablo etc. As parents it is our responsibility to know where our children are and to provide for their proper supervision when we are not at home, especially on Friday and Saturday nights. Steps are also being taken at the present time by the Community Service District and the Country Club to increase patrol coverage and the County Sheriff's Department is being contacted for help. Please report any serious incidents directly to the Sheriff's Department from now on in order to bring these problem youngsters under control.

Speaking of children—School has started and more children are walking and riding bikes along our roads. Construction vehicle traffic is increasing here in Diablo daily; little can be done to control these drivers, except perhaps a word of caution to your contractor from you that own property and are having custom homes built. Those of us who live here now and travel to and from home daily should try to remember to drive more slowly. Remember the days of the serious 55 mile speed limit. We all got where we were going—it just took longer. Try driving 15 miles an hour where it says to—for our children's sake!

In closing, I want to say how wonderful it was to see the 350 residents of Diablo and guests turn out to enjoy being social and eating ice cream on a summer evening, August 21. Dedicating our new Post Office building was the main reason for the party but also we took the time to view a marvelous slide collection showing the early days of Diablo's history compiled by Egon Pedersen. My personal thanks to the many people who helped plan the evening, Frank Schmitt and the Board of Directors of the Country Club for use of their facilities and the distinguished barbershop quartet who graciously donated their talents for the evening—Bob Cuenin, Frank Nageotte, Al Rubey, and Chuck Hillman accompanied on the banjo by Stan Thomas and Marsh Freeman, and Margaret Freeman on the washboard. Even the weatherman cooperated to provide one of Diablo's special balmy summer evenings. For those of you who were away on vacation, there's talk of planning another summer function next year, with more advance notice. Also, we're going to ask Egon if he might show slides again—on a cozy winter evening in February, perhaps, for those who missed this showing or had small children tugging toward the ice cream table instead.

Carol Seonyers.

Mt. Diablo Property Owners Association Corporate Seal, 1929, with Bob Nilssen. Bob is 1994 President, below.

A 1970s letter from the first woman president of the DPOA. Note kiosk design, problems with vandalism, music at Post Office dedication.

The devil stamp was originally used by Colonel Butler of Green Gates—2067 Alameda Diablo—on all his correspondence. It was given to Postmaster Bettye Johanson by Butler's wife Nell when he died. Sandy Patterson had the inspiration to incorporate the design on the 75th Anniversary Commerative Postmark at left.

DIABLO POST OFFICE – AUGUST 1974

Diablo Post Office workers Diana Chavez, left, and Sandy Patterson will help celebrate the post office's 75th anniversary Wednesday.

"The people who come here to get their mail are just like family," she says. "They stop in and tell me how their day is going, or what their kids are doing."

— Sandy Patterson, post office worker

DIABLO CELEBRATES

THE DIABLO POST OFFICE has found a new home. A number of Diablo residents were on hand recently to inaugurate the new facility with a slide show, car exhibit and old-fashioned ice cream social. In its 60-year history, the post office has been housed in a stock barn, a golf clubhouse and a one-time dairy milk house. —THE VALLEY PIONEER

OUR NEW POST OFFICE

From the days that Diablo Country Club was lovely spreading farm land country, and horses and cattle grazed these hillsides surrounding our beautiful country club, we have come a long way. So it is finally time that our quaint antique former milk house (Diablo Post Office) is shutting its doors forever and will no longer receive the U.S. Mail. We have advanced so far from the days of the Overland Mail and the Pony Express. But Diablo is ever growing and forever improving its facilities.

Today, our Postmistress, Mrs. Bettye Johanson and her very able assistant Sandy Edwards, are happy to serve all of Diablo in a first rate Post Office with all the modern facilities of the best of the U.S. Post Offices throughout our state. Yes, Bettye and Sandy are girls who love their country flavor. Each is deeply knowledgeable in horses and our mail system as well. So no two ladies could better represent our area, than these two.

Each family will have two keys to open their boxes. Now, don't try to duplicate your key somewhere else. This is illegal anyway, and no machine will take a postal key. If you should lose yours, report it to our Postmistress. Fifty cents will purchase another key. Your postal box number is the same as always. The advantage is, you no longer have to remember how to dial your box number (how very convenient!).

Now, let us all be proud of this new post office. No longer can we treat it as we did when it was the Pro Shop. That means, golfers must leave their cleats at the door (Oriental or Dutch fashion). This is a small favor to ask, and people who care for property abide by these rules.

Good luck, Bettye & Sandy; we from the Inferno wish you both happy days!

A welcome opening party, August 21, officially launched our new Post Office.

—Inferno Editor
Peggy Baender

Mary Lou Hodgson, Postmaster, Diablo, 1985-93.

Jim Stone recounts Diablo Post Office's unique history at 75th Anniversary, far right.

THE DIABLO TRIANGLE

Ownership of the "point" at the entrance to Diablo had been argued often among the Club, the Diablo Property Owners Association and the Diablo Community Service District. With no clear title, the question of maintenance, beautification and utilities was also open to debate.

The imposing brick marker at the entrance is on property owned by Janet (Mrs. William) Cronin, a resident since 1958 and Club member since 1948. However, the marker was designed and built by Masud Mehran, who lived across the street from the Cronins.

In 1959, the Club decided to resurface Alameda Diablo and Club House Road as a way to enhance its visibility. Shortly thereafter, Masud, the newly elected President of the DPOA, decided it would be chi-chi to have an eye-catching sign at the entrance to Diablo. He hired an architect to design one and a brick mason to build it. "I wanted to do something for the community and the Club," said Masud. "The DPOA was barely making it and was charging members only $10 a year, hardly enough to pay for paper and postage, so I contributed the $250-300 it cost to erect the brick marker."

An agreement signed by Masud and Bill Cronin and dated March 19, 1959 states:

"DIABLO PROPERTIES ASSOCIATION

You are hereby given permission to erect and maintain a sign on my property, as discussed, for a 12-month period commencing April 1, 1960. It is also understood the plans, as to size and location, must have my prior approval before erection. In the event this permission is not renewed in writing at the end of the year, said approval for the sign will revert to a month-to-month basis. In any event, your Association when notified in writing by me, will promptly remove and restore the property to the condition it was at the time said sign was erected. Any costs so incurred in removing the sign will be paid for by the Association." (signed)

William F. Cronin

Masud Mehran, President

It is clear from the text that the DPOA was to maintain the triangle. A similar agreement was made by William F. Cronin and Janet T. Cronin with Robert Tiernan, President, DPOA, on April 30, 1967 to permit EBMUD to install a water meter on the property. It states in part: "The agreement is given on the same basis as that granted formerly in the case of the non-existing sign."

The one-year stipulation and the phrase, "if not renewed in writing said approval will revert to a month-to-month basis," were both repeated in the 1967 document. There is no record about who was

Diablo's entrance triangle. COURTESY LARRY IVES.

The Cronin family: Peter, Janie, Janet, Bill, Jenifer and Tim. (circa 1961)
COURTESY JANET CRONIN.

to pay the water or electric bills to illuminate the sign. Bill Cronin was the first President of the DCSD in 1969, and that perhaps explains why a public body paid the water and electric bills during the '70s for a private activity!

Bill always took pride in his property and was an avid gardener. Within a few years after the brick sign was built, he became disenchanted with the upkeep (or lack of same) by the DPOA and reached an agreement with the Club. In return for maintaining the triangle, he was allowed to store his golf cart at the Club without charge. When Bill no longer wished to maintain the triangle, the Club took over in 1977. Ten years later, the Club gave up and again the DPOA took over.

In 1990, inspired by Susan Scherer of the Diablo Women's Garden Club, the DPOA relandscaped the triangle and fenced it. The Association then turned to the Club for help. The Club minutes of July 25, 1990 state: "Mr. Eorio, DPOA President, requested financial assistance to fund a landscaping project at the entry to Diablo. The $12,000 project would cover the corner around the brick sign. The Club was asked to either provide the maintenance or contribute to the costs. The Board approved a donation of $2,500 for the landscaping project. The contribution is large because the Club does not want to be involved in contributing to the maintenance, neither with direct labor nor with funding."

Researching who is responsible for maintaining the Diablo triangle has been a walk through quicksand. A mixed past and a murky future are revealed. In the absence of a legal agreement, the greeting "Diablo—Diablo Country Club—Private Grounds," is here today, but may be gone tomorrow.

A week after this message was published in the June '93 *Inferno*, Marilee Headen called to say, "The triangle mystery is solved." In 1986, when she was on the DPOA Board, she negotiated an easement agreement between Janet Cronin and the DPOA regarding the triangle. She received the Citizen of the Year Award in 1987 for her efforts.

Amara Koss, DPOA President, was called. She checked with the Recorder's Office in Martinez, and reported, "There is an agreement on file dated March 19, 1987. It provides an easement for planting, placement, repairing, maintenance, and replacement of signs and incidental purposes." At the same time, the Club agreed to participate with the DPOA in maintaining the triangle. Problem solved, at least for now!

On its trek to responsibility, Diablo has been infused with the spirited support of its residents. No community could ask for more.

THE CONTEXT The Cold War is over. After nearly 50 years of tension, the West has won. Communism has failed both as a form of government and as an economic system. The open market and democracy reign. Free trade, worldwide, is supplanting regional and national trading.

Gorbachev has led the breakup of the Soviet State, touting *perestroika* (reform) and *glasnost* (openness). Yeltsin follows "Gorby" in the reform battle.

The U.S. is recovering from a recession but California is at the back of the line because of defense cuts, the closing of military bases, immigration from Mexico and the Pacific Rim, and devastating earthquakes.

Bill Clinton is in the White House, the first Democrat in 12 years. Hillary is an activist First Lady in the tradition of Eleanor Roosevelt. Health care for everyone is the issue of the day. Pete Wilson, a Republican Govenor, spars with a Democratic, Willie Brown, legislature. The professional sports scene is dominated by stars making over a million dollars a year, while the homeless crowd the core of our cities.

All around the world, golf has taken over as the most popular sport, so too at Diablo. A new generation is buying homes in Diablo and their children are giving new life to Junior Golf, Junior Tennis and reinvigorating the swimming team.

Golf course reconstruction.

Chapter XII — Epilogue: The Nineties

"Twenty years ago golf was played by few and scoffed at by many. Today it is an insepa-rable part of our lives. America, and particularly California, is the golfing playground of the universe," said the editor of the Green Book of Golf in 1923. It is even more true today than it was in the '20s.

GOLF COURSE RECONSTRUCTION With a 2.5 million dollar price, the Club has a new golf course and five renovated tennis courts. Nearly half the amount was spent on a new golf course automatic irrigation system and a new drainage system. New golf paths cost $400,000, bunkers $250,000 and drain lines $65,000. These extensive improvements, akin to a new course, were accomplished over a nine-month period without having to close down the course—no mean achievement.

President John Demgen said to the membership at an informal "progress report" meeting, "In effect, we now have a new clubhouse, golf course and tennis courts along with an 82-year heritage—an almost unbeatable combination." (1)

Water, a problem at Diablo since day one in 1912, has been solved but at a high price. While other clubs have springs, lakes, rivers or wells to water their courses, Diablo is dependent on EBMUD to the tune of $150,000 per year. "Otherwise," reported General Manager Tom Marquoit, "our maintenance costs are in line with those of other clubs in the West. Our new maintenance methods also will contribute to lower maintenance costs—procedures like thatching, slicing, sweeping, blowing and spiking aerate the soil and allow the water to get to the roots quickly." The maintenance staff has undergone a retraining program and is divided into teams that are responsible for a specific set of holes, thus contributing to accountability.

THE GOLD PUTTER Diablo's first annual men's invitational golf tournament was Labor Day weekend, 1955.(3) The innovators were Jack Pingree, Bill Houston, Buzz Knowlton, Phil Kane, and Spence Archer. In 1963 the tournament was named the Gold Putter and is an established Diablo tradition. The name Gold Putter was Bill Winslow's creative touch as the chairman of the 1963 event, won by Jack Pingree and his guest Don Doten. The entry fee then was $25. Today it is $675.00.

The September 1993 "Putter" got off to the tune of bagpipes as ninety-seven teams took to the links for a "Scotch" shootout. Ed and Mike Dolinar won the first flight and George Padis and John Sitter outchipped Jay Lipscomb and his partner, Dennis Watson, to win the second flight.

Next was the Long Drive Contest. John Connell led with a blast of 309-yards followed by John Peck, with 295-yards. The low five advanced to the finals. Senior Division Champion, Jim Locker, started the competition with a drive of 229. Craig Tysdale got off a blast of 276-yards followed by Julian Steadman with a 277-yard launch. It was now down to John P. and John C. John P. put a ball safely in the fairway, and John C. was now in the spotlight. Unfortunately, he couldn't get one ball between the lines, thus John Peck for the second time was the Gold Putter Long Drive Champion.

Then came the "Horse Race." First Race #16. Fifteen teams entered the starting gate, nine stumbled. Second Race #17. Six teams advanced for the second race of the day. Morgan and Okamoto off the race track, Padis and Sitter foiled at the finish line. Third Race #18. Larsen and Phayer hit a "small bucket," but could not get one in bounds. Bredehoft and Kilburn also tried to give it away. In the meantime, the teams of Newlin-Stefani and Schick-Roth took to the reins. Newlin and Stefani made the green in 3, while the other two horses were gasping for air. Schick and Roth out of the bunker, off the fence, short of the green, skull over the green, long back to the green, how many shots is that? Bredehoft and Kilburn oops, oops, oops, putt, putt, putt, how many shots is that? "Who are those guys, Sundance?"

When the final putt was made, Tom Newlin and Dave Stefani crossed the finish first. In second place, Bob Schick and Jack Roth edged out Ron Bredehoft and Tom Kilburn. It wasn't pretty, but they finished!

Friday was "The Start." With everyone teeing up in high spirits for great scores, the course was in for a long day (wrong).

Jim McEuen and Craig Andersen took the early lead in the Gold Flight with -11 followed closely

YOU CAN'T GET AWAY FROM IT

Jack James

What are golfers? Athletes? Socialites? Confirmed Addicts? Victims of the hoof and mouth disease—hoof around all day and talk about it all night! Can one ever get away from them?

No, one cannot, for the simple reason that golfers are like the poor—always with us. Golf has become more than the national pastime, supplanting baseball and draw poker. It is now a universal state of mind, a perpetual habit and invariable topic of conversation. In the words of the once-popular ballad, everybody's doing it!

Golf originated in Scotland. Now there are more golfers in America than there are Scotsmen in Scotland. When Americans go in for something, we go in up to our necks. The first pajamas were worn in India. Now the pajama industry is one of the cornerstones of our national prosperity. So it is with golf, which has become as much a part of our daily life as our pajamas.(2)

The famous course at St. Andrews, Scotland, where golf began, opposite page, top.

Phil Kane of Silver Seniors fame, shown above.

COURTESY OF JACK HUGHES.

by Bill and Steve Ikard with -9. For Jim and Craig, Saturday again was a blowout with another good round of -10, a total of 21 under and a 7-stroke lead into the last round. With both balls counting, that blowout turned into almost a flat tire by Sunday. Jim and Craig in the morning round shot a 3-over to finish the tournament -18. Knowing they had to play, Gary Larsen and Larry Phayer made a great run for it finishing -6 for a total of -17, just one shot behind Jim and Craig. Jim couldn't look at the scoreboard, but with all the handshakes he knew they'd won.

The Green Flight was so close it was hard to tell who had the lead until the final day. The last day 12 teams had a chance to win. Coming down the stretch were Mark and Monte (Blues Brothers) Mullins with a stretch drive of -8, for a total of -10 to nose out Rob Olson and Stanley Pasarell by one shot to claim the Green Flight Championship. The Silver Flight had all kinds of ups and downs. Again, on the last day with both balls counting, Fred Dillett and Bob Martin ran away with the low round of the day with an amazing -12. Peter Hayman and Bill Crane also played well the last day. They passed the other teams to capture the Gross Division by 5 points, thus winning the championship.

SILVER SENIORS TOURNAMENT The Silver Seniors is different from the Seniors group. Silver Seniors is a two-day invitational in June for men 55 or over. It was first organized by Jim Hague and Bill Houston in 1987. "We go 22 deep," said Phil Kane in an interview, "meaning the first 22 teams receive prizes. All the prizes are set out on a table and each team gets its 'pick of the table.' We also give prizes for every 3-par both days."

The Club serves breakfast and lunch and there is a dinner dance the second night. The Silver Seniors Tournament is so popular, the tournament committee established a lottery to select the teams to play. Members' applications are tossed on a table and selected at random. The 64 members and their guests are picked by lottery play. Those who participated in the lottery and were not selected are guaranteed a place the following year. "That way," said Phil, "nobody misses a second year."

SENIORS When Hal Saur took over the Seniors group from Bill Bailey in '85, he thought it was a one-year assignment. "And here I am still doing it," he said laughing, "but now we've got a fourth of the members participating in our three in-house tournaments and five home and away tournaments with Claremont, Crow Canyon, Orinda, Round Hill and Sequoyah."

Hal keeps stats on each player's participation and his wins. At the annual finale luncheon, the low point players receive prizes with the lowest scorer receiving a silver tray.

BORN TO FLY

Bill Bailey started flying at age 15. At 16 he had his license. In 1928 at 18 he was flying U.S. mail from Houston to New Orleans in an open cockpit, single engine Pitcairn biplane.

Flying the mail was dangerous business. There were no weather stations, no radio beams, no beacons, no modern flying instruments in the cockpit. Pilots flew blind—strictly by "the seats of their pants," often calling farmers enroute to get weather reports. The pilots were an exclusive clique and believed that what they did was 80% luck and 20% skill.

Of the 40 civilian pilots like Bill who were flying the mail in 1928, 31 were killed before private airlines took over the job. Because flying the mail was so hazardous, pilots earned $800 to $1,000 a month—a lot of money at the time.

After completing an MD degree in obstetrics, Bill and his wife Helen, also a medical doctor, practiced in Houston. He said, "I delivered a bunch of babies. But my heart was in the air." He joined the Army Air Corps in 1940, flying B24s, B17s, B25s—all bombers—and C47 transports. For 28 years he was the Air Force's expert in schooling pilots and he continued to fly until he retired in '63. Bill still is jet qualified. Surely a man born to fly.

Colonel Bill's last base was Oakland and that brought him to the Club, which he and Helen joined in 1973. Bill had known Jack Prescott in the military service. Now Jack was the Club tournament chairman and said to Bill, "Why don't you get a committee together and start a Seniors group for guys 50 or older?" Bill responded, "OK, but I don't want a committee. They just get in your hair. I'll do it myself."

He did and the group grew each year, competing within the Club as well as against other clubs. Hal Saur took over the chair in the middle '80s when Bill's health forced him into a less active role.

But all his life Bill's heart was in the air. He said, "It's good to be around old time flyers. There aren't many of us left. When you're flying you're so free and unfettered. You're on your own, totally responsible and in command."

Lt. Colonel William W. Bailey—pioneer pilot, obstetrician, Air Force training expert, ardent golfer.

Hal Saur, leader of Seniors group, shown above.

It rained!

Dave Staub's sand-blast on #13.

SCOTCH CLUB The first annual Scotch Club Invitational was held on April 25-27, 1994. The idea was borrowed from the San Gabriel Country Club, which celebrated its 69th year of Scotch Club play last year. A field of 64 teams were entered in Diablo's inaugural, many from other clubs. The first day was medal play qualifying for all teams. The 16 lowest net medal scores qualified for the championship flight, held on the second day.

The Board hopes the Scotch Club Invitational will grow in popularity until it becomes a regular tournament equal to the Gold Putter and the Silver Seniors.

A GOLFING LIFE (4)

by Rob Meyers

"A few of us let golf approach the center of our lives, determining our free time, idle reading and shopping desires. But the thought of a life comprised entirely and focused on golf makes the mind reel and thoughts appear like, 'Only in heaven . . .'

"Well, a few minutes with Diablo Country Club head pro Paul Wilcox, Jr. and the envy can rise to titanic proportions.

"'I've got to say it seems like a charmed life,' said Paul. 'I've had ups and down, but I'm grateful to golf for giving me the game to play and the people to meet. I'm really fortunate to know a lot of great people. Golf is a game with ethics and most of its players are nice people. That's what I appreciate most.'

"Paul grew up in the shadow of the Richmond County Club and at an early age became a fixture on the practice greens. 'Back then, everything was big and wonderful. People like Sam Snead, Byron Nelson, Patty Berg, the best of 'em came to play when I was a little kid. I was there when Patty Berg set the course record, I went and got her a new shirt when she ruined one just before that round. I met her years later and reminded her of that. We had a laugh or two. What a great lady.' Paul reminisced.

"At the age of seven local newspapers ran a story comparing his swing to that of golf legend Sam Snead. Even then Paul knew golf was it for him. He started attending junior tournaments, taking lessons and competing in tournaments.

"After college, thinking golf offered no real income potential, he went into lithography, selling scorecards to golf courses. One day he arrived to sell scorecards to the newly opened Franklin Canyon

Golf Course and found his old friend Pat Markovich of the Richmond Country Club. After a few meetings to get him to buy the cards, Pat said he never would buy them but wanted Paul to come to work for him. That was all it took. Hooked for life.

"In 1977, while staying with friends in Pebble Beach, a young Australian golfer appeared looking for some way to get to play the various cathedrals of American golf on the Monterey Peninsula. For two weeks Wilcox golfed with the 'great white shark' Greg Norman at all the great courses.

"On the last day they played the Bayonet Course at Ford Ord. On one of the par 3s they were facing a shot of 210-yards into a strong wind. "It's howling and Greg hits a low 3 iron to 8-feet. I'm feeling weak from the last two weeks and I rip a driver as hard as I can. It sticks two feet from the pin and Norman turns to me and says, 'From now on you're The Dart. Danny the Dart.' It didn't matter that I'm not a Danny, the name has stuck. The phone rings and half the time it's, 'Hey, Dart!'

"As good as golf has been to Paul, it almost took his life. Coming out of a pro shop door in 1960 he was hit by a driver to the side of the head. He took the blow from a full swing and it took hours of surgery to bring him back. 'I'm still a little apprehensive around the pro shop door. I always look,' added Paul.

"Now as he has settled into his work at Diablo, we asked him to outline his goals for the future. 'The senior tour,' he chimed. As if you couldn't guess."

DWGG June 15, 16, 17, 1994, Diablo Women's Golf Group celebrated its 40th birthday with an annual invitational tournament. "Everyone refers to this event as 'The Classic,'" said Jody Dennison, the current captain, "a name that evolved from the unparalleled success of the tournament. It's two and a half days of golf—nine holes the first day and 18 the next two, bringing together 128 players."

Besides DWGG's in-house tournaments scheduled throughout the year—Partner's Match Play, Handicap, Captain's, Club Championship—a major interest of DWGG is to promote golf for women. The group is active in the Women's Golf Association of Northern California and supports its charity *Guide Dogs for the Blind*. Each spring, DWGG sponsors a Guide Dogs for the Blind Tournament for members that typically raises $5,000.

Vi Oakley, a DWGG member since 1959, remembered when the annual invitational was in mid-July. "One of these times—maybe the last July tournament before moving it to June—it was 105

THE VALLEY PIONEER Wednesday, July 16, 1969

Diablo Golf Winners

THE FOUR TOP WINNERS in the annual Diablo Country Club invitational golf tournament are, from left, Mrs. Thomas Osborne of Lafayette, Orinda Country Club; Mrs. William C. Howard of Oakland, Diablo Country Club; Mrs. Irving Seely of Lafayette Diablo Country Club; and Margaret Wall Black of Walnut Creek, Lake Chabot Country Club. The 18-hole, two-day match was shotgun-started both Thursday and Friday. "Diablo County Fair" was this year's theme and participants enjoyed continental breakfasts and picnic lunches both days. There was a dinner Thursday night and a banquet luncheon Friday following the awards presentations. A total of 148 ladies entered, comprising 37 teams of four.

Wednesday
July 16, 1969

'WRANGLERS' WIN INVITATIONAL

The Women's 18-Hole Golf Group of Diablo Country Club held its Annual Invitational on July 10 and 11, using the best first and second ball for scoring, with the third best ball breaking ties.

The foursomes, designated by titles which carried out the group's County Fair theme, posted the following results: The "Thoroughbreds," consisting of Mmes. William Howard, Diablo; Irving Seely, Diablo; Thomas Osborne, Orinda; and Margaret Black, Chabot; came in first with a score of 250.

In second place were the "Wranglers" with a score of 251. This foursome consisted of Mmes. Howard Lamb, Diablo; James Howe, Diablo; Ruth Stefanski, Merced; and H.H. Lockyer, Merced.

The "Pacers", made up of Mmes. Jack Hughes, Diablo; Robert Wolf, Diablo; Howard Crandall, Orinda; and James Boyce, Orinda; took third place honors with a 253.

The quartet of Mmes. Robert Wall, Diablo; Jack Pingree, Diablo; William Conroy, Hacienda; and Wesley Bailey, Round Hill; calling themselves the "Jelly Makers," scored a 255 for fourth place in the tourney.

Mmes. Jack Dana, Diablo; George Shank, Diablo; Roy Moffitt, Round Hill; and Douglas Ramsey, Meadow; playing under the name of "Horse Traders," combined efforts for a 256 and fifth place.

The "Trotters," with a 257, took the sixth spot. The team consisted of Mmes. Tom Elmore, Diablo; David Lamson, Diablo; Robert Steger, Orinda; and J. Kusserow, Pasa Tiempo.

"Natural Golfers"
Snead - age 39,
Wilcox - age 7.

degrees in the shade and players were dropping like flies. I survived, just barely, by keeping wet towels on my head. Didn't look pretty but they kept me in the game." Another memory is sitting around the pool celebrating the end of a successful tournament. "After a few drinks," she said, "people got kittenish and started pushing each other into the tempting cool pool. They tried to throw me in but I was too quick for them."

Lilan "Li" Kane, a member since DWGG's inception in 1954, was playing with Betty Crane and Harriet Bowman when all three of them birded the eighth hole. Miriam Hughes—whose husband Jack was President in 1977—said, "All those years, everything that went on was exciting because it was so new to me." The DWGG remains exciting to this day.

THE HOLYNINERS (5) The group began in 1955 as a subgroup of the DWGG. It was Barbara Kusserow Hall's idea and Marge Dagget was first captain of the 50-member group. They played nine holes and therein follows a partial explanation of their name "'Niners." But what about the word Holy? It's a spin-off of Diablo (Devil) and is represented on the 'Niners logo by a little girl holding a golf club with a halo above her head.

The Holyniners are the only group in the 82-year history of the Club to receive the Helfrich Award. In 1956 they were honored for "assisting in the renovation of the *Men's* locker room" (!!!), hoping thereby to draw attention to the need to restore the *Women's* locker room. Several years later, when the main bar and dining room were closed for refurbishing, the Holyniners had lunch in the self-same Men's locker room. A record crowd of 'Niners was on hand for this event.

The Holyniners held their first invitational in 1958 and the following year, the first member of the current 'Niners joined—Joan Filice.

The September '62 Annual Invitational Tournament hosted six clubs and over 150 golfers. Joanne Loveland and Ginny Rei joined in 1965—both are current 'Niners. A popular event was the Little/Big Sister Tournament. This competition was to help the Holyniners "get the competitive edge." Each was paired with a DWGG golfer who referred to her partner as "my little sister." In the late '60s the practice began of putting players' names in a hat and drawing threesomes as a way to play with different golfers once a month. Later they established that any time one of them chipped into a hole, she won a pair of golf socks. Another novel idea was winning a golf ball whenever a 'Niner finished with fewer than 15 putts.

Vi Oakley's last outing, above.

Audrey Barrie at the Holyniner's Invitational.

Max Gray demonstrates an 80s President's 90s Swing.

Bud is on the right—the golfer everyone wanted to beat, top photo.

Bud is second from left, in lower photo.

Sally Pianalto, Suzanne Fraser and Carol Jones joined in the early '70s—all still players. The Holyniners planted a tree in 1973 in honor of Benjie Hendricks, a long-time Club member and Diablo resident. (Her husband Joe was Club President in 1953.) In 1977 Carol Jones joined Sally Pianalto as co-captain, and Irene Smiley was Secretary and *Inferno* representative. Then the Little/Big Sister Tournament was renamed Devil/Devilette.

In 1980, the 'Niners won the Team Play Competition, which involved besting five other clubs. Later a 'Niner foursome won the Crow Canyon Invitational and repeated the next year. 'Niners and their guests—131 in all—inaugurated the Pink Putter Invitational in 1983. Several years later, Anne Timmermans suggested a Friendship Poster Board—on which each Holyniner who played with someone new entered a mark. At the end of the year, the one playing with the most other 'Niners won the Friendship Prize.

As the '90s opened, Holyniners could be readily identified by their unique uniform—white tops with red shorts, slacks, skirts—and their annual Christmas contribution of over 50 packages of food and toys to the Battered Women's Shelter.

CHAMPION OF CHAMPIONS George F. Shank (Bud) won the Club men's Championship six times: 1954, '56, '58, '64, '68 and '71. He won the U.S. National Seniors Open in 1964 and lost the State Amateur Championship in 1967 to Dick Lotz.

Bud holds Diablo's all-time best golf score, a 62.

Bud and Muir touring China—at the Great Wall—1985.

A SALUTE TO AL McCARRON (6)

by Larry Ives

Al McCarron, a member since 1969, is well known among Diablo's golfing community. He hits the ball straight and long. Al celebrated his eighty-fifth birthday on December 27, 1990.

Strangely enough, Al didn't play golf until he was fifty years old. His early athletic years were taken up by baseball. He pitched for Washington State until his graduation in 1930.

Al comes from a family of golfers including his wife Ruth, three sons, Joe II, Scott, Barry and two grandsons. Joe II is a three handicap. Scott is not handicapped, but showing late interest in golf. Barry and grandsons Scott and Joe are scratch handicaps. Grandson Scott is the Club Champion at both Rancho Murieta and Silverado.

Most golfers in their seventies and older hope to have a lucky day and shoot their age once. Al shoots his so often that he doesn't keep records. He has been known to shoot as many as six under his age, at least once in a tournament. The feat is all the more remarkable when one realizes Al has endured a host of medical problems. When one asks Al McCarron how things are or how do you feel—his most usual answer is, "Everything is just great."

A SALUTE TO DICK GRAHAM (7)

by Larry Ives

Dick started in golf as a 12-year old caddy in Salt Lake City. The Graham family moved to the Bay Area in 1929 and Dick joined the Club in 1961.

Dick was bit by the bug in Salt Lake City and has played golf continuously to this day. He had been known throughout the Bay Area as a fine golfer for more than five decades. He played in the State Amateur twenty times and in many other tournaments such as the San Francisco, Hayward City, Berkeley City, Commuters, Tilden Park, Oak Knoll, and Regional Park Championships. He qualified for the playoffs to the National Seniors Championship at the San Francisco Club in 1979.

Graham recalled a game played against Ken Venturi in Harding Park in the early 1950s. This was

Al who shoots his age every time he shoots his handicap, opposite top.

Dick Graham who won one hell of a lot of tournaments, opposite bottom.

Jim McMurtrey in full swing, below.

Courtesy of Jack Hughes.

the San Francisco Championship and was Venturi's last year as an amateur. Dick stated that "He shot one of his best games ever in the worst conditions he had ever played in—wind and rain—and was still out of the match at the fifteenth hole." Venturi had an eagle, five birdies and two bogies for five under par. Graham did beat Harvie Ward, who was also in the foursome. Heywood, a San Francisco reporter, later wrote that "Graham would have beaten any other player in the tournament in match play."

Graham, who won tournaments at Berkeley City, Commuters Open and Tilden Park, continued his winning ways when he joined Diablo. He won two Club championships, 1962 and 1978, and twice won the President's Cup in 1967 and 1968.

Dick remembered perhaps his career best game shot in December 1975 on the Diablo course. Teamed with Bob Read, and playing against George Padis and Byron Lewis, Dick shot a 63. His round included birdies on holes, 1, 2, 4, 9, 10, 11, 13 and 17. He barely missed a birdie on 18. This is a modern day course record exceeded only by Bud Shank's 62 shot before the sprinkling system was installed.

DIABLO BASKS IN REFLECTED GLORY AS MCMURTREY IS LOW SCORING AMATEUR IN USGA SENIOR OPEN (8)

by Barry Redfearne

Jim McMurtrey, a Club member since 1979, knows the exhilaration of superior performance, of claiming the reward for his best effort. He fired a final round 73 to win the coveted title of "Low Amateur" in the nationally televised U.S.G.A. Senior Open on July 2, 1989 at Laurel Valley Country Club in Ligonier, Pennsylvania.

Jim is the first to acknowledge the keenness of the competition which made his victory all the sweeter. He was exempt from qualifying for the event by virtue of being a semi-finalist in last year's U.S.G.A. Senior Amateur. Of the 150 players who qualified at this year's Senior Open, 54 were exempt and only 5 were amateurs.

McMurtrey, like the rest of us, is spoiled by the Bay Area's moderate clime and found the heat and humidity oppressive so he elected to practice Monday and Tuesday and rest on Wednesday. The tournament started Thursday and for the first two days Jim was paired with Dale Douglass and Miller Barber, both former winners of this event.

Jim remembered standing on the 1st tee that first day of tournament play. "I was a little nervous. Looking down the fairway and seeing crowds on both sides all the way down to the green where spectators were four or five deep is very impressive." Of the four rounds of play, Jim said, "I played great the first day—hit 14 greens but bogied the last hole which is an easy birdie hole, to shoot 73. The next day I played badly but putted great. I was one over through 12 but ran out of gas and shot 77. The third day I shot 77 after being two over through 16 and tripled 17. The final day, all I could think about was shooting near par to beat Fred Boydston, who was four strokes ahead. I shot 73 after hitting 13 greens with one double bogie."

Jim accompanied Pro winner Orville Moody to the winner's circle where he was awarded a gold medal. However, he can't rest on his laurels since he is not exempt from next year's Senior Open unless he makes the top four at the Senior Amateur to be held in September at Lockinvar Country Club in Houston.

JUNIOR GOLF In the long history of the Club, there has always been a special place for youngsters playing golf. Their place is strong and growing in the '90s, thanks to the leadership of coaches Dave White and Bill Mills. Twenty boys, aged 11-19, play 10 matches at home and 10 away with other clubs from San Jose to Santa Rosa. The play is under the auspices of the East Bay League of Junior Golfers. In addition to League play, a Junior Club Championship is held in August. Play is in three formats: scramble (two-man best ball) handicap, and scratch (no handicap) whereby the "true" champion is determined. Parents are invited to play on the championship day and to join the kids' fun at the ice cream social that follows.

Notable Juniors with a bright future are: Tyler and Brett Brown, Jeff Mills, Scott Puccinelli, Lance Silva, Brent Soura, Steve Spangler and Lance Torey. Coaches Dave and Bill are justifiably proud of all 20 of "their boys."

Dave White (right) and Bill Mills (left), coaches.

Eric Nystrom putting for par, above.

Jason Minor, proud owner of a hole-in-one, at right.

Stockton, Ca. *Record*, May 22, 1961.

TO WINNERS, THE SPOILS — The big winners in the Oakmoore Invitational Pro-Amateur tournament flashed winning smiles yesterday along with Stan Moore, sponsor of the tournament and owner of the private course. Members of the winning pro-amateur team, with a 252 two best-ball total for 36 holes, are Howie Williams (left) of Stockton Golf and Country Club, Moore, pro Billy Casper of Apple Valley, Mark Fields of Salinas and Bud Shank of Diablo Country Club. Casper also was the lowest scoring professional. He shot a three-under-par 69 yesterday to post a 140 two-day total for 36 holes.

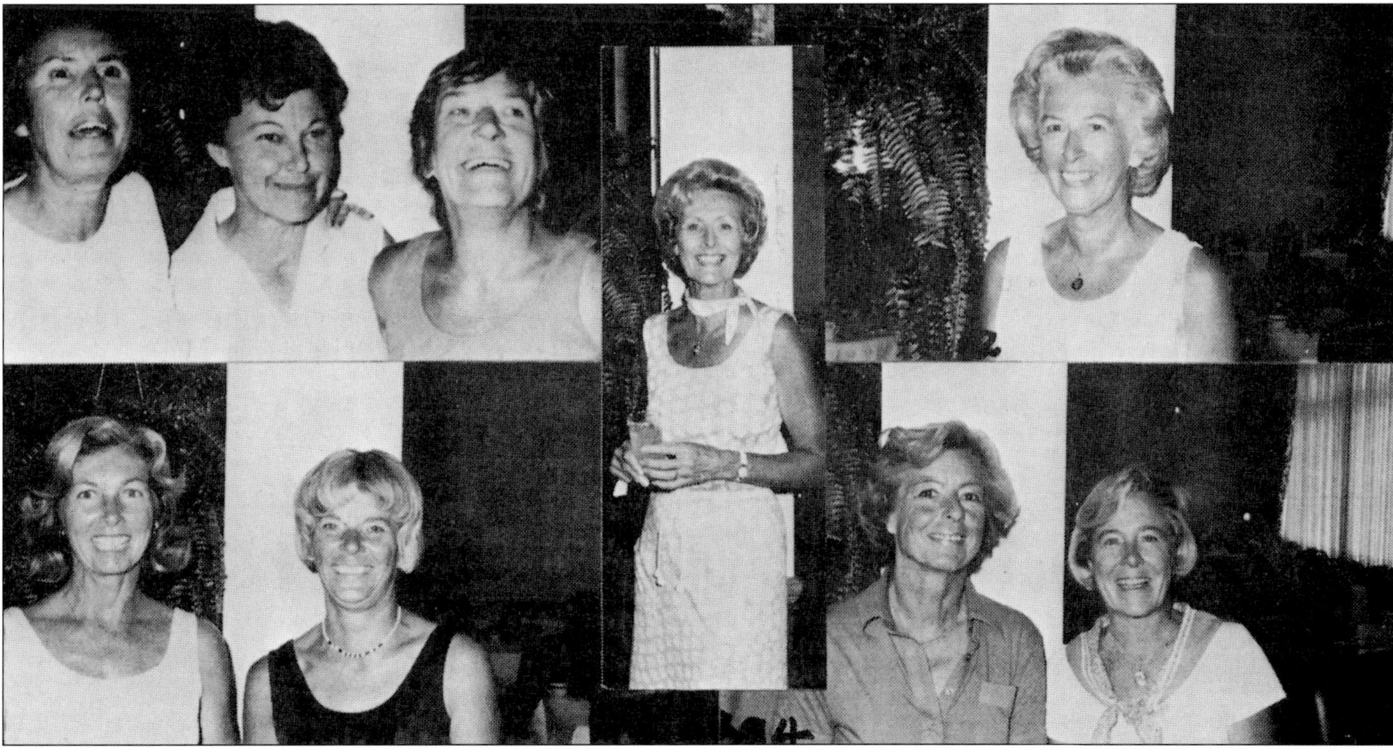

WOMEN'S GOLF INVITATIONAL JULY 7TH-8TH 1977

There is no doubt that the "Happiness is" theme fitted the occasion to a tee. The weather was lovely; the ball rolled on and on and on, making you feel almost like a Pro; the food was in good taste; the selection of rewards was excellent (take a good look at the workwomanship on those tee prizes); and, ultimately, you couldn't have asked for better company. All facets of the tournament, inside and out, ran so smoothly that they belied the fact that so many people worked so hard and skillfully to create that very impression. Well organized, our Invitational was truly a delightful success. Here's **Jean**, Invitational Chairman, and the women in the committees who planned the event: 1. **Ruth Seely, Dolores McCoskey, Vivian Farrell,** Tournament Chairmen, Jean Vendt; 2. **Joan Ullery and Donna Henney** (absent), Decorations; 3. **Gene Snyder, Mary Lynn Peck,** Prizes; 4. **Lee Kane, Jan Samuel,** Invitations.

DIABLO LAKE REVISITED (9) May 23, 1993 was the date, upper Alameda Diablo the place, Diablo's 1st Annual Dads' and Children's Fishing Derby and Fish Fry the occasion, and Byron and Katie Washom the host and hostess, assisted by five-year old Spencer.

This addition to the traditions of Diablo was Byron's brainchild. He commented, "Our moms are always doing things with our kids. It was time dads did something." With the rains this year, that something became obvious; return to the tradition of Diablo Lake as the center of action! Byron filled the now private three-acre lake with 150 pounds of catfish (75 @ two pounds each) plus one five-pounder to be the prize catch of the day.

With 30 dads and 40 plus juniors in the 5-10-year old category invited, careful planning was needed, with an emphasis on safety. Byron sent a letter with detailed instructions:

Item: When you rig your rod or purchase tackle, remember we are fishing for catfish and they are a bottom fish.

Item: Have a one-ounce sinker set at the end of the line and your medium fish hook tied about 18 inches above the sinker.

Item: There will be three varieties of bait—worms, chicken liver and "can't miss" catfish bait.

Item: Unless your child is an experienced caster, I suggest fathers do the shoreline casting since this is when most snagging and tangling occur.

The water was calm and cool, light southwest winds, sun just right—ideal fishing conditions. Dads, some fishing for the first time, and sons and daughers, were casting from the south shore. One reeled in an old glove. The rest, including Steve Headen with David and Travis, plus Tom, Scotty, Andy Suitor, Byron, and Caitlan Cella, paid no attention. They just kept fishing, fishing, fishing.

Fishing boys and fishing girls were not limited to shoreline casting. Six boats were plying the lake. Rob Scharnell with Kirsten and Kendra were in one. Don and Tanis Wallunas and Mark and Alexis Jones in another. Waiting their turn were Bob and Ian Markstein, Jim and Jason Minor, Benny Mills, Cliff Malone and Evan.

Enthusiastically, the boatmen paddled, trolled, and cast. Jeff Haug with Tommy and Charlie operated from a dock on the west bank that could be reached only by boat. They may have had a better location but the fish didn't know it. Even Wes Coy, our Deputy Sheriff, with sons, Nicholas and Adam, couldn't arrest the fish.

Byron and Spencer Washom, above.

Waiting for the fish on shore, inset opposite page.

No catches, no bites, no catfish in sight! It's been speculated that the fish had seen Byron's instructions and were themselves enjoying the revival of Diablo Lake and decided not to put in an appearance—too comfortable, no doubt, in their new home. Jeff Miller remarked to his two boys, Colin and Jordon, "Think how much bigger they'll be next year!"

MEMORIES Many dads like Dave Birka-White, Dan Coleman and Ravi Lai wondered how the lake today compared with yesteryear. Mike Cortese told Jeni, his 12-year old daughter, how the lake looked when he first saw it. "I remember because it was my birthday, August 4 and I was 7," he said. "The lake was larger then than it is now." Harry Baggett, whose daughter, Suzanne, used to swim her horse across it said, "But see how the trees and foliage have grown. There's a lot more than shows in old pictures. In fact, the banks and beaches are so overgrown, the water space appears smaller than it really is."

Byron pointed out the big oak tree near the edge of the water on the east side of the lake where the tire swing used to be. It was marked by a piece of the old rope that somehow remained. In its time, the swing arced to about the middle of the lake. The snack shack used to be nearby. The Washoms had erected their own snack shack—a colorful, portable stall sheltering plates of finger food to keep body and soul together before the celebrated fish fry.

Thus the first of its kind Diablo Fishing Derby and Fish Fry became a barbecue of hamburgers and franks by chefs Pete Burman and son, Kody; Bob Field and son, Blake; John Wilhelmy and sons, Chris, Sean and Patrick. After the barbecue, as in the old days, swimming took over. Colin Miller led the way—jumping into the water with everyone following, including dads.

An old tradition was revived and a 1993 fishing derby for dads and their small fry was established, thanks to Byron and Katie Washom.

GOEF, ANDREW AND KATIE: FISHERMEN ALL! The 2nd Fishing Derby and Fish Fry was even more successful than the opening one. More dads and kids were on hand, and fish were actually caught and fried—a total of 25!

Juanita and Mannie Del Arroz, new neighbors of the Washom's, co-sponsored the event, thus increasing the lake frontage fishing area.

Goef Gonzales caught the first fish after 10 minutes of patient effort. He was quickly followed by Andrew Gardner who caught the second one, and then Katie Mills' patience paid off with a catch of six sunfish! Her older brother Ben brought in three. The bait of choice was night crawlers supplied by the Washoms. Still to be accounted for are the 60 snickering catfish from last year, 15 black bass added this year, and the remaining 375 sunfish from the 400 Byron planted this spring.

As Katie Washom said, "These kids amazed their parents by their interest and patience. Only when the aroma from the barbecue wafted their way did they pull in their lines." The 25 fish were cleaned, fried and served as an hors d'oeuvre by Tom Kurtenbach as the hamburger, hot dog, chicken barbecue got underway on a sunny funfilled Sunday, May 22, 1994 afternoon.

PRESIDENT JOHN DEMGEN'S VISION

"I'm a golfer, Joan's a tennis player and our three kids were swimmers. We arrived in Danville looking for a place that could accommodate our interests. When we saw Diablo twelve years ago, we fell in love with it—a Club that had everything we wanted, plus something special—character, style, grace, beauty. In addition to these qualities, Diablo has a history and a heritage.

"Once we joined, we got to know people and were impressed by the breadth of the membership—the span in ages, ideas, interests, businesses. I thought, "Here's a place where you either sit on the sidelines and "watch the Fords go by" or you get involved and try to make a difference.

"Joan and I decided, "Let's make a difference," so we became active with the swim team and co-chaired the swimming committee one year. Then I chaired the membership committee. At that time we'd average losing two members a month but always had two or more in the wings. I was appointed to the Board of Directors to complete a resigned Director's term. When I began the second year of my second term, I agreed to be President.

"To some, being President now is to do so at the worst time. I disagree. It's a challenge and I thrive on challenges. I see it as a window of opportunity to: plan new strategies; try out innovative ideas; realign resources; strenghten our strengths.

"I challenge the members to be more supportive of the Club and more active in its affairs. Diablo has such great potential and a rich resource in its 600+ members that together we can do anything we want. But first we need to agree on what our priorities are, evaluate them realistically, then organize to get the jobs done. That's why I've set our sights on these goals as our 1994 Priorities:

1994 BOARD PRIORITIES

1. Improve the utilization of the Club.
2. Enhance the quality of our communication between members, employees and Directors.
3. Develop a clear understanding by members of the Club's budget, our financial practices and the opportunities to reduce costs and improve revenue.
4. Increase the demand for new members.

"Driving into Yosemite Valley" Courtesy of *The Green Book of Golf.*

"I like to think my experience in organizing people and solving problems in business is what the Club needs. Being President also allows me to repay the wonderful experiences our family has enjoyed.

"LOOKING AHEAD What will the Club be like in the year 2000? That's a good question because these are demanding, uncertain times. We need to continue to expand the breadth of our membership—golf *and* tennis, for one can't succeed without the other. I see the swim team and other clubhouse programs as the bridges connecting golf and tennis.

"To specifically address the question about the 21st century, the Club will be older, naturally, but more importantly 'people different.' Our Club Historian said it succinctly: 'Now we wake up to the sound of a Japanese clock radio, put on warm-ups made in Korea or Taiwan and see our Club parking lot dominated by German-made Mercedes and BMWs. The communication highway has begun. On TV the news also is reported in Spanish, one-third of California's children are Spanish-speaking, and a quarter or more of our college students are Asians. In our local restaurants we find Sushi bars, Thai cafes, Mandarin take-outs, pizza parlors galore and new burrito cafes. This influx of other cultures is the tip of the iceberg. Club and Community of the 21st century must be prepared to deal with a polyglot of international trends and migration patterns. We of the year 2000 will share a common multicultural mix of people with their varied cultures, languages and traditions. The global village will be at hand.'

"And Diablo will be a better Club if we continue to: maintain, respect and expand our multiple interests; focus on the essentials that make a club a club; make decisions that balance the interest of the many with those of the few; openly communicate through a two-way exchange that respects each member's interests and provides a forum for each member's input.

"We will continue to obtain new members and keep present ones. The surest way to achieve this goal is to have each person feel his/her ideas are valued and keep them in touch with the realities of our joint investment. I think of our 600+ members as consultants who provide input, who understand our problems, the why of our decisions, who are a cohesive force that gives Diablo its reason for being.

"We have a new clubhouse, golf course, and tennis courts—all sustained by an 82-year heritage. Our legacy has survived bankruptcies, two world wars, the great depression, inflation and recessions.

"I know of no club that has the assets Diablo possesses. I'm optimistic about the year 2000. With our talented members and employees we can achieve whatever we set our minds and hearts to doing."

AFTERWORD

Readers may not be aware of our efforts to corroborate people's recollections and reflections as described and interpreted in *Diablo's Legacy*. We have relied on Denzin's[1] concept of triangulation in order to ascertain what is real (factual) from the imagined and partially or faultily recalled. Denzin says a primary tactic for verifying information is to have multiple sources of data (informants, records, pictures), and several methods of data collection (observations, interviews, informal conversations).

The data reported in these 12 chapters have been verified by at least three persons, three documents, or in combination. In two instances what we were told did not meet the triangulation test and has been so noted in the text.

In these ways, this historical account of Club and Community has sought to meet the researcher's time-honored criteria of credibility (validity) and dependability (reliability).

Historians grapple with the question: does man make history or does history make man? *Diablo's Legacy* argues that man makes history.

The perspectives, observations, experiences and recollections reported are testimony of the struggle of a social institution—the Diablo Country Club—to survive through wars, bankruptcies, depression, recessions and inflation. In this sense, it is the story of every social institution. Likewise, the history of the Community—its struggle to be and to have a voice of its own—is the story of every community.

What one learns from these pages are lessons from the past that are applicable to the present and future.

FOOTNOTES

Sheriff Coy's sons, Nick and Adam, above.

Jonathan Del Arroz.

CHAPTER I PRELUDE TO DEVELOPMENT

(1) Eddy, E.D. (1931). *An Appreciation of Mt. Diablo Country Club*. Goodhue-Kitchener.

(2) *Contra Costa Chronicle*, Leonora Fink, "Mt. Diablo Mountain House," February, 1967.

(3) Nancie Burgess Shaw, "Pre-War Developments," December, 1940, unpublished manuscript.

(4) Robert O'Brien (1948). *This Is San Francisco*. N.Y.: McGraw-Hill.

(5) Colton did the count-down in the fatal duel between U.S. Senator David Broderick and California Supreme Court Chief Justice David Terry. The ill-fated duel that ended Broderick's life took place on the sand dunes of S.F. bay on a gray dawn of September, 1859. This account is taken from Bill Grandy (1965). *History of Diablo Country Club* . Private publishing.

(6) Bill Grandy (1965). *History of Diablo Country Club*. Private publishing.

(7) *Contra Costa Gazette*, undated, 1880.

(8) George C. Collier (December 17, 1976). *Diablo Country Club*. Unpublished manuscript.

(9) *Inferno*, December, 1958.

(10) George C. Collier (December 17, 1976). *Diablo Country Club*. Unpublished manuscript.

(11) *Contra Costa News*, Special Edition, July 1, 1897.

CHAPTER II WWI—FORE & AFT

(1) Prohibition lasted 14 years—January 16, 1920 to December 5, 1933.

(2) Blackmur, Arnold (1981). *In Old Diablo*. Redwood City, Ca.: Ampex.

(3) In *Memoirs* Burgess gives the date of 1913, but that is incorrect in view of subsequent events. Nancie Burgess Shaw said on many occasions, "The book is full of errors." This date is one of them.

(4) The Olympic Club of San Francisco also was interested in buying the Oakwood Farm as a summer club and a group from the Olympic Club visited the area. *Blackmur*, page 9.

(5) Eddy, E.D. (1931). *An Appreciation of Mt. Diablo Country Club.* Goodhue-Kitchener. Page 3, places the opening of the Club as 1916, but supplies no supporting references. The Club was not incorporated until 1919. Articles of Incorporation, #1482, December 3, 1919, *Archives,* C.C. Co.

(6) George C. Collier (December 17, 1976). *Diablo Country Club.* Unpublished manuscript. Collier also states that technically, the Oakwood Farm was purchased by Burgess' Mt. Diablo Park Company. Once organized, commission quickly followed. See Articles of Incorporation #931. April 19, 1912, *Archives,* C.C. Co. The earliest reference to the Club was "Mt. Diablo Park Club," the year of founding, 1912.

(7) Blackmur, Arnold (1981). *In Old Diablo.* Redwood City, Ca.: Ampex.

(8) The Farmhouse became the Inn during the 1912-19 period because that was Burgess' plan. There were ten bedrooms on the second floor which were rented to travelers and visitors, as well as Club members. From 1920-48, the Inn was the clubhouse.

(9) *San Ramon Valley Times,* "25 Years Ago." *Valley Pioneer,* August 24, 1966.

(10) Blackmur, page 24.

(11) George C. Collier (December 17, 1976) *Diablo Country Club* (unpublished manuscript)

CHAPTER III THE ROARING '20S

(1) These 160 acres are mentioned often when property surrounding the Club is discussed. It is the hilly land serviced by the extension of Alameda Diablo in the '70s. Diablo Lake was a part of the 160. The dedicated horse trail through Diablo to the trail maintained by the State Park goes through the 160. Another way to place it is to "Stand on the 15th green, look up to the top of Mt. Diablo, the 160 acres would be approximately in the middle of this line." (*Inferno,* May, 1956)

(2) "In 1925, the prizes consisted of 100 live bunnies." (*Oakland Tribune,* April, 1969) Benji Hendricks said, "We're not allowed to have bunnies anymore. One year it rained and they moved the hunt and the rabbits into the dining room at the Club, and that was the end."

(3) In 1979, Bill Rei acquired the Club's insurance contract and he asked Cecil to take him on an inspection of the property. Rei remarked, "When we got into the Chalet basement I was flabbergasted. There was this enormous steam furnace for such a small building and it had more pipes and valves than a submarine. Fortunately, Cecil knew the thing inside out."

(4) In Blackmur's (1981) *In Old Diablo* and Tatum's (1993) *Old Times of Contra Costa, Clubhouse* is used for what is referred to in this book as the *Casino* or *Recreation Hall* (more properly the *Men's Casino*). Our designation Clubhouse for the former Oakwood farmhouse is based on numerous interviews with those who lived in Diablo or worked at the Club during the '20s, '30s, '40s. The confusion stems from Robert Burgess himself who refers to the Oakwood farmhouse as the Inn in his *Memoirs.* See also the map on page 9. Shortly after Burgess left Diablo in 1919, the farm-

Pete & Vanessa Lunardi, top.

Emily, John & Liz Holt, Mike Miller & Brittany

Erin Parker.

Blake & dad Bobby Field, left.

house ceased to be the Inn and became the Clubhouse. It remained so for 28 years until Larry Curtola remodeled it as his home in 1948. He then built a large addition to the Men's Casino and renamed it the Clubhouse.

In Bill Grandy's *History of Diablo Country Club,* there is a picture on the cover showing the Casino. He says, "Picture of Casino which was the Diablo Country Club in 1918-19." This is added confirmation of what others interviewed have said: the Casino was the Clubhouse at the very beginning but the Inn (Oakwood farmhouse) became the Clubhouse from the '20s through 1948 when the Club was purchased by Curtola.

(5) The Caldecott tunnel opened in 1937, named for its chief engineer and was built by forming a special district.

(6) The Oakland Antioch line was one of the most attractive railroads of the time. Each car had its own distinctive features. All had lots of stained glass with clerestory windows.

(7) Henry Roberts (1923). *The Green Book of Golf.* San Francisco: Private Printing. John Poulos, a club member since 1978, lent Larry Ives this book, which had been willed to John by his father-in-law. It is a treasure of golf memorabilia.

CHAPTER IV THE DEPRESSION '30S

(1) National Recovery Administration, Public Works Admin., Works Progress Admin., National Youth Admin., Federal Housing Admin., Home Owners Loan Coporation.

(2) Leigh joined the Club in 1968 and moved into the Halls' summer home at 1778 Club House Road. In 1976 he moved to 28 Campo Pelota next to Marshall and Margaret, who bought their home at 36 Campo Pelota and joined the Club in 1966.

(3) Sessions S. Wheeler and William W. Bliss (1992). *Tahoe Heritage,* Reno: University of Nevada.

(4) Semmes Gordon put the author in touch with Carrol Wilson, a most remarkable man. He has worked at Hills Brothers for 70 years and still works two days a week. In our conversation he recalled all those Diablo events everyone else remembered—Easter bunnies, Fouth of July fireworks, and swim meets, plus the Lake, the golf course, water problems, *et al.*

(5) George Thebolt is the father of JoAnn Berridge, a UC Berkeley doctoral candidate enrolled in the author's *Qualitative Research and Evaluation* class, Spring semester, 1994.

(6) *1935 Annual Report to Members of the Claremont Country Club* by V.S. Hardy, President, "The Directors have not reached a conclusion as to the purchase of the Mt. Diablo Country Club properties . . ."

(7) George Hall lent the author his father's *Book of Bylaws* and *Minutes of Diablo Properties, Inc., Stock Certificate Register,* and *Book of Correspondence, 1939-1943.* The author is also indebted to Elijah Poxson for a legal and financial analysis of these papers and to Steve Jones, who "found" George Hall in the first place.

(8) Articles of Incorporation, #5839, January 29, 1937, *Archives,* C.C. Co.

(9) George C. Collier (December 17, 1976). *Diablo Country Club.* Unpublished manuscript.

CHAPTER V THE WAR-TORN '40S

(1) Seabees stands for Navy Construction Batallions: *C* = sea, *B* = bees.

(2) Rose couldn't remember the other names, now two with Teller eliminated. Bill Harford, long-time business manager of the Lawrence Livermore Lab, is sure the group was Berkeley faculty.

Henry McDonald, long-time Lawrence Livermore Lab Electronics Engineering expert, proved to be the most knowledgeable person about the personnel most likely to be at this luncheon meeting. Given the time frame, late '41 to early '42 when the decision to go ahead with the bomb already had been made, he believed the next question had to be how to use the calutron technology to enrich the uranium. The experts on that were Oppenheimer, Lawrence, Alvarez, and McMillan—all of U.C. Berkeley.

(3) Lucky Strikes were the most popular brand of cigarettes and were packaged in green. The manufacturer decided to change the package to white and advertised, "Lucky Strike Green has gone to war."

(4) Paul Fussell (1989). *Wartime.* Oxford: Oxford University Press.

(5) *Ibid*

(6) Kamikaze means "God wind."

(7) The officers were Dr. Bud Scroins (Indiana), Dr. John Carmody (Worchester), Harold Moon and Vern Scarbough both of Charlotte, and John Tierney.

(8) Winn Haagensen lead me to Lois Lippincott.

(9) These incidents coincide with the history of Camps Parks and Shoemaker in Pleasanton. After Camp Parks was commissioned on January 19, 1943 (construction had begun in November, '42 and completed the following April), it was the largest Navy Seabee station. Technically known as a "replacement depot," its mission was to provide "rest and recuperation after the arduous ordeals of Seabees' work in war zones." It was disestablished January 1, 1946. Five years later, it became Parks Air Force Base, and in 1959, Army.

The Seabees' R and R Base (Parks) was adjacent to Camp Shoemaker and an integral part of it. Shoemaker was the Navy's Training and Distribution Center, meaning point of embarcation for sea duty. Later it became a separation center. Shoemaker had a large Naval Hospital, completed in 1944. The camp was disestablished January 1, 1946.

From the March 15, 1943, minutes, Board of Directors, Diablo Properties, Inc.: "110 members of Diablo Country Club have indicated a willingness to pay $5 a month each as a standby charge for the maintenance of the Club for the duration of the war, the Club, however, to be closed during that period. The revenue from this source, supplemented *by the rental for the Chalet now being received from Navy and civilian personnel connected with the Camp now being constructed near Livermore, (Shoemaker and Parks) would be sufficient to permit the Club to operate on a break-even basis . . .*" According to military tradition, it was the perogative of local commanders to make arrangements to billet their personnel at nearby establishments and agencies when the base had no quarters or the available quarters were inade-

Sarah, Mike & John Cortese, top.

Zach Cadet with Ian & Bob Markstein.

quate. From this and Hall's minutes, it is clear the Navy used the Club during WWII, and in that sense "took it over" during the '42-'44 period.

The Walnut Kernel, "25th" Anniversary Historical Progress Edition stated, "Gas rationing and other World War II emerging curtailments gradually brought the activities of the Mt. Diablo Country Club to a halt. The U.S. Navy occupied the club facilities for government use from 1942-44."

In a letter dated January 14, 1994, Charles L. Morey III wrote, "My father Charles L. Morey, Jr. did indeed grow up in Diablo and lived there during the war in the family home (2139 Alameda Diablo). He was a Lt. Commander in the Supply Corps." In a follow-up telephone conversation, he said, "The Diablo Navy man I recall Dad talking most about was Al Layton."

John Wright with Sam & Casey.

(10) Blackmur relates this same incident from an interview with Joe Ferreira

(11) Minutes of Directors' meeting, April 29, 1948, signed jointly by Herbert E. Hall, Secretary, and Joseph L. Alioto, Secretary. From Herb Halls *Book of Minutes*.

(12) *Ibid*, April 21, 1943.

CHAPTER VI THE NIFTY '50S

(1) *Inferno*, January, 1957.

(2) *Ibid*, January, 1957.

(3) *Ibid*, November, 1957.

(4) *Ibid*, March, 1958.

(5) *Ibid*, December, 1959.

(6) *Ibid*, November, 1959.

(7) *Ibid*, December, 1959.

(8) *Ibid*, April, 1956.

(9) *Ibid*, December, 1955.

(10) *Ibid*, October, 1955.

(11) *Ibid*, January, 1957.

(12) *Ibid*, April, 1956.

(13) *Ibid*, May, 1956.

CHAPTER VII THE STRIDENT '60S

(1) *Inferno*, May, 1960.

(2) *Ibid*, March, 1961.

(3) The intent was to purchase a part of the Rei property on Club House Road that adjoins the Club parking lot. But despite numerous attempts, no deal was ever agreed to.

(4) *Inferno*, June, 1965.

(5) *Ibid*, June, 1960.

(6) *Ibid*, October, 1968.

(7) *Ibid*, 'September, 1964

CHAPTER VIII THE INFLATED '70S

(1) SLA stands for Symbionese Liberation Army, a leftist radical group. With them Patti took the name "Tonya." The SLA was responsible for the assassination of Marcus Foster, Oakland's first African-American Superintendent of Schools.

Monte Hall, a Diablo member, then a special agent with the FBI, was assigned the case. His partner arrested Patti and Monte arrested the Harris duo.

(2) Minutes, Board of Directors, April, 1977.

(3) List of Helfrich Winners is in the Appendix.

(4) *Inferno*, June, 1976.

(5) As the decade of the '70s closed, interest in tennis gradually declined; both nationally and at Diablo.

(6) *Inferno*, September, 1993.

(7) On August 8, 1993, Mugs wrote: "Jim—Marsh is a little concerned that you are overstating his role because for so many years Bob Tiernan was Mr. Tennis as far as we were concerned."

(8) *Inferno*, December, 1990.

(9) *Ibid*, October, 1990.

(10) *Ibid*, June, 1990.

CHAPTER IX THE ENTERPRISING '80S

(1) April 2, 1985, memo to members, "What to do about Diablo Clubhouse" from 18 "Members Organizing this Letter." It is signed by 289 "Members Supporting this Position."

CHAPTER X TWENTY FROM THE '20S

(1) The selection of the "20" homes was made on the basis of particularly interesting architectural or landscaping style, prominence of owners, location of the property, or stories told about the residence. The numerically-conscious reader realizes the number of homes has been stretched to 22 and that nine actually were built prior to the '20s. Initially we were going to exclude the Field (Burgess) and Minor (Inn) houses since they were featured elsewhere in the book. But they are well worth a closer look.

Katie with her first of six catches, and her dad Sam Mills & Ben, top.

Charlie, Jeff, & Tommy Haug.

Paul & Mary Ngs and nephew Douglas Mui.

CHAPTER XII EPILOGUE: THE '90S

(1) The tennis courts are blessed with Sherry Endicott who was appointed tennis pro in 1989.

(2) Henry Roberts (1923). *The Green Book of Golf.* San Francisco: Private Printing.

(3) *Inferno,* October, 1993.

(4) *The Tee Times,* Vol. 1, Number 2, (October, 1993).

(5) Sherry Smith, Holyniner *Inferno* correspondent did the research for this summation.

(6) *Inferno,* February, 1991.

(7) *Ibid,* April, 1991.

(8) *Ibid,* August, 1989.

(9) *Ibid,* July, 1993.

AFTERWORD

(1) Norman K. Denzin (1978). "Strategies of Multiple Triangulation," *The Research Act: A Theoretical Introduction to Sociological Methods.* New York: McGraw-Hill.

Blackmur, Arnold (1981). *In Old Diablo.* Redwood City, Ca.: Ampex.

Burgess, Robert Noble (1964). *Memoirs.* Santa Barbara, Ca.: Private Printing.

Collier, George. C. (December 17, 1976). *Diablo Country Club.* Unpublished manuscript.

Eddy, E.D. (1931). *An Appreciation of Mt. Diablo Country Club.* Goodhue-Kitchener.

Fuller, Barbara (1992). *Sharing a Vision: The History of the Orinda Country Club.* McNaughton and Gunn.

Fussell, Paul (1989). *Wartime.* New York: Oxford.

Grandy, Bill (Nov., 1968) *History of Diablo Country Club.* Publisher unknown. Presented to members at Anniversary Party.

Green, Bernard (1982). *The Timetables of History.* New York: Simon/Schuster.

Jones, Vergie V. (1987). *Historical Persons and Places . . . in San Ramon Valley.* Alamo, Ca.: Morris Burt.

Roberts, Henry (1923). *The Green Book of Golf.* San Francisco: Private Printing.

Sorrick, Muir (1970). *The History of Orinda: Gateway to Contra Costa County.* San Francisco: Lawton and Kennedy.

Stone, James C. and DeNivi, Donald P. (1971) *Portraits of the American University.* San Francisco: Jossey-Bass.

Tatum, Robert (1993). *Old Time in Contra Costa.* Pittsburg, Ca.: Highland.

APPENDIX

APPENDIX A—CLUB PRESIDENTS

1912-19	R N Burgess, Founder
1923	George W. McNear
1937-41	Herbert E. Hall
1936, 42	V. E. Breeden
1948	Laurence Curtola
1949	Herbert E. Hall
1950	R. D. Fish
1951, 52, 57	W. K. Van Bokkelen
1953	Joe Hendricks
1954	Lester Foley
1955	Allan Hart
1956	Jack Herzig
1958	Bailey Justice
1959	DeWitt Krueger
1960	John Enright
1961, 62, 79, 80	William Houston, Sr.
1963	Louis Schrepel
1964	Robert Foley
1965	Hal Morgan
1966	Jack Pingree
1967	J. G. Knowlton
1968	Arthur Brunckhorst
1969	William Shipley
1970	Rett Turner
1971-72	Spencer Archer
1973	Henry Steinbach
1974	Frank Schmitt
1975	George Padis
1976	Clifford Gant
1977	Fred Bennett, Jack Hughes
1978	James Hague
1981	Jim McEuen
1982	David Cox
1983	Max Gray
1984-86	Lynn McCoskey
1987	Neils Lawson
1987-88	Michael Stead
1989	Charles Henry
1990-91	David Cox
1991	William Houston, Jr.
1993	John McGlynn
1994	John Demgen

APPENDIX B—DIABLO POSTMASTERS

1916-18	John N. Curtis
1918-40	Edwin Lee Cooper
1940-55	Helen A. Cooper
1955-69	Ethyl M. Stott
1969-82	Bettye B. Johanson
1983-85	Ron Elizondo
1985-93	Mary Lou Hodgson
1993-	Cathy Cantu-Ott

Cliff & Evan Malone.

Geof & Tim Gonzalez — The first catch of the day, top.

Andrew — who caught the 2nd fish with Graham & daddy Paul Gardner.

APPENDIX C—PRESIDENTS OF THE DIABLO PROPERTY OWNERS ASSOCIATION SINCE 1965

1966	Edward La Cava	1979	Robert Schepman
1967	Robert Tiernan	1980	Joseph Hohenrieder
1968	Lloyd Ives	1981	Henry Timmermans
1969	Joseph Kriz	1982	Thomas Pelandini
1970	Richard Johnson	1983	Jerry Chaine
1971	Marshall Freeman	1984	Donald Thiele
1972	Stephen Jones	1985-86	Duane Papierniak
1973	William Daegling	1987-88	Roger Wilkie
1974	Carol Sconyers	1989-90	Jeffrey Eorio
1975	Gary Elgaaen and	1991	Ravi Lai
	Dolph Senasac	1992	Jeffrey Haug
1976	Donald Hoffman	1993	Amara Koss
1977	Donald Johnson	1994	Robert Nilssen
1978	Arnold Blackmur		

APPENDIX D—PRESIDENTS OF THE DIABLO COMMUNITY SERVICE DISTRICT

1968-74	William Cronin
1974-76	Paul Cortese
1976-78	John Olander
1978-80	James Stone
1980-82	Lloyd Ives
1982-84	Stephen Jones
1984-87	John Oliver
1987-88	Thomas Pelandini
1989-90	David Kipp
1990-93	Thomas Pelandini
1993-	Richard Swanson

Legal Advisor: Richard Breitwieser, 1968-
General Manager: Lloyd Ives, 1969-71;
Richard Breitwieser, 1972-

APPENDIX E — CITIZEN OF THE YEAR AWARD WINNERS GIVEN BY THE DIABLO PROPERTY OWNERS ASSOCIATION

1971	Lloyd Ives
1972	John Imrie
1973	Robert Tiernan
1974	Robert Wall
1975	Paul Cortese
1976	Stephen Jones
1977	John Olander
1978	Barbara Hale
1979	William Hale
1980	Philip Hammond
1981	Arnold Blackmur
	Theodore Petersen
1982	James C. Stone
1983	Penny McFarland
1984	Robert Miller
1985	Kim Gilman
1986	Mary Lahti
1987	Marilee Headen
	John Oliver
1988	Deni Oliver
1989	Bill McFarland
1990	Nancy Rubey
1991	Cliff Malone
	Byron Washom
1992	Jocelyn Comegys
1993	Jeffrey K. Haug

APPENDIX F — HELFRICH AWARD WINNERS

"To the member who has given unselfishly to make Diablo a better place to have fun."

1955	Bailey Justice
1956	Marge Daggett
1957	Lucille Armstrong
1959	Joe and Benji Hendricks
1960	DeWitt Krueger
1961	Buzz Knowlton
1962	W.K. Houston
1965	Spencer Archer
1966	Carl Vendt
1967	Leo Calestini
1968	Robert Foley
1969	Bill Owsley
1970	Lloyd Rossi
1971	Bill Cronin
1972	Bob and Lila Hart
1973	Henry Steinbach
1974	Bob Wall and John Price
1975	Frank Schmitt
1979	Phil Hammond
1980	Jim McEuen
1981	Larry Curtola
1982	Rudy Fruscella
1983	Vincent Smith
1984	Ann and Bob Jones
1985	Monna Olson and Audrey Barrie
1986	Hildegard Frederick
1987	Frank Clapp
1988	Ginger Miller
1989	Dan McDonnell
1991	Ed Henney
1992	Dave White
1993	Russ Blomberg

The days total catch of 25.

APPENDIX G—INFERNO EDITORS

1955-57	Bill Helfrich
1958	Walt Mallally and Bob Barry
1959-67	Spence Archer
1968-73	Millie Knowlton
1973-74	Peggy Baender and Adeline (Ad) Schmitt
1974-77	Peggy Baender and Monna Olson
1978-84	Monna Olson and Dolores McCoskey
1984-87	Mona Olson and Audrey Barrie
1987-88	Audrey Barrie, Emily Pitcher, Anne Timmermans, Barry Redfearne
1988-91	Audrey Barrie, Larry Ives, Anne Timmermans
1991-92	Roseanne Ogles, Larry Ives, Jan McGlynn
1993-94	Carol Jones and Mary Lou McDonnel

Pete & Cody Burman.

APPENDIX H—DEVIL'S ADVOCATE EDITORS

1979-81	Tom Pelandini
1982-86	Roberta Seabury
1987	Nanci Hirsch
1988	Jean Blackmur and Sue Guinivere
1989	Jean Blackmur, Sue Guinivere, Elizabeth Birka-White
1990-	Elizabeth Birka-White

APPENDIX I—GOLF PROS

William Hackney
Jim Smith
Jock Whitney
Arthur Winting
Pat Patton
Johnny Juris
Norm Tauscher
Ron Patton
Lyle Wehrman
George Winn
John Madonna
Bob Wynn
Paul Wilcox

APPENDIX J—TENNIS PROS

1961-79	Dick Overstreet	1988-89	Brad Reiser
1980-87	Jon Toney	1989-	Sherry Endicott

APPENDIX K—SAN RAMON VALLEY AREA PLANNING COMMISSION APPOINTEES FROM DIABLO

1979-81	John Olander
1982-87	Jim Stone
1987-89	Marshall Freeman

APPENDIX L—SAN RAMON VALLEY FIRE PROTECTION DISTRICT DIRECTORS FROM DIABLO

1984-	Tom Seabury

APPENDIX M—GOLF RECORDS

1962	Bud Shank—All time best men's golf score—62.
1963	Dick Graham—Modern men's golf record—63.
1974	Tom Edwards—Golf Champion and Tennis Champion (men's) in the same year.

APPENDIX N—MEN'S GOLF TOURNAMENTS

March	Scramble	July	The Grinder
April	4-Man Team Championship	Aug	Scramble
April	Scotch Tournament	Aug	Special Event
April	President's Cup	Sept	Gold Putter
May	Oldsmobile Scramble	Sept	Club Championship
June	YMCA Pro-Am	Oct	Director's Cup
June	Silver Seniors	Oct	Rigney Invitational
July	2-Man Championship	Nov	Scramble

Hilda San Juan, Katie Washom, Pat Joseph holding in his arms Patrick Joseph, top.

Thomas, Erin & Tom Parker, below.

Grandpa Dud Fabrique and Jonathan Wallunas.

1994 MIXED TOURNAMENTS

March	Mystery Mixer	July	Mixed Invitational
April	Guide Dogs	Oct	Mr. & Mrs. Championship
July	Flag Day	Nov	Turkey Shoot

OUTSIDE GOLF TOURNAMENTS

May	Crondolet	Sept	St. Isidore's
June	Junior Achievement	Sept	Children's Hospital
June	Summitt Medical	Oct	De La Salle
June	Danville Rotary		

HOLYSMOKER

May, July, Sept

EAST BAY GOLF LEAGUE

March	At Sequoyah	June	At Discovery Bay
March	At Castlewood	June	Castlewood
April	Sequoyah	July	Contra Costa
April	At Richmond	July	At Crow Canyon
May	Round Hill	Aug	At Round Hill
May	At Contra Costa	Aug	Discovery Bay
May	Richmond	Aug	Crow Canyon

SENIOR SCHEDULE

March	Senior Warm-up	July	Summer Shoot-Out
April	Claremont	Aug	Sequoyah
April	Orinda	Aug	Claremont
May	Crow Canyon	Sept	Round Hill
June	Crow Canyon	Oct	Sequoyah
June	Round Hill	Oct	Senior Finale
July	Orinda		

APPENDIX O

DIABLO WOMEN'S GOLF GROUP

March	Mystery Tournament
April	Guide Dogs Tournament
May	Spring Handicap
June	Invitational Wednesday - Practice Round/Dinner
June	Diablo Classic
July	Captain's Tournament
Aug	WGANC Open Day
Sept	Championship Tournament
Oct	Halloween Tournament with Holyniners
Nov	Turkey Shoot

HOLYNINERS

March	New Member/Old Member Tournament
April	Match Play
May	Special Tournament
May	Holy Smoker
July	Diablo Invitational
July	Holy Smoker
Aug	Championship Tournament
Sept	Holy Smoker - Guest Event
Oct	Halloween Tournament with DWGG

Kirk & Kylie Duthie, Caitlin & Brian Cella.

Tom Kurtenbach who cleaned and cooked the 25.

Diablo's popular '90s Tennis Pro, Sherry Endicott.

APPENDIX P— SHERRY ENDICOTT'S TENNIS PROGRAM

MEN'S

1. Century Cup Tournament
2. Doubles Championship
3. Silver Racquet
4. Singles Championship
5. Gentlemen's Cup League

WOMEN'S

1. Luncheon & Tennis
2. Sherry's Camp
3. Singles Championship
4. Ladies' Invitational
5. Ladies' Awards Luncheon
6. Leagues
   5 teams in Spring League
   1 Bay Area Ladies' League
   3 USTA Teams
   5 Fall League Teams
   1 Summer League Team
7. Doubles Ladder
8. Doubles Circuit
9. Singles Mania

MIXED

1. Valentine Tournament
2. Kick Off Cocktails
3. St. Patrick Tournament
4. John Newcomb Clinic
5. Cocktails Jr. Summer Sign-up
6. Cinco Tournament
7. Mixed Golf/Tennis Tournament
8. Celebration Dance
9. Turkey Tournament
10. Mixed USTA League

JUNIORS

1. John Newcomb Tournament
2. Jr. Summer Leagues
3. Jr. Championships
4. Jr. Award Banquet

INDEX

Abbotts, The, 169
Abbott, Cynthia, 74
Abbott, Myra Mae, 74
Abbott, Sam, 29, 81, 169
Abbott, Suzette, 74
Abbott, Samuel, 164
Ahoe, Harry, 88
Alamassy, John, 96
Alexanderson, Phylis, 148
Alioto, Joseph L., 69
Alioto, Michele, 165
Aliotos, The, 165
Andersen, Craig, 196
Anderson, Don, 73
Andrews, Bob, 102
Andrews, Emily, 102
Anzio, 67
Applegarth, George A., 162
Archer, Spence, 111, 117, 128, 196, 223
Archer, Spencer, 80, 119, 220, 222
Armstrong, Lou, 81, 108–109, 143
Armstrong, Lucille, 109, 175, 222
Armstrong, Robert, 80
Arroz, Jonathan Del, 213
Arroz, Mannie Del, 209
Ault, Major, 67
Baender, Peggy, 117, 191, 223
Baggett, Bill, 102
Baggett, Harry, 209
Baggett, Sue, 120
Bailey, Bill, 87, 197–198
Bailey, Wesley, 201
Baker, Floyd, 98
Baldwin, John, 177
Baldwin, Suzy, 161
Ballard, Rig, 80
Barber, Jerry, 119
Barber, Miller, 205
Barone, John, 80, 84
Barrie, Audrey, 117, 151, 202, 222–223
Barrie, Don, 142
Barrons, Monique, 98
Barry, Bob, 117, 223
Bartell, Dick, 79
Bates, Nancy Witter, 44
Batts, Kay, 20
Beardslee, Jenifer, 156
Bedsworth, Jay, 110
Bell, Bee, 64–65
Bennett, Fred, 116, 130, 144, 220
Benton, Arthur, 143
Berg, Patty, 199
Berryhill, Jim, 81
Birka-White, Dave, 209
Birka-White, Elizabeth, 161, 223
Black, Margaret, 200–201
Blackmur, Arnold, 132, 184–185, 221–222
Blackmur, Jean, 223
Blemer, John, 65, 76, 79
Bliss, Bill, 39, 42
Bliss, Helen, 66
Blomberg, Russ, 222
Blumhardt, Mark, 120
Bowman, Harriet, 202
Bowman, Reg, 80
Boyce, James, 201
Boyd, John, 5, 9
Boyd, Louis, 173
Boydston, Fred, 206
Boynton, Claude, 54
Bray, Frank, 176–177
Bredehoft, Ron, 196
Breeden, Jim, 67
Breeden, V. E., 45, 47, 68, 220
Breitwieser, Gail, 76
Breitwieser, Richard, 176–177, 179, 185, 221
Brown, Brett, 206
Brunckhorst, Arthur, 80, 220
Bull, E. B., 11
Bull, Edwin, 167
Burgess, Edward, 6, 19
Burgess, Elizabeth Ann, 6, 19
Burgess, Reverend Joshua, 6
Burgess, RN, 5–6, 8, 10, 14, 19–20, 141, 157, 167, 176, 220
Burman, Cody, 223
Burman, Pete, 209, 223
Butler, Colonel, 190
Cadet, Zach, 216
Calestini, Leo, 222
Cameron, William, 4
Cantu-Ott, Cathy, 188, 220
Carlyle, Henry, 45
Carlyles, The, 171
Casper, Billy, 207
Cella, Brian, 226
Cella, Caitlan, 208, 226
Chaine, Jerry, 221
Chandler, Mathew, 136
Chandler, Matt, 142
Chaplin, Charley, 29
Chavez, Diana, 188, 190
Church, Thomas, 162
Clapp, Frank, 222
Clarks, The, 95
Coleman, Dan, 209
Collins, Robert, 80
Colton, David, 4
Comegys, Jocelyn, 222
Conklin, Vern, 41
Connell, John, 196
Connors, Ed, 81
Conroy, William, 201
Cook, Dan, 5, 8, 168, 173
Cook, Seth, 5, 8, 11, 173, 187
Cooper, E. L., 11, 32
Cooper, Edwin, 186, 220
Cooper, Helen A., 220
Corcoran, Erin, 98
Corcoran, Tim, 120
Corcoran, Tom, 120
Corlett, Thomas, 172
Cortese, John, 216, 221–222
Cortese, Mike, 209, 216
Cortese, Paul, 114, 116, 130, 132, 144–145, 184–185, 221–222
Corteses, The, 174
Cox, David, 220
Cox, Elizabeth Ann Burgess, 6, 19
Coy, Wes, 177, 208
Craig, E. G., 137–138, 142
Crandall, Howard, 201
Crane, Betty, 202
Crane, Bill, 197
Cronin, Bill, 120, 148, 157, 177, 179, 192–193, 221, 222
Cronin, F., 177, 179, 192
Cronin, Jan, 102
Cronin, Janet, 157, 192–193
Crosby, Bing, 111
Cross, Jenni, 118
Cuenin, Bob, 99, 102, 106, 123, 166, 177, 189
Cuenin, Jinny, 102, 123, 166
Cuenin, Mary, 102
Cuenins, The, 95, 123, 166
Curtis, John, 186, 220
Curtiss, John, 14
Curtola, Betty, 20, 72, 83, 86, 108, 181
Curtola, Larry, 20, 68–72, 78, 83, 85–88, 90–91, 129, 145, 148, 168, 173, 179, 181–182, 184, 186, 188, 220, 222
Daegling, William, 221
Daggett, Majorie, 117, 202
Dana, Jack, 201
Datwyler, Ellie, 175
Davies, Caroline, 20
Davies, Joe, 23
Davies, Rod, 20
Davis, Hamilton, 59
Davis, Julie, 98
Davis, Nell, 59
De Chene, Bob, 102
De Chene, Liz, 102
De Chenes, The, 95
De John, Bob, 102, 116
De Johns, The, 95
Demgen, John, 195, 210, 220
Dengel, John, 106
Dennison, Jody, 200
Dietrich, Stojkovich, 101
Dillett, Fred, 197
Ditto, Jean, 102, 153
Ditto, Sam, 102, 121, 153
Ditzler, Hugh, 66
Dolge, William, 30
Dolgin, Judge, 137
Dolinar, Mike, 196
Dollar, Stanley, 45
Donleys, The, 171
Doten, Don, 196
Douglass, Dale, 205
Dozier, Pete, 73
Dwyer, Tom, 110
Dykes, Bernice
Eddy, E. D., 51
Edwards, Dave, 121
Edwards, Debbie, 98
Edwards, Sandy, 191
Edwards, Tom, 39–40, 61, 67
Eisenhower, Dwight, 111
Elgaaen, Gary, 221
Elgaaen, Kathy, 122
Elgaan, Kirsten, 120
Elisondo, Ron, 188, 220
Elliot, Charles, 30, 163
Elliot, Mary Mills, 163
Elmore, Tom, 201
Endicott, Sherry, 227
Enright, Fran, 19, 88
Enright, John, 84, 88, 102, 220
Eorio, Jeffrey, 221
Erickson, Karin, 121
Ernst, Diane, 120
Eschen, Chester, 81, 156
Eschen, Mary, 156
Fabrique, Dud, 225
Farmer, John, 45
Farmer, Peter, 45
Farrell, Vivian, 207
Ferreira, Fritz, 63, 69
Ferreira, Joe, 60, 64
Ferreira, Rose, 39, 42, 60, 67
Ferrell, Sandy, 65
Ferroggiaro, Fred, 68
Field, Bob, 162, 209, 215
Fields, Mark, 207
Filice, Gennaro, 85
Filice, Joan, 202
Fimrites, Les, 80
Firestone, Leonard, 111
Fish, Anne, 8
Fish, Mary, 86
Fish, R. D., 86, 220
Fisks, R. D., 83
Flores, Tom, 71
Foley, Aida, 86
Foley, Les, 86, 220
Foley, Robert, 220, 222
Ford, Patty, 73
Fortado, George, 168
Fowler, Marty, 142
Fraser, Ken, 136, 142
Fraser, Suzanne, 203
Frederick, Hildegard, 222
Freeman, Bill, 27, 39–40, 102, 106, 117, 184, 185
Freeman, Elizabeth, 23, 26–27, 39–41, 106
Freeman, Ginny, 165
Freeman, Kim, 125
Freeman, Leigh, 23, 27, 39, 165
Freeman, Margaret (Mugs), 102, 122, 189
Freeman, Marshall, 23, 27, 39, 102, 121–127, 152, 184–185, 189, 221, 224
Freeman, Patty, 123, 125
Freeman, Steve, 102, 125
Freeman, Susan, 165
Friden, Jane, 105, 155
Friden, Ted, 102

Frost, Jim, 107
Fruscella, Rudy, 222
Fryer, Charles, 182
Fryer, Gil, 120
Fuller, Thomas, 181
Gallagher, Henry, 70, 81
Galvin, Lorna, 118
Gant, Cliff, 114, 130, 135, 142, 220
Gardner, Andrew, 209, 221
Gardner, Paul, 221
Garons, The, 175
Gibson, Helen, 59
Gibson, Read, 59
Giffin, Bren, 73
Gilbert, Brad, 99
Gilman, Kim, 222
Gonzales, Goef, 209
Gonzalez, Tim, 221
Gordon, Kin, 102
Gordon, Mary Jane, 121
Gordon, Peggy, 98, 123, 161
Gordon, Semmes, 98, 121, 123, 152, 161
Gordon, Tripp, 95, 99–100
Gosslin, Eileen, 108–109
Graham, Dick, 119, 204–205
Greenwood, Bob, 42
Gray, Max, 202
Guinivere, Rex, 171
Guinivere, Sue, 223
Guinivere, Suzanne, 133
Guiniveres, The, 171
Gwynns, Charles, 80
Hackney, William, 223
Hagopian, Connie, 20
Hagstrom, Emil, 63, 155
Hagstrom, Esther, 155
Hague, Jeanne, 108
Hague, Jim, 116, 119, 130, 145, 197, 220
Hakman, Dave, 73
Hale, Barbara, 67, 69, 105, 113, 222
Hale, Bill, 25, 39, 45, 67, 69, 158, 176, 185, 222
Hale, Bob, 45, 67
Hale, John, 26, 39, 45, 48, 185, 222
Hale, William, 30, 44, 55, 67, 158, 184, 222
Hall, Barbara Kusserow, 202
Hall, Betty, 74
Hall, David, 45, 74
Hall, George, 39, 45, 64, 74, 220
Hall, Herb, 27–28, 45–46, 68–69, 155, 165
Hall, Herbert, 45, 47, 55, 68, 74, 220
Hall, Susan, 27–28, 45, 69, 74, 165
Hall, Suzette, 74
Halls, The, 40, 69, 164–165
Hammond, Ben, 95
Hammond, Philip, 222
Hansen, Kristen, 98
Hare, Shirley, 52, 159
Hares, The, 159
Hart, Allan, 220
Hart, Lila, 222
Haug, Jeff, 208, 218, 221–222
Haug, Tommy, 208, 218
Hawleys, Stuart, 156
Hayes, Gabby, 171
Hayman, Peter, 197
Headen, Marilee, 193, 222
Headen, Steve, 208
Headstrom, Al, 20
Hearn, Beth, 23, 41, 67, 143, 160, 184
Hearn, Norman J., 67, 143
Hearn, Penny, 67, 73
Hearns, The, 26, 31, 66, 159–160
Hearst, Phoebe, 10
Hearst, William Randolph, 9–11, 14, 18, 141
Helfrich, Bill, 87, 117, 128, 223
Helfrich, Frances, 95–96, 98, 101–102
Helfrich, Margaret, 159
Hendricks, Benji, 75, 83, 86, 143, 166, 203, 222
Hendricks, Candy, 73
Hendricks, Jay, 75
Hendricks, Joe, 55, 75–76, 83–84, 86–87, 166, 203, 220, 222
Henney, Donna, 207
Henney, Ed, 222
Henry, Bert, 59
Henry, Charles, 59, 220
Herzig, Jack, 220
Hillman, Charles, 112, 189
Hills, Herbert, 42, 45, 47, 54–55, 64, 68, 159
Hirsch, Bob, 120
Hirsch, Nanci, 223
Hodgson, Mary Lou, 188, 191, 220
Hoffman, Donald, 184–185, 221
Hohenrieder, Joseph, 221
Holden, Arthur, 105
Holt, Liz, 214
Holts, The, 175
Hornby, Starr, 171
Houston, Bill, 90–92, 129, 196–197
Houston, W. K., 222
Houston, William, 220
Howard, Charlie, 181
Howard, R. Frazer, 105
Howard, William, 200–201
Howe, James, 201
Hudson, Larry, 107
Hughes, Jack, 116, 130, 144, 201–202, 220
Hughes, Miriam, 202
Humphrey, Marge, 72
Hunt, Elizabeth, 159
Hunt, Lee, 142
Hunts, The, 42, 48, 155, 159
Ikard, Steve, 197
Imrie, John, 177, 179, 222
Ives, Cheri, 151
Ives, Chris, 72, 118
Ives, Connie, 151
Ives, Larry, 20, 32, 51, 135, 148, 151–152, 177, 179, 204, 223
Ives, Lloyd, 148, 178, 221–222
Jackson, Evelyn, 117
James, Jack, 196, 201, 220
Jensens, The, 155, 157
Johanson, Bettye, 72, 188, 190–191, 220
John, Jenkin, 155, 175
Johnson, Art, 119, 135
Johnson, Donald, 221
Johnson, Karen, 120
Johnson, Richard, 221
Johnsons, The, 156
Jones, Alexis, 208
Jones, Bob, 130, 142, 208, 222
Jones, Brooke, 121
Jones, Carol, 54, 143, 203, 223
Jones, Gloria, 20
Jones, Harman, 54
Jones, Lisa, 121
Jones, Lowrey, 118
Jones, Stephen, 130, 132, 184–185, 188, 221–222
Joseph, Pat, 224
Juris, Johnny, 67, 75, 223
Justice, Bailey, 83–84, 86–87, 220, 222
Justice, Marie, 83, 86
Kahl, Ernest, 51–52
Kahls, The, 166
Kane, Lee, 207
Kane, Lilan, 105
Kane, Phil, 93, 196–197
Kilburn, Tom, 196
Kinkel, Don, 123, 152, 169
Kinkel, Marjorie, 152, 169
Kipp, David, 121, 221
Kirkland, B. O., 80
Knoedler, Peter, 167, 184–185
Knowland, Bill, 75, 184
Knowland, Russ, 75
Knowlton, Buzz, 83–84–91, 93, 108–109, 118, 196, 222
Knowlton, Gary, 96
Knowlton, J. G., 220
Knowlton, Millie, 93, 108–109, 117, 128, 223
Koss, Amara, 193, 221
Kriz, Joseph, 148, 179, 221
Krueger, Carol, 83, 88, 108
Krueger, DeWitt, 79, 83–84, 88, 107–108, 129, 220, 222
Kurtenbach, Tom, 210, 226
Kusserow, J., 201
La Cava, Connie, 102, 126, 164
La Cava, Edward, 99, 164, 179, 221
La Cava, Nikki, 126
La Cava, Steffi, 102, 121, 126
La Cava, Vince, 95–96
La Cava, Ward, 95–96, 99, 103
Lahti, Mary, 222
Lai, Ravi, 209, 221
Lamb, Howard, 201
Lamson, Dave, 119, 142, 201
Landry, Jane, 121
Larsen, Gary, 197
Lawrence, Ernest G., 60
Lawson, Neils, 148, 220
Lawson, Niles, 136
Layton, Al, 92, 94–95, 102–103, 177
Layton, Kathy, 94
Leach, Abe, 32
Leach, Frank A., 32
Lee, Jack, 164
Leonard, Paul, 120
Lewis, Byron, 205
Lindsay, Larry, 120
Lindsey, Todd, 120
Lingle, Mervin, 117
Lion, Edgar H., 54
Lippincott, Lois Blemer, 65, 71
Lipscomb, Jay, 196
Lloyd, Harold, 29
Locker, Jim, 196
Lockyer, H. H., 201
Lotter, Will, 96
Lotz, Dick, 203
Loveland, Joanne, 202
Lubbock, Dan, 121
Lunardi, Vanessa, 214
MacHugh, Frank, 88
Madonna, John, 223
Magrath, Nancy, 145
Mainhardt, Bob, 69
Mainhardt, Corky, 101
Mallally, Walt, 223
Malone, Cliff, 208, 220, 222
Malone, Evan, 208, 220
Mandley, Jim, 124, 126, 152
Markovich, Pat, 200
Marks, Diana, 120
Markstein, Bob, 156, 208, 216
Markstein, Brenda, 156
Markstein, Ian, 208, 216
Marquoit, Tom, 195
Martin, Baxter, 102
Martin, Bob, 197
Martins, H. I., 80
Maybeck, Bernard, 158–159
Mayne, Cliff, 66
McCann, Frank P., 47, 68
McCarron, Al, 148, 204
McCoskey, Dolores, 207, 223
McCoskey, Lynn, 133, 135–136, 138, 141–142, 220
McDonald, Hank, 102
McDonald, Marian, 102, 121
McDonnel, Mary Lou, 223
McDonnell, Dan, 222
McEuen, Jim, 196, 220, 222
McFarland, Bill, 222
McFarland, Penny, 222
McGaw, Ed, 68
McGlynn, Jan, 151, 223
McGlynn, John, 220
McKesson, Billie, 102
McKesson, Ken, 102
McMurtrey, Jim, 205
McNear, George, 18, 30, 220
McSherry, Elizabeth, 148
Mehran, Alex, 96, 101
Mehran, Casey, 95
Mehran, Henry, 11
Mehran, Maryam, 102
Mehran, Masud, 192
Mehrans, The, 155
Melvin, Henry, 155, 175
Meyer, Bobbie, 102
Meyer, Jeff, 120
Meyer, John, 102, 120
Meyers, Rob, 199
Milks, The, 159
Miller, Colin, 209
Miller, Ginger, 222
Miller, Jeff, 166, 209
Miller, Karen, 166
Miller, Mike, 214
Miller, Patty, 166
Miller, Robert, 222
Mills, Benny, 208
Mills, Bill, 206
Mills, Jeff, 206, 218
Mills, Katie, 209
Mills, Sam, 218
Minor, Jason, 206, 208
Minor, Shelley, 173
Minors, The, 132, 173
Moffitt, Roy, 201
Mohr, Arthur, 177, 179
Moody, Orville, 206
Moore, Lawrence L., 80
Moore, Stan, 207
Morey, Charles, 30, 59, 171, 187
Morey, Dr. Charles, 30, 171
Morey, Wilhemina, 105
Morgan, Hal, 93, 220
Morrison, Kathy, 73
Moulds, Ann, 102
Moulds, Liz, 102
Moye, Pat, 122
Mui, Douglas, 219
Mullaly, Walt, 117

Mullins, Mark, 197
Mullins, Monte, 197
Nageotte, Frank, 189
Nageotte, Judy, 120
Nelson, Byron, 199
Neufelds, 144
Nevelle, Jack, 9
Neufeld, Dan, 142
Newlin, Tom, 196
Ngs, Mary, 219
Nichols, Henry, 45, 169
Nilssen, Bob, 189, 221
Nilssen, Lynn, 121
Noeckers, Carl, 80
Norman, Greg, 200
Noyes, Beth, 118
Nystrom, Eric, 206
Oakley, Vi, 200, 202
Ogles, Roseanne, 151, 223
Okell, Shirley, 28
Olander, John, 184–185, 221, 222, 224
Oliver, A. Leslie, 45, 47, 55, 68
Oliver, Deni, 222
Oliver, John, 221–222
Oliver, Letts, 11, 62, 157, 167
Oliver, William, 11, 155, 167, 222
Oliverios, Viva, 120
Olson, Carl, 142, 222
Olson, Monna, 117, 222–223
Olson, Rob, 197
Olson, Todd, 120
Osborne, Thomas, 200–201
Osmer, John, 120–122, 152
Osmer, Mark, 120
Osmer, Shirley, 120, 122, 152
Osmers, The, 95, 152–153
Overstreet, Dick, 92–95, 97, 99, 102, 121, 126, 224
Overstreet, Ricky, 100
Owsley, Bill, 65, 73, 75–76, 83, 85, 107, 222
Owsley, Fran, 75
Owsley, Josh, 75
Owsley, Pam, 77
Padis, George, 120, 153, 196, 205, 220
Papierniak, Duane, 221
Parker, Erin, 215, 224
Parker, Tom, 224
Parks, Doris, 114
Parks, Ed, 113–114
Parsons, Dave, 127
Pasarell, Stanley, 197
Patten, Ron
Patterson, Sandy, 188, 190
Patton, Pat, 38, 58, 223
Patton, Ron, 58, 77, 79, 106–107, 223
Pearce, Solon, 51–52
Peck, Bill, 116
Peck, John, 106, 196
Peck, Mary Lynn, 109, 207
Pedersen, Egon, 189
Pedersen, Kim, 168
Pedersens, The, 167–168, 188
Peds, John, 102
Pelandini, Sandi, 158
Pelandini, Tom, 158, 221, 223
Petersen, Dorothy, 65, 131, 143
Petersen, Robert, 63
Petersen, Ted, 189, 222
Peterson, Jeryco, 135, 137
Peterson, Sally, 102
Phayer, Larry, 197
Phillips, Kady Lou, 59
Phillips, Ralph, 59
Pianalto, Abe, 142
Pianalto, John, 120
Pianalto, Sally, 203
Pigeon, Darlene, 95
Pigeon, Frank, 102
Pigeon, Kristy, 95, 97
Pingree, Jack, 111, 196, 201, 220
Pitcher, Emily, 223
Potter, Grace, 42
Potts, William, 136, 142
Poulos, John, 32
Powells, Glen, 80
Pratt, Carol, 54
Pratt, Maude, 109, 130, 143
Pratt, Roy, 48
Prescott, Jack, 198
Preston, Robert, 111
Price, John, 88, 117, 143, 222
Priewe, Don, 80, 99
Priewes, 95, 123
Prince, Jim, 80
Prouty, Robin, 72
Puccinelli, Scott, 206
Rader, Ken, 120
Ragusa, Joe, 177, 179, 184–185
Ramsey, Douglas, 201
Read, Bob, 8, 205
Reagan, Ronald, 104
Redfearne, Barry, 205, 223
Redfearne, Liz, 120
Redmond, Debbie, 101
Redmond, George, 102
Redmond, Jackie, 102
Reed, Ben, 72, 95
Reed, Daphne, 73, 75
Reed, Suzan
Rei, Ben, 120
Rei, Benji, 100
Rei, Bill, 94, 98, 102, 123, 163
Rei, Ginny, 94, 102, 163, 202
Rei, Tim, 102, 144
Reimer, Henry, 169
Reiser, Brad, 224
Rhind, Julie, 132, 169
Rhind, Ridley, 132, 169
Richards, The, 148
Rigney, Bill, 110–111, 118–119
Ristenpart, Johnny, 45
Roberts, Earlene, 172
Roberts, John, 106, 148, 172
Rossi, Frank, 83–84, 222
Rossi, Lloyd, 78–79, 107, 119, 129, 222
Rossi, Mildred, 83
Roth, Jack, 196
Rubey, Al, 148, 179, 189
Rubey, Nancy, 120, 153, 222
Rubey, Reed, 95
Russell, John, 20
Ryan, Paul, 144, 164
Ryan, Vern, 144
Ryder, Cecil, 27, 39–41, 64, 66, 145, 181
Samuel, Jan, 207
San Juan, Hilda, 224
Sander, John F., 65
Sander, Maureen, 65
Saur, Hal, 197–198
Scharnell, Deborah, 102, 172
Scharnell, Rob, 102, 172, 208
Schepman, Robert, 221
Scherer, Susan, 193
Schick, Bob, 196
Schmitt, Adaline, 117
Schmitt, Frank, 102, 112, 145, 153, 188–189, 220, 222
Schneider, Lee, 152
Schoenfeld, Ed, 119
Schrepel, Lou, 84, 220
Sconyers, Carol, 98, 102, 132, 188, 221
Sconyers, Devin, 95, 100
Sconyers, Hal, 98, 102, 148, 153
Sconyers, Susan, 102, 165
Sconyers, Terry, 102
Seaborg, Glenn, 60
Seabury, Roberta, 223
Seabury, Tom, 223
Seeleys, Robert, 80
Seely, Bob, 84
Seely, Irving, 200–201
Seely, Ruth, 207
Senasac, Dolf, 184–185
Senasac, Nona R., 184
Shank, Bud, 79, 107, 119, 203, 205, 207
Shank, George, 78, 119, 201, 203
Shaw, Nancie Burgess, 18–20
Shearers, The, 174
Shipley, Tom, 120
Shipley, William, 220
Silva, Lance, 206
Sitter, John, 196
Slavonia, Joel, 120
Smiley, Brian, 120
Smith, Hal, 188
Smith, Harold, 130
Smith, Jim, 223
Smith, V. O., 142
Smith, Vincent, 222
Snead, Sam, 199
Snyder, Gene, 207
Sorensen, Bob, 121
Sorensen, Greta, 121
Sorensen, Gretchen, 98
Soulé, Lee, 19
Soura, Brent, 206
Spangler, Steve, 206
Spicer, Ann, 98
Stapler, Mike, 27, 105
Stapler, Myra Mae Hall, 23, 27, 68
Staub, Dave, 199
Stead, Mike, 136, 220
Steadman, Julian, 196
Stefani, Dave, 196
Stefanski, Ruth, 201
Steger, Robert, 201
Steinbach, Henry, 220, 222
Stewart, Alex, 77
Stockton, Gilbert, 96
Stone, Ashley, 73, 155
Stone, Brett, 73, 94–96, 102
Stone, Dorothy, 87
Stone, Jim, 62, 81, 94, 98, 123, 127, 177, 179, 184–185, 191, 221–222, 224
Stott, Ethyl, 186, 220
Suitor, Andy, 208
Surano, Kris, 98
Suttons, Tom, 81
Swallow, George, 138, 159
Swanson, Richard, 185, 221
Swenson, Josh, 120
Taapken, John, 101
Tantau, Clarence, 47
Tauscher, Norm, 85, 223
Taylor, Wakefield, 177
Teller, Ed, 60
Thebolt, George, 45
Thiele, Donald, 221
Thode, Chuck, 102
Thomas, Alice, 22–23, 26, 105, 143, 160
Thomas, Bill, 23, 27–28, 39, 41, 45, 58, 143, 160
Thomas, Eric, 102
Thomas, Fred, 22–23, 26–27, 143, 160
Thomas, Missy, 120
Thomas, Stan, 102, 189
Thompson, Neil, 148
Tiernan, Lyn, 102, 126
Tiernan, Robert102, 123, 126, , 148, 150, 152, 177–179, 184–185, 192, 221–222
Tierney, Gene, 64
Timmermans, Anne, 138, 151, 203, 223
Timmermans, Harry, 135, 136, 142, 221
Tinneys, The, 166
Toney, 95–96, 99, 101–102, 152–153, 224
Toney, Jack, 102, 152–153
Toney, Jill, 102, 152–153
Toney, John, 99, 101–102, 152
Toney, Jon, 95–96, 102, 153, 224
Toney, Mel, 102, 153
Toney, Melissa, 95–96, 101–102, 153
Torey, Lance, 206
Turner, Lou, 127
Turner, Rett, 106, 127, 220
Tysdale, Craig, 196
Udall, Fred, 80, 106
Udelhoven, Jerry, 98
Ullery, Joan, 207
Unger, Beverly, 148
Van Bokkelen, Bill, 83, 85, 86, 182, 220
Van Bokkelen, Billie, 83, 86
Vendt, Carl, 222
Vendt, Jean, 207
Venos, Ken, 226
Venturi, Ken, 204
Vergez, Johnny, 79
Waldo, Marian, 66
Walker, Frank, 80, 83
Wall, Bob, 117, 130, 188, 179, 201, 222
Wallunas, Jonathan, 225
Ward, Harvie, 205
Warren, Bill, 75, 80
Washom, Byron, 208–210, 222
Washom, Katie, 208–210, 224
Washom, Spencer, 208
Watson, Dennis, 196
Watson, William, 32
Wehrman, Lyle, 106, 119, 149, 186, 223
Weinmann, Teller, 29
Weitzberg, Abe, 102
Welch, Pat, 73
Wendt, Alice
White, Dave, 206, 222
White, Tim, 120
Whitney, Jock, 29, 223
Wilcox, Paul, 199, 223
Wilhelmy, John, 209
Wilkie, Roger, 221
Williams, Howie, 207
Wilson, Carrol, 42
Winn, George, 119, 223
Winslow, Bill, 80, 196
Winting, Arthur, 223
Wise, Winifred Gray, 52
Wolf, Robert, 201
Wood, Charlotte, 11
Wright, Charlotte, 26, 39
Wright, John, 217
Wright, Maynard, 26, 38–39
Wynn, Bob, 223